The Art and Politics
of College Teaching

PETER LANG
New York • Washington, D.C./Baltimore • Bern
Frankfurt am Main • Berlin • Brussels • Vienna • Oxford

The Art and Politics of College Teaching

A Practical Guide for the Beginning Professor

SECOND EDITION

Edited by
Karl D. Hostetler, R. McLaran Sawyer,
and Keith W. Prichard

PETER LANG
New York • Washington, D.C./Baltimore • Bern
Frankfurt am Main • Berlin • Brussels • Vienna • Oxford

Library of Congress Cataloging-in-Publication Data

The art and politics of college teaching: a practical guide
for the beginning professor / edited by Karl D. Hostetler,
R. McLaran Sawyer, and Keith W. Prichard.—2nd ed.
p. cm.
Includes bibliographical references.
1. College teaching—United States. 2. College teachers—United States.
I. Sawyer, R. M. (Robert McLaran). II. Prichard, Keith W.
III. Hostetler, Karl D.
LB2331 .A648   378.1'25'0973—dc21   00-049727
ISBN 0-8204-5204-1

Die Deutsche Bibliothek-CIP-Einheitsaufnahme

The art and politics of college teaching: a practical guide
for the beginning professor / ed. by Karl D. Hostetler,
R. McLaran Sawyer, and Keith W. Prichard—2. ed.
–New York; Washington, D.C./Baltimore; Bern;
Frankfurt am Main; Berlin; Brussels; Vienna; Oxford: Lang.
ISBN 0-8204-5204-1

Cover design by Dutton & Sherman Design

The paper in this book meets the guidelines for permanence and durability
of the Committee on Production Guidelines for Book Longevity
of the Council of Library Resources.

Printed in the United States of America

Table of Contents

Foreword   1
    Gene A. Budig, former Chancellor,
    University of Kansas

Introduction   5
    Karl Hostetler, Keith Prichard, and
    R. McLaran Sawyer

**Part I   Role Expectations for Beginning Professors
               at Eight Institutions of Higher Education   17**

The Making of a Scholarly Career at a Major Research University   19
    Dean K. Whitla

Meeting Expectations for Research, Teaching, and Service at the
    Comprehensive Public University: The Dominance
    of the Discipline   29
    Kenneth E. Andersen

Teaching at a Small Liberal Arts College   39
    Anthony S. Abbott

Building a Future at "the Premiere Teaching University"
    in the Midwest   47
    Roy Weaver

Role Expectations for the New and Not-So-New Professors at
    Grambling State University   55
    Lamore J. Carter

Women's Education at Women's Colleges: Responsibilities
    and Challenges for New Faculty Members   61
    Mary E. Kitterman

Expectations for New Professors at Fresno Pacific College:
       A Religiously Oriented Institution   67
       Norman Rempel
Perspectives on Values Needed for Teaching at the
       Two-Year College   77
       David H. Bergquist

**Part II   Step-by-Step Analysis of Career Patterns for
         Faculty Members   85**
Getting the Job: Anxiety and Aspirin   87
       *Karl Hostetler, Keith Prichard, and
       R. McLaran Sawyer*
Getting the Job: With a Little Bit of Luck . . . and a Whole
       Lot of Forethought   93
       Linda Haverty
The Complexities of the Job Search Multiplied by Two   107
       Constance J. Pollard and Richard R. Pollard
Accepting the Job: The Die Is Cast   119
       *Karl Hostetler, Keith Prichard, and
       R. McLaran Sawyer*
The Decisions, Dilemmas, and Opportunities Involved in
       Accepting a Non-Tenure Track Appointment   125
       Jay W. Rojewski
Benefits   133
       Gregory P. Clayton
Making the Transition: Demands and Decisions of the First
       Months on the Job   141
       *Karl Hostetler, Keith Prichard, and
       R. McLaran Sawyer*
On Becoming a Professor: Identity and Responsibility in the
       Student-to-Professor Transition   163
       Linda J. Koenig
Getting Along with Colleagues: A Cultural Perspective   171
       Gargi Roysircar Sodowsky
Creating the New Course: Putting the Show on the Road   179
       *Karl Hostetler, Keith Prichard, and
       R. McLaran Sawyer*
Navigating the Wood: An Essay on Course Planning   191
       Anthony S. Abbott

Some Considerations for the University Teaching Faculty   199
    Dean K. Whitla

Research Agenda for the Beginner: When Your Feet Hit
    the Ground, Start Running   207
    Karl Hostetler, Keith Prichard, and
    R. McLaran Sawyer

Scholarly Publications: It's Still Publish or Perish   217
    John A. Glover

Promotion and Tenure: Keys to the Kingdom   227
    Karl Hostetler, Keith Prichard, and
    R. McLaran Sawyer

Promotion and Tenure   235
    Paul E. Kelly

Committees, Associations, and Organizations:
    The Fine Art of Networking   245
    Karl Hostetler, Keith Prichard, and
    R. McLaran Sawyer

Gaining National Recognition: A Place in the Sun   253
    Karl Hostetler, Keith Prichard, and
    R. McLaran Sawyer

Leaving Gracefully or Not So Gracefully   261
    Karl Hostetler, Keith Prichard, and
    R. McLaran Sawyer

Part III   Legal and Ethical Issues for Faculty   275

Legal Rights and Responsibilities of College Faculty   277
    Donald E. Uerling

Academic Freedom and College Teaching   289
    Robert M. O'Neil

Affirmative Action: Myths and Realities   301
    Mark R. Killenbeck

Ethics of the Profession: Complexities of Collegiality,
    Professionalism, Morality, and Virtue   323
    Karl Hostetler

Contributors   341

Foreword

Gene A. Budig
former Chancellor University of Kansas

Teaching at the college or university level is one of the most rewarding careers an individual can choose. After years of arduous (and costly) study, the newly minted Ph.D. is ready to embark on the long-sought career. Academic departments and advisors will often provide guidance for that initial job search, but traditionally one learns how to conduct a career by observation, exploration, and pure chance. Colleagues and mentors can—and will—be helpful, and so will this volume of essays.

Professors Hostetler, Sawyer, and Prichard and their contributors have provided a superb handbook for the aspiring faculty member and, indeed, for the veteran as well. It is a practical, pragmatic, and candid guide from women and men who have the experience to address their topics authoritatively. They also all share a genuine interest in the well-being and success of their junior colleagues, a desire to help them achieve their potential as teachers and scholars. The collegial spirit from which this volume springs is characteristic of American higher education. There is competition in the academic world, certainly, but there is also a higher degree of collegiality than in perhaps any other profession: a shared commitment to our common goals of teaching, research, and service.

This is not to say that the beginning professor will find a life of ease and comfort. Those very faculty who offer welcome and assistance must also judge the contributions of their new colleagues and make difficult decisions on promotion and tenure within a few years. They have shown their faith in the potential of the new professor through the selection and appointment of this candidate, but it is the task of the new professor to demonstrate that this faith is justified. That justification may take different forms, depending on the type of institution one has joined. The eight institutional statements in Part I demonstrate the variety among institutions of higher education and the differing ways they look upon the new faculty member. There may be little expectation of research and publication or great expectations indeed. There will doubtless be demands for service, great or lesser, depending on institutional style. There will certainly be a demand for skill in the classroom and in other interactions with students.

These expectations can be daunting, but they are certainly not out of reach. Graduate study weeds out the unqualified. It instills an understanding of and appreciation for research and scholarly endeavor. In most cases, it provides an apprenticeship in teaching, with critical supervision by committed teachers. And today there are ample opportunities for graduate students to experience the necessary, if often tedious, committee work that is service to one's institution. Examples of successful careers are readily at hand among the faculty with whom one has worked as a student. It is difficult to complete graduate study without having gathered at least anecdotal information about academic careers. This volume distills the experiences of many successful academics in the hope that it will ease the path through the critical first years in the profession.

Because of retirements, American higher education will be faced over the next decade with an enormous demand for new college and university faculty. This is a great challenge for doctorate-granting universities, to which higher education looks for tomorrow's faculty. It will also be a challenge to all hiring institutions for they will have many new colleagues to nurture, evaluate, and assimilate into their own institutional cultures.

And while these challenges are being met, higher education faces other, more difficult, challenges. Minority enrollments, particularly in graduate and professional schools, have declined in absolute numbers over the past decade, even as the minority population in the United States has increased. This trend must be countered. Black, Hispanic, and Native American youth must be brought into higher education in vastly increased numbers. They must be persuaded and encouraged to complete not only an undergraduate degree but graduate and professional degrees as well. Higher education must work with schools to bring this about so that the professoriate will begin to reflect the marvelous diversity of our nation. To do otherwise would be unconscionable.

As technology continues to advance at a bewildering rate, colleges and universities must learn to take advantage of those advances. And in doing so, it may be that the nature of the college experience will change—

for students and faculty alike. The history of American higher education since 1945 has been one of constant evolution and will take all of higher education in directions we cannot now foresee with any certainty.

What will not change is the essential interaction between students and faculty, the interaction between educated men and women and those who aspire to that status. There will be a greater need than ever for bright, committed, mature individuals who understand the importance of higher education and wish to participate in it as members of our faculties. These new professors must be teachers and, in the appropriate settings, scholars and researchers. For the past half century, it has been taken for granted that most advances in knowledge, whether in science, technology, the humanities and social sciences, will occur on our college and university campuses. The need for continued advances in knowledge is all around us, and increasingly it will be higher education which is expected to meet that need. That means people: women and men whose lives are committed to the classroom, the laboratory, the library, who understand the unique rewards which a career in academe provides.

This volume will serve such individuals well. It will help ease the transition from student to colleague. It offers prudent advice on shaping and building a career in higher education. I wish it had been available 25 years ago.

Introduction

Our intention in this book is to offer new (and perhaps not-so-new) professors some guidance in dealing with the complexities of their profession. We hope that such analysis and advice as we and our contributors offer will be helpful to professors in a wide range of fields and institutions. We believe there is a gap between what graduate schools prepare students for and what colleges and universities expect of new faculty members. This book tries to do something to fill that gap.

The book is divided into three parts. In this introduction, we say a bit about the point and content of each of these parts.

Part I

One thing that should be understood is that institutions of higher education differ in the demands they make upon their faculty. In Part I, expectations for faculty at eight different institutions are described. As you will see, the expectations differ, sometimes considerably. It behooves candidates to be aware of this variety as they seek out professorial appointments so that they can improve their chances of finding a position in which they can be happy and successful.

But it also behooves new professors to be aware of the wider intellectual, social, political context in which colleges and universities are located. Institutional policies about faculty expectations and educational mission are not simply internal matters. The days when colleges and universities could insulate themselves from their broader context are gone; faculty, students, government, and the public at large demand that postsecondary institutions be responsive to the needs and desires of the "outside" world. And colleges and universities have been responsive. However, these demands are many and varied, and this explains, at least in part, the variation in expectations among institutions, for they respond to different demands and in different ways to those demands. This also does something to explain the shifting ground of expectations within institutions. In some places, this shift is less dramatic and rapid than in others. Yet, as our initial eight essays show, in none of these institutions are expectations completely fixed. No doubt, some of this vagueness is attributable to the vagueness inherent in standards of performance for teaching, research, and service. Still, some can be attributed to the difficulty of the struggle to develop balanced and appropriate responses to the many complex and often competing demands with which institutions of higher learning must deal.

The upshot is that understanding and dealing with faculty expectations may be facilitated if new professors have at least some sense of the wider forces and issues that affect those expectations. We wish to offer some thoughts about that before we address the eight institutions described in the Part I essays.

This matter is complex, of course, and we cannot claim to offer an exhaustive analysis. Nor do we claim to offer an explanation for the contemporary situation. However, perhaps we can at least present a fruitful if incomplete description of the situation that might offer some amount of insight.

Institutions of higher education in the United States exist in a historical, social context that embodies particular traditions as to knowledge, and, in turn, traditions as to the role of colleges and universities as developers, protectors, and dispensers of that knowledge. We can describe the variety and tensions among expectations for professors by considering this to be a manifestation of the tensions within this tradition about knowledge, in particular, the tension between theory and practice with which Western culture has grappled since at least the time of Plato and Aristotle.

Our modern notion of theory has its roots in the ancient Greek notion of *theoria* (although our contemporary notion differs considerably from the Greek). For the Greeks, *theoria* is "the highest manner of being human," and it involves "sharing in the total order" of what exists.[1] This is different from practical knowledge, knowledge of how to lead a good life in the everyday world. Although practical knowledge was a true form of knowledge, Aristotle esteemed it less, because it was not knowledge of the unchanging.

This sort of distinction has appeared in modern times in the form of "pure" theory versus "applied" theory. In the minds of some people, "pure" theory is superior to "applied" theory; or, if the division is not necessarily between better and worse, at least these are different realms, and there may be a division of roles so far as who should do the work in the one realm or the other. Historically, the role of colleges and universities was to be developers of "pure" theory, unsullied by the messy, distracting problems of practice. Application of such theory to such problems was to be left to others.

However, this arrangement did not find easy acceptance in this country. As Richard Hofstadter argues, there is an anti-intellectual tradition in this country that is suspicious of "theorists."[2] Valued is the person of action, the person who can get things done, preferably without the benefit of theory or "book learning." Also, there has been criticism from within the intellectual community itself. Pragmatic philosophers have attacked the theory/practice distinction. John Dewey, for example, challenged the distinction between pure and applied science and the supposed superiority of pure research.[3]

For whatever reason, there was a shift in perception of the role of the college and university around the end of the nineteenth century. Hofstadter cites the example of the University of Wisconsin, which "had gathered some distinguished scholars, who were concentrating on social and economic problems, notably on those of the state and municipality."[4]

Here we see a conscious attempt to shift the role of the university toward developing and utilizing practical knowledge that has direct social benefits. This role is much in evidence today. Probably stimulated by several wars and other salient social problems and crises, the federal government and other public and private agencies have actively sought college and universities to help solve pressing social problems. There is a strong push for postsecondary institutions to produce students who do not just know "theory" but who are vocationally prepared to get things done.

This shift has impacted the lives of professors and institutions in profound ways. People wanted research that was application oriented and were willing to pay for it. Competition for grant dollars began. Premium research universities began to emerge. However, virtually all institutions of medium and large size were drawn into the revolution of rising expectations. Even those that did not win in the grant competition were expected to do more. There was a general increase in intensity, if that is the proper word. Application-oriented research became the common denominator by which institutions were evaluated. The top-producing institutions were, indeed, "in the club." Others sought to enter if at all possible.

Of course, there are departments or sections of the faculty who do not have the practical orientation of some of their colleagues. However, with the push toward producing "useful" knowledge, even for those professors who are not expected to be "practical"—such as philosophy professors or professors of music or music history—there has been increasing expectation to do *something* "productive," to show people something concrete. It is not enough to contemplate the total order of the universe and engage one's students in that.

However, this trend has prompted shifts of focus even within these more esoteric disciplines. For instance, one sees more and more professional philosophers addressing themselves to questions of practice. Work in medical and business ethics provides some prominent examples. And there is a concomitant recognition among some "practitioners" that philosophy does have something "practical" to offer.

Conflicts and tensions remain, however. In fields where there is a strong push toward application, "pure" theorists sometimes have a hard time surviving. For instance, in education, specialists in philosophy of education and history of education are a vanishing species. Furthermore, the emphasis on application has prompted something of a status revolution. Those professors who can and do produce good work which is perceived to be rather straightforwardly practical, for example, in such areas as chemistry, physics, biology, and computer science, have been able to demand higher salaries and other fringe benefits that their colleagues in other fields are not able to demand.

This competition for status is not lost on professors. Consider American philosopher Richard Rorty's rather acerbic commentary that "highbrows" in the academy

> do not get grants; they have disciplines rather than research teams; they inhabit whatever mansions may still be tucked away among the academic skyscrapers. Their more businesslike colleagues treat them alternately with the deference due from tradesmen to the clergy, and the contempt the successful feel for the shabby genteel.[5]

We should be careful not to overgeneralize the effects of the trend toward "practical" knowledge, for institutions have responded to it differently. To analyze these different reactions, it is useful to return to Aristotle. Until now we have glossed over a distinction within Aristotle's conception of practical knowledge. What we have been emphasizing is really just one sort of practical knowledge, what can be called technical or productive knowledge. This is knowledge of the technical means that will most efficiently and effectively produce some desired end.

But Aristotle posited another sort of practical knowledge in the everyday world, knowledge that had to do with "right living." For Aristotle, technical knowledge is not enough. For example, technical knowledge can be used for bad things as well as good. The technical knowledge of the scientist can be used to destroy people as well as to make their lives better. What is needed is knowledge of how to distinguish right uses of science or other technical knowledge from bad uses. One needs to have knowledge of what actions are conducive to an ethically worthwhile life for oneself and other human beings.

In the past, colleges and universities have been places that were to produce "gentlemen" who knew about "right living" in the sense of having the manners suitable to their "station" and who had a sense of *noblesse oblige*. This is not what Aristotle meant by knowledge of right living. His idea was more along the lines of the German notion of *Bildung*, cultivation, "the properly human way of developing one's natural talents and capacities."[6] This cultivation was not merely according to one's station or particular desires. It was to be cultivation as a human being (hence the need for *theoria*). Furthermore, this cultivation was not intellectual merely, although there certainly was that dimension. Yet cultivation came through action in the world, though not action in the technical sense that would excuse any behavior so long as it produced the desired end. The idea was that one's actions are not ethically neutral. One cannot separate one's technical activities from one's ethical responsibilities. To be technically efficient but unjust in one's actions does something unfortunate to oneself as a person.

It seems that some institutions respond to the trend toward practical knowledge by emphasizing this sort of cultivation of character. The aim is not so much to produce technical knowledge but to produce good people, people who are aware of social problems such as gender or racial inequality and are trying actively to rectify those.

This division of knowledge and institutional purposes into the categories of "pure" knowledge, technical knowledge, and cultivation may help us see some structure in the faculty expectations described in the Part I essays. We do not claim to make any neat divisions here. Nor do we wish to argue for one view on knowledge or expectations being superior to the others; perhaps they all have their proper place. But perhaps as a heuristic device, this categorization offers new professors some way of thinking about institutional demands and their own beliefs and aspirations.

In looking at the institutions described in Part I, we can identify some broad categories: "student-centered" institutions (Davidson College, Grambling State University, Stephens College, Becker College, and Fresno Pacific College); "knowledge-centered" institutions (Harvard University and the University of Illinois); and an "institution in transition" (Ball State University).

Student-centered institutions are concerned primarily with student development. For professors in student-centered institutions, their role definition emphasizes a primary and continuous interest in the student. There must be an acceptance and wholehearted support of working constantly with the students. Because student development is a way of life, your personal life must become part of the college life. To be successful, the faculty member and his or her family must become part of the college.

"Knowledge" certainly is not neglected in these institutions, but teaching and student development are the priorities. Whatever scholarship is expected, this scholarship should first of all advance students' development rather than merely advance "theory." To this extent, these institutions would seem to see their role as "cultivation."

There are differences among them, though. Becker College has a very clear and explicit career orientation even though that is not its sole purpose. In a liberal arts college such as Davidson, there is more emphasis on scholarship in the tradition of *theoria* than in a religious school such as Fresno Pacific, in which cultivation is deemed to take place through deep commitment to a particular doctrinal way of life. Grambling and Stephens seem to be somewhere in the middle. Orientation to a particular sort of scholarship is expected, as well as a more definite emphasis on social action, but yet there seems to be a legacy of traditional liberal arts preparation.

At the "knowledge-centered" institutions Harvard and Illinois, students are by no means neglected, but there is at least relatively greater emphasis on "knowledge." Here, too, there are differences. As a public institution, "technical" knowledge may have somewhat more emphasis at Illinois than at a private university such as Harvard. Dr. Andersen notes, for example, that Illinois "is seeking increased ties to business and industry and fostering faculty entrepreneurship." Because it is publicly supported, Illinois may have to accommodate public demands for technical relevance of professors' work. Harvard may be at least relatively more hospitable to professors who work with "pure" scholarship.

Role expectations for those faculty members who opt to work at "institutions in transition" are defined yet differently. Here there must be a very high level of focus on the new goals rather than the old goals. There may, unfortunately, be something of a split among the faculty, and factionalism may exist for a time. There may be the moss-backs vs. the young Turks conflict. Institutions and institutional administrators may give mixed signals as to what they want. To be successful, the new faculty member must focus on new goals while not alienating the older faculty members who often have the keys to promotion and tenure. How difficult this situation is depends on the depth and breadth of the shift being attempted. This shift can be unrealistic because of: (a) a lack of financial resources to achieve what is wanted, (b) too little time for faculty to devote to making the changes, and/or (c) insufficient numbers of the new-type faculty to achieve a critical mass for change. Needless to say, this situation can be very difficult for new faculty members. But if you succeed and are instrumental in helping achieve the shift in institutional mission, you will doubtlessly be given a page in any future history of that college or university. Your picture may hang in the faculty room or in the president's office!

No matter the type of institution at which you find a home, sage advice appears to be that you should: (a) find a mentor that fits the institutional goals and is a heavy hitter on the faculty to guide you along the first year or two, (b) be a success from the first day you appear on the job, (c) set a standard for yourself of being an excellent classroom teacher, and (d) let your expectations exceed those of being a good graduate student.

Your best chance of success will occur where: (a) the institution has clear and relatively stable expectations, (b) the older faculty members meet the current expectations, (c) new faculty members genuinely can fit the institutional expectations with their personal goals, (d) the institution provides resources and time for new faculty, and (e) there is an effective system for mentoring the work of the new faculty members.

The institutions described in Part I represent a range of institutions that is intended to give you a sense of the career options you have. Be aware, though, that this is only a small sampling, and our writers had only a short space to describe a quite complex institution. We hope that the essays give you a sense for what to look for in a faculty position, but they can offer you only a start. If you're wise, you'll carefully study whatever institutions you consider applying to.

On the other hand, in one sense we consciously took the attitude of not trying for representative views. A chief concern was to permit the reader to hear the "voice" of our writers, and we wanted to preserve the personalness of their accounts. We wanted readers to realize that academic communities are human communities that are not all of a type but are the product of the thought, action, and passion of particular people. We felt that we might lose that quality if we demanded that our essayists write only in terms of broad generalities.

One can read the eight Part I essays and readily sense the energy and drive conveyed in the role descriptions for new faculty members at these institutions. Today, there are external and internal forces that attempt to harness that energy, to dictate change for the college, the university, and their faculties. Today it is not always possible to predict the degree or direction of the change that will occur; however, that change will most certainly occur must be recognized. Part of your challenge as a new faculty member is not just to adapt yourself to institutional demands but to take your proper part in determining the future of postsecondary education.

Part II

Despite differences in the expectations institutions have of faculty, there are some quite basic career steps through which most faculty members must progress. Today's new professor may well be knowledgeable about the content of her or his academic field but be virtually unschooled in such things as teaching techniques, curriculum development, collegial relationship expectations, and the enigmatic routes to promotion and tenure. We wrote our Part II essays with the intent of offering the newcomer or prospective newcomer some realistic advice on these crucial steps and problems in building an academic career. We intentionally sought to avoid the romanticism so often used to portray the professoriate. Our essays are based not only on our experience as students and faculty members at some 14 institutions of higher learning but on conversations and discussions with a great many other professional educators at various institutions.

We realized that there was a problem of generalizability similar to that in Part I. Because of the limits of our own experience, we solicited second opinions in order to provide as much balanced advice as possible given our limited space. If contradictions exist as a result of the second opinions, so be it.

The contributors range widely with respect to age, experience, and geographical location. They come from a variety of types of institutions. And we were determined to have contributions from women faculty members and faculty members who represent ethnic minorities. Of course, we do not have representatives from all relevant groups, from for example, gay or lesbian faculty and faculty with physical disabilities. Despite this limitation, we believe that the essays will give you a helpful account of some of the opportunities and challenges that face you as you pursue a career in higher education.

No particular directions were given to the contributors. We simply asked them for candid and realistic essays that were based on their first-hand experience. For the essays on "Getting the Job," "Accepting the Job," and "Making the Transition," we sought second opinions only from faculty members who had been recently appointed as assistant professors and so had those experiences fresh in their minds.

For several topics we include only our own essay. In these instances, we felt it sufficient to present guidelines for the beginner and to create an awareness level of knowledge. Greg Clayton's essay on benefits is not really a second opinion on the matter of accepting the job, but we felt it appropriate to place it there because the type and amount of benefits an institution offers are important considerations when deciding whether to take a job there.

Part II, like Part I, is presented in narrative style because we believe that the depth of feeling and contextual complexities involved in these career steps could not be conveyed in a statistical presentation. As it is, the reader gets only a glimpse of the challenges and opportunities that await new professors as they secure a position and build a career.

Part III

We end the book with some discussion of legal and ethical aspects of being a professor. Like the career steps described in Part II, the legal and ethical basics are much the same for all professors. But unlike particular career steps, law and ethics are not just occasional concerns, relevant at some times and less so at others. Basic principles of law and ethics provide a framework for thinking about the work of professors that is always relevant. But here, too, we see an unfortunate shortfall in the education of the typical graduate student. Law and ethics provide professors some of their most fundamental protections and guidance, but rarely do doctoral students have the chance to think seriously about these dimensions of higher education. We cannot make up for that shortfall, but perhaps we can begin the discussion at least.

There are many legal and ethical issues we could talk about, of course. We include essays on two of the more visible, important, and controversial issues being debated today: affirmative action and academic freedom. But beyond their currency and controversial nature, these issues merit attention because they place before us some of the most fundamental principles of higher education: Who merits membership in the academy and why? How is merit to be understood and evaluated? What is the proper role of professors? To be political activists? Seekers of truth? Can they be both? Who should decide that? What should be the content of professors' courses? And all this leads to perhaps the most fundamental question of all: What is the proper aim of higher education?

We do not say that principles of law and ethics always must be at the forefront of professors' thinking—deciding to teach *Macbeth* rather than *King Lear* is largely a scholarly decision, for instance. But at the same time we need to be careful not to underestimate the ethical content of such decisions. The intent still is to teach *good* material, *worthwhile* material, rather than trash. Deciding to include a representative sample of authors—men and women, from a range of racial and ethnic groups—goes beyond scholarly issues to ethical issues of justice and inclusion. The opportunities and protections institutions provide professors for academic freedom and access to higher education positions are constant concerns, ones that merit vigilance. Similarly, as teachers, professors must be vigilant in order to understand and protect the freedoms and opportunities students should have.

But we want to say, too, that ethics is not just a matter of high-profile issues such as these. Being a good professor is not just a matter of avoiding illegal behavior or being on the front lines of the ethical battles over academic freedom and affirmative action. Part of being a good professor is simply being a decent person, perhaps showing courage or integrity in small, unnoticed ways in day-to-day interactions with students and colleagues. In this way, too, ethics is a constant concern; indeed, it is part of the very fabric of life in higher education.

So in addition to the essays on specific issues, in two essays some general legal and ethical issues and principles are discussed. Clearly these do not offer you answers to difficult problems, but we hope they will provide you some useful concepts and suggestions to begin dealing with them.

We hope that in sharing these essays, stories, and narratives, in the interaction and sometimes clash of opinions and second opinions, readers will come to have a feel for the real world of a professorial career, so that new professors can enter that world with open eyes and reasonable expectations and with a head start on the project of shaping a career that is enjoyable and worthwhile for themselves and those people with whom they work.

Notes

1. Hans-Georg Gadamer, *Truth and Method*, 2nd rev. ed., trans. Joel Weinsheimer and Donald Marshall (New York: Crossroad, 1989), p. 454.

2. Richard Hofstadter, *Anti-Intellectualism in American Life* (New York: Random House, Vintage Books, 1963).

3. John Dewey, *The Public and Its Problems* (Athens, Ohio: Ohio University Press, Swallow Books, 1927), p. 174.

4. Hofstadter, op. cit., p. 201.

5. Richard Rorty, *The Consequences of Pragmatism* (Minneapolis: University of Minnesota Press, 1982), p. 61.

6. Gadamer, op. cit., p. 10.

ROLE EXPECTATIONS FOR BEGINNING PROFESSORS AT EIGHT INSTITUTIONS OF HIGHER EDUCATION

The Making of a Scholarly Career at a Major Research University

Dean K. Whitla

Some wag once suggested that college teaching is the only profession in which two promotions make a career. One begins an academic career as an assistant professor, during the next three, five, seven years publishes fourteen articles, writes two books, teaches two basic courses in the department and offers a third in his or her specialty, serves on a couple of committees, and is promoted to associate professor. He/she now offers a second course in the specialty in lieu of one of the basic courses, writes another book and a few more articles (now searching for quality rather than volume), chairs a departmental committee and is promoted to full professor. It is now time for sabbatical, if it hasn't occurred before, and a period of re-examination and search for any midcareer correction which may establish the intellectual direction for the rest of the professional life. While this is far too formalistic, it is, with variations on the theme, a route taken by a number of faculty members in the major research universities of the country.1

Such a parody ignores the intellectual dedication and even the physical energy that went into these achievements. During graduate study, the goals were to master the discipline, to develop the skills of historical research or competency in economic analysis. The first of independent research tasks comes with the thesis. Many really first-rate graduate students founder at this point because the rules have all changed. In a recent discussion with a graduate student in physics, he said it was hard to see how working hard today would lead to a reward five years from now. Deferred gratification is not a cliche but a way of life. A tendency to procrastinate befalls many scholars who await the muse. Although intellectual contributions do demand a high level of creativity and insight, they also demand great dedication. Even the most gifted do not conceive of brilliant research ideas or dash off books without both serious thought and much labor.

Credo 1

The thesis must become book number one. A good publisher who will see that it is properly reviewed is also important. It is not that the thesis must be the basis of the first book, but failure to publish quickly is done at some peril. Why is this? The younger scholars are assumed to be the brighter scholars; therefore, speed is important. It comes out of a long-held belief that the gifted contributions—especially in math and the sciences—are made by the young and that the years of significant contributions are few. Therefore, the best work must come early. Incidentally, many believe that people with such gifts can be identified at an early age. This, like many truisms, is exaggerated: many mathematicians seventy years old are still making substantial contributions to the field, and more and more this will become the rule rather than the exception.

This is a demanding life even for the most able. Is it worth the chase? Indeed it is. Being a tenured faculty member at a major university in these United States is one of the finest positions one can hold. If you have the intellectual capacity and the drive to obtain a professorship, then you could have chosen other callings instead. Professional choices that could have been made range from banking to podiatry. However, if you enjoy the life of the mind; find your greatest satisfaction from reading, writing, and research; have just the touch of ham so that you can lecture with at least a modicum of pizzazz; and enjoy teaching the young, then the academic life is for you.

If this is true, then you should maximize the chances of the full professorship and a position of tenure that goes with it at a major research university as early in your career as possible. It provides great control over your life's work and gives you the highest rewards of the American educational system.

The major decision that must be made is the type of institution in which one finds compatibility. There are many subcategories, but the most important are teaching versus research and large versus small. Some people would also place geographical location high on their list; others would favor a single-sex institution, and yet others prefer colleges or universities with a religious orientation. Public versus private distinctions are very important to a few people, but those distinctions blur, especially among first-tier institutions.

Some of my friends who work in junior colleges find that these are the only places of educational ferment today and would feel I was amiss if I didn't single them out for special comment. Certainly, lots of imaginative teaching is carried out in junior and community colleges. For all of these considerations, I feel that the most important distinction in terms of your search for a life style of your choice is the distinction between institutions which emphasize teaching as the basis for promotion and those which, while appreciating teaching expertise, will not promote anyone unless they have demonstrated substantial evidence of scholarly promise and even of scholarly pre-eminence.

The rewards of each of these educational systems, though quite different, are substantial. John Monro, once Dean of Harvard College, left Harvard to direct the writing program first at Miles College and later at Tougaloo College, both small historically black colleges. He recently told me that he thought he was getting too old to teach, but then the students elected him "teacher of the year" for the third time, so he decided to continue. He was then seventy years old, and he did for free what he was once paid to do. Somebody at the luncheon said, "John, is it really true that you will come down to the campus anytime of day or night to help a student with his paper?" He replied, "Of course—it's no big deal, I just live down the road a couple of miles. If someone calls at 3:00 in the morning, I just hop in my car and just buzz down, no problem." Can there be any greater reward than the satisfaction of knowing that by giving of yourself, you have helped some student master a prose form or a way of thinking that, in turn, helps them develop their self-esteem and take their rightful place in the world? This personal form of engagement in the lives of students and personal sacrifice can and does take place in all kinds of educational institutions. The likelihood of that happening is simply greater in the typically small teaching colleges of the country. If that is your style, there can be no better calling.

David Riesman, who has given a great deal of thought to higher education and written extensively on these issues, would mention that burnout at such institutions can be a problem. At the University of California at Santa Cruz and Hampshire College, where faculty teach small courses and make themselves very available to students, teachers can have trouble surviving students' capacity to absorb endless hours of faculty time and energy. The most consuming are those places which want you to engage in this form of individual mentoring and still be a published scholar—

those places are doubly seductive. They invite the full engagement of both student and faculty: the hours are long, the rewards high, but for some the price is too dear.

In research institutions, publication plays a major part in advancement. It is very taxing as you begin your career to prepare articles for the better journals and at the same time prepare your first set of lectures. Just last week, a young assistant professor was describing her first year as a teacher; she found teaching three courses inordinately difficult. An economist's phrase probably describes it best—this is a period when one is building capital. The energy that you put into getting your lecture notes in first-class shape is worth it. You will be drawing on them for some time; it is a capital investment which will pay high dividends. At the same time you must be getting your research underway and turning your thesis into your first book. Some of the world's best work has been accomplished under pressure—didn't Handel write the *Messiah* in under a month?

Some people feel that the promotions are given to those who befriend the authorities. There is no denying that some of this exists. However, as I have watched academic appointments being made for years, it is merit that is rewarded, more than in most forms of human endeavor. One can remember a few cases where the promotion was based on promise rather than on proof of ability. But if your list of publications is slight, don't count on a promotion, even if you are considered the department's best teacher. Teaching helps, but it is not sufficient.

At Harvard, tenure is granted by a very thorough review system, called the Ad Hoc process. As a matter of fact, at times it seems so laborious that good candidates can be lost. It begins with the department chair, who requests permission from the Dean of the Faculty for the privilege of conducting a search for a senior appointment. The request is generally granted because the department has a space according to the Groustein formula, which allocates tenured slots to each department on a replacement schedule. At the moment many departments have openings that need to be filled. A list of the leading scholars around the world in this field, actually specialties within the field, is compiled. If there is an inside candidate, his or her name is added to the list. This list is circulated to other leading figures in the field for ranking. The central question is "Who will in the next 20 years make the greatest contribution to the field?" An Ad Hoc committee is then chosen to evaluate the top-ranked candidate. The Ad Hoc committee consists of two departmental members, two from a related field, two from other universities, and the dean of the faculty, with the president as the chair. All of the scholarly work is thoroughly reviewed; departmental letters are invited from all senior members of the department, and these are considered along with documentation from other universities. The committee then advises the president, who, in his wisdom, ultimately makes all tenure decisions.

Harvard grew from a small college on the banks of the Charles to a major university through the bold strokes of President Charles William Eliot, who gave the university his brilliant leadership for 40 years. One major innovation that Eliot made followed the recommendation of a professor, George Ticknor, who, upon returning from a sabbatical in Germany, advocated the establishment of departments. The departmental structure was instrumental in raising the level of scholarship in America, for then judgments about faculty appointments were not based primarily on service to the community but on research and scholarship as well; these qualities were judged by faculty knowledgeable in the discipline. In fact, in honor of the growth in scholarship, the portrait of Theodore Richards, who was awarded the Nobel Prize in 1904, hangs in the Harvard faculty room.

Under President Derek Bok, a requirement was instituted that for every Ad Hoc candidate, the level of teaching effectiveness as well as research must be documented. It is difficult to make the case that the increase in the quality of teaching has improved at Harvard solely because of this requirement, for it is only one of several recent efforts to improve teaching that have been made. There is, on the other hand, no evidence that this effort has reduced the quality of research at the institution, which still does and most likely always will give the greater accolades to research than teaching. One is tempted, however, to cite by name those members of the faculty who excel in both research and teaching. For them, the university reserves its highest attributions.

How does one achieve such lofty goals? It is appropriate to begin with research. Many approaches are fruitful. For example, some people believe that tunnel vision is important, knowing more and more about your chosen topic until, even though only in a limited domain, one is acknowledged as the ultimate expert. This can indeed be effective and a satisfying approach. Another alternative is to bring a breadth of scholarship to one's research. Often exciting developments have resulted from the cross-fertilization of fields. More than ever, virtually all research is incorporating ideas from an international perspective.

Some people are loners; others can think only when there is a crowd of research assistants around them. Some work at night, others early in the morning. The flexibility of the academic schedule requires a personal discipline that some people find difficult to achieve. We all know too many whose great book has not been written and never will be. After a while self-defeating behaviors begin to take over, and people understandably get defensive about their lack of progress. Should this begin to happen to you, take active steps to correct it. Forcing oneself into a routine, doing research and writing at the same time in the same place every day is helpful for many. Force yourself to write so many pages each day before you stop. George Bernard Shaw describes his own progress in just these terms; during his early years he wrote ten pages of foolscap a day. He would even stop in the middle of a sentence when he came to the end of the last page. Many a serious scholar advocates writing whether you feel it is good or bad, whether you feel under the weather or buoyant. When you reread those pages, you will find that the bad is not as poor as you thought; unfortunately, neither does your best writing seem as brilliant. There are some excellent discussions of research style; read several. They might help you develop your own.

Credo 2

Keep yourself professionally well informed. Sometimes one becomes so engaged in one's own research that one doesn't realize that the field has leapfrogged your efforts. There is nothing more sad than watching a once-gifted colleague become more and more out of touch with the field and grasp the aging lecture notes more furtively. One of my brilliant colleagues, as he neared seventy, simply refused to update his lectures. When students criticized his course, he simply refused to teach it any more, offering instead only a small graduate seminar. However, another colleague, admittedly a bit of an insomniac, reads a book a day. He is a model for all of us.

The competition for first-rate scholars is already substantial and will grow. Bill Bowen has predicted that the number of new professors needed during the next decade is very substantial. The faculty members who were part of the great expansion that took place in the fifties and sixties are now at the age of retirement; these positions will be filled with the new hires. The only question is whether they will be newly minted Ph.D.s or whether they come from a roster of experienced teachers whose career trajectories were broken because of the absence of tenure openings during the eighties. Should you fall into the latter category, if you have had a series of teaching positions of a year or two or three and need to get back on track to be competitive for tenure at a research university, then it is important for you to update your dossier with a new book or major research effort. The Bunting Institute is one of the places that has provided just such opportunities for women. One of their emphases has been on those whose careers have been interrupted by families. Some new research, a new book, several new articles have given a number of women a career boost.

Credo 3

Book number two must follow within 3 to 5 years. You cannot afford to be known as the person that used every idea you had in your first book. Incidentally, there are some rules of thumb about the value of articles; many people feel that seven articles in refereed journals equal one book. There must be a significant amount of output, but it is the quality of the scholarship which influences the field and is rewarded by the system.

In a recent discussion with a chairman of a leading chemistry department, I was told that there was a bidding war for the four top newly minted Ph.D.s in organic chemistry last year, not for salary but for the amount to be allocated to laboratory costs. The bidding was running, when I last heard, at nearly $500,000. At Harvard, the lab equipment is in place when a new assistant professor of chemistry arrives, and his or her teaching load is kept light the first year so that serious research can be gotten underway at the very beginning of a professional career. Even with this support, it is difficult to become one of the world's greatest chemists in seven years—when tenure decisions are made.

Stephen J. Gould has stated it clearly: The tenure decision at Harvard will always be made on the quality of the research. It is difficult to imagine any major research university not retaining research as its first priority in the appointment process. On the other hand, it does seem that serving the community is getting more recognition these days. Teaching, supervising graduate students, raising research money, being a substantial contributor to committee work are all important. Especially, teaching is viewed with increasing favor. The reasons are several. Students are increasingly demanding better instruction, and, frankly, they are getting. it. The nostalgic image of a student sitting on one end of a log with Mark Hopkins on the other has always been one of the myths of higher education. Those opportunities do exist for students, though not because institutional structures typically create them—they are very expensive—but seldom does any student ask for that level of interpersonal interaction with faculty. When students do, it is surprisingly often granted.

If students, in general, seek better instruction, the faculty will deliver, and the administration will tend to place greater value on the teaching process. Student course evaluations, which call to everyone's attention the quality of instruction which faculty members provide, bring increasing recognition to teaching.

Credo 4

Become the best teacher you can. Over the several years that I have served with the Harvard-Danforth Center for Teaching and Learning, it became increasingly evident to me that all faculty members should analyze their teaching methods, styles, and content. Many of Harvard's most famous scholars have also been the institution's best teachers. Famous names like Agassiz, Emerson, James, and Kittridge brought stimulating classes to thousands of Harvard students.

What could be more satisfying than to be a teacher, to be one of those chosen to transmit the thought, knowledge, and culture of one's generation to the next? To create a new generation of thinkers who will build on the very best of one's ideas, to do it well, is one of life's finest achievements.

There are other reasons why values other than research are becoming more important in the appointment process. It is increasingly difficult to recruit faculty of great stature by simply issuing an invitation. Twenty years ago there were only 10 or 15 institutions that actively recruited the great scholarly minds; that number has now grown to 100 universities. Why should a distinguished historian or physicist want to uproot his or her family and pay for expensive housing changes simply to be with colleagues with whom he or she can now so easily communicate by fax or electronic mail? With two-career families, the task of finding the spouse a comparable position exacerbates the problem, especially if both are academicians and teach in the same discipline.

A third reason is that institutions would like to feel that faculty owe them some loyalty; the loyalty should not simply belong to the discipline. Are you a psychologist who could as easily be at Berkeley, Rice, or Chicago, or do you feel you are a professor at Berkeley who happens to be a psychologist? When the going gets tough, will you roll up your sleeves and help solve the problem or will you accept another position, where you are not distracted from your "work"?

Credo 5

Find a mentor, preferably several. Seldom are individuals so gifted in their research, writing, or teaching that they can rely on their own judgment alone. Colleagues, research assistants, postdocs can provide useful sounding boards for ideas and arguments. In some fields at some universities, it is assumed that one needs a sponsor to advance through the departmental steps. Seldom are departments dominated by such an autocrat; if you happen to find yourself in such a situation, be vociferous in your complaints and find another position.

A final note: the research university is one of the great institutional creations of the century. It is an honor to be part of an organization which encourages freedom of thought, rewards its participants generously, protects its scholars from inappropriate harassment, gives dignity to the life of the mind, and trains others to follow the high road. This is an institution that we want to be part of and, in turn, to which we want to contribute.

Note

1. There are, of course, some gifted individuals who receive tenure through other routes. One at Harvard who heard a different drummer was David Riesman, whose seminal work, *The Lonely Crowd*, coauthored with Nathan Glazer and Reuel Denney, gave him national recognition. Like his initial work, his later contributions have been stellar.

Meeting Expectations for Research, Teaching, and Service at the Comprehensive Public University: The Dominance of the Discipline

Kenneth E. Andersen

Exciting but daunting challenges confront the new faculty member at a major comprehensive university with its emphasis on research and scholarly contributions. Demands for early, demonstrable achievements of high quality with promise of a national reputation in the discipline face a new faculty member from first reading of the job listing through the selection process and, most notably, during the six-year period in which a recommendation for tenure must be approved or a terminal contract issued. New faculty at Illinois have already been tested in graduate or postdoctoral programs or prior positions and demonstrated a high probability of success in an institution of this type.

The department, college, and campus want the new faculty member to gain tenure. In providing start-up funds and continuing support for scholarly and creative work, including a major research library, modest teaching loads as compared to many institutions, support for travel, and a relatively consistent stream of evaluation, untenured faculty receive major investments of funds, time of colleagues, and support of various kinds. When comparative decisions are made about resources, untenured faculty are often given an edge. Yes, the standards for promotion and tenure are high. Recognized, high-quality scholarly contributions to the discipline are required. Solid, even excellent, teaching and service are not sufficient. Indeed, the level of recognized disciplinary impact demanded in order to be tenured has reached a point at which there is increasing concern about the demands placed upon the individual. There is growing agreement within the academy and among the public that quality of and commit-ment to teaching must receive greater attention. This demand adds to rather than replaces the demand for research productivity and scholarly and creative activities.

This essay examines the challenges posed to untenured faculty at a comprehensive public university. While reflecting the specifics of a par-ticular campus, the expectations are those of a class of public universities recognized nationally as centers of research and scholarship. Following an overview of the institution, the essay characterizes the years leading to a decision on tenure, summarizes the tenure decision process, and con-cludes with a brief overview of posttenure years.

The Institution

As a comprehensive public university, the campus offers a startling range of 145 undergraduate programs of study and graduate and professional degrees in 150 fields. The University of Illinois at Urbana-Champaign, a land-grant institution, stands among the top dozen—the top five public—universities nationally in rankings of graduate programs, a measure of the quality of the research, scholarship, and creative activities of its faculty. The campus has the third-largest collection among academic libraries nationally. The staff includes more than 2,700 faculty, 2,500 graduate assistants, 2,000 professional and administrative staff, and 5,300 sup-port staff. The enrollment is approximately 35,000, including 9,000 gradu-ate and professional students. Undergraduates have strong academic records: 25 percent of the freshmen rank in the 98th percentile nation-ally on the ACT or SAT; two thirds graduated in the top 10 percent of their high school class.

The campus budget totals over $705 million, with the state providing $258.7 million, federal appropriations $16.2 million, contracts and grants $164.9 million, institutional funds, including indirect costs recovered from contracts, $50.5 million, student tuition and fees $75.3 million, and stu-dent aid and auxiliary enterprises $17.6 million. The percentage of the budget derived from the state has declined for several years. Two decades of tight state budgets have constrained everything: salaries, operating funds, the library, and undergraduate education reforms. External funds, normally restricted, are the major source for the research enterprise.

A campus of this size is highly decentralized. Decisions about hiring, course offerings, curriculum, admission of graduate students, and pro-gram emphasis are made at the departmental level and then reviewed through a succession of levels. Once funds are assigned, budgets are a unit responsibility.

The publicly stated goal of this university is one shared by several comparable institutions, i.e., to become the best public university in the nation. As a public institution, resources are tied to state revenues and the priority accorded to education. Given limited resources, the campus pursues a strategy of supporting the highest-quality units, strengthening units with promise of achieving greater disciplinary stature, and maintaining or reducing support for units of lesser quality or ones less central to its mission. Good ideas inevitably outrun resources. Given the anticipated limits of future state support, the resistance of the federal government to expanding resources going to higher education, and the resistance to tax increases, the institution will continue to refine its strategy of maximizing quality.

In recent years the campus has made major commitments to greater recognition of the importance of teaching, enhancement of undergraduate education, a revitalized general education program, increased enrollment of minority students, increased employment of minority faculty, and provision for greater assurance of success for minority students and faculty. The campus is seeking increased ties to business and industry and fostering faculty entrepreneurship. The coming decade promises a major turnover in faculty with a large number of retirements requiring replacement of a high proportion of the faculty and adding faculty in areas of growing enrollment. Several studies suggest shortages of faculty, which already exist in some areas, will be a major problem for most disciplines in the next decade.

Thus, younger faculty will find themselves in an established institution which is facing a number of resource limitations, one seeking to develop new directions and new means of obtaining resources while building on and preserving its strengths, one in which the professoriate is undergoing significant changes as long-established senior faculty are replaced with new faculty members. Standards for promotion and tenure, steadily rising for the past fifteen years, will continue to be quite demanding in terms of research productivity, quality of creative activity, and accountability for teaching. And they will find themselves at a worldclass university committed to remaining one, with outstanding colleagues in every field and an astonishing array of available cultural, scholarly, and scientific resources. It is an exciting arena in which to work.

Locating a Position and Getting Started

New faculty at a major research university usually find the demands placed upon them to be similar to those placed upon their dissertation adviser. The emphasis is upon working at the cutting edge of the discipline in a highly specialized area. In a sense there will be less adjustment in habit patterns than if the individual had chosen a position at a liberal arts college or one with less emphasis upon research. Applicants are committing themselves to a level of scholarship and research productivity sufficient to develop a national reputation in the discipline. Granted, not all achieve that standard, but it is the norm against which individuals measure themselves and their colleagues.

Applicants use the on-campus interview to obtain an understanding of the expectations they must meet. Many units provide detailed guidelines relative to weighting of various elements in tenure decisions. For example, creative arts units may provide indices for the measurement of quality relative to public exhibitions of art, the role of external evaluations, expectations in terms of rate of performance or production, participation in professional activities, and service to the unit and to the profession. Discussions with younger faculty reveal their perceptions of the climate in the unit, the support given to younger faculty, the "real" standards for promotion and tenure. Other important questions focus on the normal teaching load, the basis for adjustments of that load, availability of research assistants, secretarial support, etc. Individuals needing extensive support in terms of equipment and laboratory facilities investigate support to be provided directly as well as availability of external sources. More items are negotiable before an offer is accepted than afterwards.

Getting a good start is essential. Quality teaching demands attention and effort. Because the same or similar teaching schedule often holds for a few years, preparation time invested initially can be used as a reserve in the future when research activities and departmental responsibilities consume more time. Early recognition as a good teacher by colleagues and students is very helpful in building a record for tenure. If problems are detected through student evaluations or feedback from colleagues, there is an opportunity to make adjustments, restructure courses, and work with colleagues and mentors to improve teaching. Although excellent teaching alone will not lead to tenure, it is a major asset.

The nature of the discipline determines the speed with which the individual can move forward on a program of research. If extensive equipment and facilities are needed, the candidate must develop grant applications and acquire equipment and staff to get the lab up and running. The faculty member may continue to publish with the dissertation adviser or previous research team, but the individual must develop a research program which is independent of the dissertation adviser and former colleagues or be perceived as a leader of the research enterprise. Individuals hired by their own graduate department often find that developing an independent research program is difficult because graduate advisers or others may be alienated by moves toward independent scholarship, and external referees may not perceive the person as having established an independent research program.

The first year should be a reality check. Newcomers should watch the promotion and evaluation process, observing who is promoted and why. Understandings as to the demands of the position need to be validated. A heavy load of service responsibilities or an overload of teaching responsibilities is to be avoided because those who fulfill urgently needed functions are often denigrated for not having the right priorities when tenure decisions are made.

But the first year also involves the excitement of having full responsibility for one's own classes, teaching advanced courses in one's specialty, working with graduate students, getting to know colleagues, exploring the campus, and getting settled in a new community and environment. And after the grind of graduate school, some time to enjoy a degree of freedom is warranted. But a tenurable record must be built.

Building the Tenurable Record

As noted, tenure requires evidence that the individual's teaching, research, and service are leading to a national reputation within the discipline. In a sense, members of the discipline are as much, or more, one's colleagues as others in a large department or sister department on campus.

The importance of teaching performance in tenure decisions is growing. Student and peer evaluations of teaching performance are required in promotion papers. Reviewers raise questions when teaching is rated below the average of the campus or unit. Because teaching is an activity not easily evaluated by external reviewers (unlike scholarly and some service contributions), judgments internal to the department and campus are important. Strong teaching evaluations can overcome some limitations in research productivity, providing the existing research is of good quality. Further, strong teaching attracts students, particularly the very good graduate students from whom one learns as one teaches.

Service, unless required by the nature of the position, is given less weight in the tenure decision. Many reviewers believe service, particularly to the campus or college, should normally be deferred until tenured. A limited amount of service to the unit should be accepted and discharged effectively. Service to the discipline directly tied to scholarship such as serving on editorial boards or review panels, is desirable, but service should not interfere with one's own scholarship and publication.

Significant research and scholarly or creative activity are demanded of every Illinois faculty member. Quality is normally assessed through judgments of publication outlet, refereed or invited; impact upon other researchers in the same specialty; and specific comparisons vis-a-vis other researchers in the same area. External referees are used to make these assessments. In these assessments, the discipline plays a powerful role in determining the template used. Creative efforts may be evaluated in terms of prizes won, quality of museums or exhibitions, inclusion of work in published books or other outlets, critical commentary, success in getting grants and commissions. In some humanistic disciplines, a scholarly book, not a textbook, published by a scholarly press with favorable reviews is the standard. In philosophy, a relatively few published papers and pages of high quality are adequate. In the social sciences, a series of articles related to one or two major research themes is required.

Untenured faculty have resources available in their colleagues. Many are interested in coauthoring articles and undertaking joint research. More senior colleagues advise on such issues as departmental standards and normal progress. A mentor, a wise counselor, may be needed to interpret the interstices of the tenure process. Some department heads are quite helpful in guiding junior colleagues; others are indifferent or resist such activity. Annual evaluations of merit, the basis for salary increments, may be shared with the faculty member. If not, questions can be raised. The university requires a formal letter of evaluation addressing the issue of progress toward a tenurable record, indicating strengths and weaknesses in the third year of the probationary period.

Some departments are quite responsible about counseling the faculty member at risk in the tenure process. Often they assist in locating another position when it becomes clear that a tenurable record is not developing. Occasionally, a unit exploits faculty, making use of their teaching or service skills, knowing a tenurable record is not being developed. The faculty member may receive what is perceived as an unfair, abrupt notification of a terminal contract.

Decisions not to promote made at the departmental level are essentially irreversible on appeal, whether within or beyond the campus. Public efforts to fight the termination tend to jeopardize future employment at an appropriate institution. The discipline (the department) is dominant. If the research and teaching record does not satisfy the disciplinary unit or if the external letters of reference are not strong and essentially unanimous in praising the research, tenure is denied. If the unit is satisfied, the test becomes whether other reviewers are convinced of the strength of the case: "Is the argument presented in the promotion papers convincing?"

The Promotion Process

The actual promotion process from its inception to formal notice of promotion takes an academic, sometimes a calendar, year. By early fall the departmental review begins. Departmental bylaws usually prescribe the process and the committee(s) involved in consideration for tenure. Initial reviews may be conducted by the full professors, the tenured faculty, a standing or special committee. A complete curriculum vita listing courses taught, theses directed, publications, grants received, service responsibilities, convention papers, invited lectures, and seminars is examined as well as student and peer teaching assessments. External offers received often are a factor.

Following a favorable preliminary review as a potential candidate for promotion, or, rarely, as part of that initial review, letters are solicited from external disciplinary referees. Referees are not to be dissertation advisers, coauthors, or persons who have worked closely with the candidate. A portion of the external evaluators may be suggested by the faculty member, but others must be selected by the department. Copies of all letters received, favorable and unfavorable, and sample letters soliciting the evaluations must be included in the promotion papers as well as a brief description of the referees' academic qualifications. Usually the external reviews complete the file, and a final determination is made. A negative recommendation means a terminal contract for a person in the sixth year of employment. If an individual appears not likely to be recommended for tenure in the sixth year, the department may still issue a terminal contract or open discussion with the individual about his future. There is no guarantee of six years of employment.

If the recommendation is favorable, one person, often the head, normally prepares the promotion papers. Skillful preparation of promotion papers is an important factor in the success of problematic cases because the papers become the argument for promotion in the remaining stages of review. The candidate reviews the factual material for accuracy, but evaluations by the external referees, the department, and department head are confidential to the degree permitted by law. Committee votes at every level are included in the promotion papers.

Tenure recommendations are next reviewed by the college. In accordance with college bylaws, the promotion is reviewed by a faculty committee. Although procedures vary, if the promotion is questioned, additional information and, often, discussion with a unit representative are sought as part of the review process or any appeal of a negative decision. The dean typically accepts the committee's recommendation.

Colleges forward recommendations to the office of the vice chancellor for academic affairs. Recommendations are reviewed by the campus promotion and tenure committee (faculty appointed by the vice chancellor), the dean of the graduate college (who is also the vice chancellor for research), and staff members of the two vice chancellors. The campus committee will question a number of tenure recommendations, and additional information will be solicited. The vice chancellor for academic affairs makes the final determination. Some colleges typically have all recommendations for promotion accepted; others do not. Appeals of negative decisions are not uncommon, and either the original faculty committee or a new, smaller committee is appointed to advise the vice chancellor. Although campus recommendations are reviewed by the vice president for academic affairs and become effective upon approval by the board of trustees acting on the president's recommendation, the vice chancellor's decision is essentially final.

This extensive process is designed to assure the quality of the faculty and reasonably comparable standards by assessing the degree to which a convincing argument for a developing national reputation for contributions to knowledge within a discipline is made. Faculty and key administrators give extensive time and energy to the process and guard zealously their role in determining who will become a tenured colleague.

The Tenured Faculty Member

The granting of tenure marks the end of the preliminary stage of a career often lasting 30 to 40 or more years. Granting tenure commits institutional resources that can total millions of dollars in salary and support. The balance among teaching, research, and service will vary over time, but faculty are expected to remain active researchers or creative artists. Tenured faculty are free to undertake projects with greater risk of failure and long payoff periods and expected to devote more time to governance and service activities.

Not all achieve the ideal to the fullest measure. If they did, we would raise the goal to a higher level. However, those who fall significantly below the standard for the unit and the discipline will suffer in terms of salary, prestige, and research support and be denied promotion to full professor. Outside offers come to those with strong disciplinary reputations.

Within limits, external offers are met with competitive counteroffers for strong faculty. Salaries in universities of this type essentially have no cap and there is always competition for new space, laboratory facilities, and additional graduate students. The ideal of the contributing researcher and teacher-scholar remains the model; activities and individuals fitting the model are supported.

Summary

With the comprehensive public university's commitment to research and transmission of knowledge to others, the impact of the individual on her or his discipline is the key to the respect and authority that person commands across the campus. Quality instruction, drawing upon the best of current research and scholarship, will be respected. A few will gain recognition for the quality of their contribution rendered in service and administrative roles. However, achievement in research and scholarly endeavor, including work in the creative and performing arts, remains the *sine qua non* of the ideal faculty member's career at Illinois.

Although this essay stresses the size of the hurdles, it is important to remember that faculty at Illinois have tremendous institutional support in the library, laboratories, equipment and staff provided and in one's colleagues. Further, the campus community provides an astonishing array of outstanding artistic performances, often by world-renowned faculty colleagues and lectures by visiting and local scholars working at the cutting edge of almost every domain of knowledge. It offers interaction with top graduate students of almost every nationality and superb undergraduate students. This mix and their own intellectual talents insure that most tenure-track faculty become tenured members of the professoriate, spending some or all of their careers at the university.

Teaching at a Small Liberal Arts College

Anthony S. Abbott

The pleasures and rewards of teaching at a small liberal arts college can be enormous, but you will not experience those pleasures and rewards unless you understand what the institution expects of the young teacher and possess the particular skills necessary for success at such an institution. I have taught at Davidson College, a small liberal arts institution in North Carolina, for 25 years. I have interviewed hundreds of candidates for jobs at Davidson; I have seen many young professors come and go, and I believe that almost every unhappy situation stems from the failure of the candidate and the institution to address these two requirements honestly and realistically.

Small liberal arts colleges are deep wells. They expect scholarly achievement, excellent classroom teaching, loyalty to and love of the institution, good counseling skills, energy, imagination, collegiality, understanding of the values of the college and community, patience, hard work, personality, and tact. This may sound like a list of the characteristics of superman or superwoman, but it is not presented entirely in jest. Versatility is the keynote of what small liberal arts colleges expect. The more things you can do, the more they will love you. The more things you can do well, the more they will honor you.

Teaching

Let's begin with the single most important factor: *You must be an excellent classroom teacher.* The small liberal arts college has one major product to sell: small classes taught by excellent teachers. Don't go to the big universities, admissions officers will say, where you will have 200 people in your introductory economics course, or you will be taught calculus or composition by graduate students. At our college, they will say, full professors share in the teaching of lower-level courses. You will have only 15 students in writing courses and no more than 25 or 30 in your other classes. You will be a somebody. You will count.

If the student is to be a somebody, then the teacher must have the ability to make her feel like one. There is no place to hide a bad teacher at a small liberal arts college. Many departments have only four or five faculty members, and each faculty member must teach his share of the department's courses. One bad teacher can ruin a department's reputation and send students scurrying to other majors and even to other schools.

What do students expect? First, they expect competence in the field, and although they do not always know specifically how to measure competence, they sense it. They sense it by the way a teacher talks, by style, by assurance, and by comparisons with other teachers. If six different instructors are teaching composition, you can bet that the students will be comparing notes. Second, they expect you to be interesting. A frequent student complaint about teachers is that they are boring. Teaching undergraduates is not like teaching graduate students; they do not come already motivated to study. Often the single most important thing an undergraduate teacher can do is to arouse student interest in a field to which the student has not yet been exposed. The successful teacher at the liberal arts college must interest nonmajors as well as majors and must frequently have the ability to turn students around who did not like a particular subject in high school.

Students also place a high premium on fairness. Most colleges permit students to evaluate their professors at the end of courses and use those evaluations as part of the salary and promotion procedure. Some faculty members resent those evaluations, dismissing them as popularity polls, but it is not the easy teachers who get the best evaluations. Frequently the most demanding teachers are most highly regarded by the students. The crucial issue is fairness. Does the teacher give assignments of a reasonable length? Are tests and examinations based on material assigned? Does the professor grade according to standards the student can understand? Are there sufficient written comments on papers and tests for the student to know why she received a particular grade? Do professors get written work back to students before they assign another piece of work? These are all elements of what the student would call fairness.

Another crucial factor is the teacher's ability both to lecture and to lead discussions. The nature of the small liberal arts college is such that a high premium is placed on class size, and professors who lecture day after day when they could be engaging the students in the discussion of texts are not likely to appeal to many students unless they are brilliant lecturers. Even in such unusual cases the student can still argue, "I would have gone to a big university if I just wanted to hear lectures."

Finally, there is the whole issue of personality. Most of the great teachers have been characters, widely remembered by generations of alumni for particular habits, traits, gestures, and statements that set them apart from their fellows. Some have been quiet and intense, others flamboyant and theatrical. I once had a math teacher who taught us the Pythagorean Theorem standing on his head so that we would never forget it and another teacher who drew a line with a piece of chalk all the way around the room to illustrate the concept of infinity. It is not these particular actions that made such men and women great teachers but an intense love both for their subjects and their students that allowed them to become completely uninhibited in the classroom, so driven were they by their tasks. Students who sense their teachers' love for their subjects and their willingness to be themselves in their teaching of those subjects work harder and with more enthusiasm.

Scholarship

The small liberal arts college has traditionally been the domain of the memorable teacher. Teaching has always come first, and only in recent years has the pressure to publish affected teachers at many of these institutions. Scholarship has historically had an ambiguous role at most liberal arts colleges, playing a secondary position not only to teaching but also frequently to contributions to college and community life. The outstanding teacher who was also a valuable committee member and an elder in the local church could get by without publishing many articles. But that seems to have changed, especially at high-prestige institutions like Williams, Amherst, Carleton, Swarthmore, Davidson, and Wesleyan. One reason for the change is the competition between the small colleges and universities for the best young teachers coming out of graduate school. They have come to understand the important relationship between active scholarship and engaged and exciting teaching. They have begun to convince their job candidates that they do indeed care about scholarship and that they not only support it but encourage it through sabbatical leaves, summer grants, and lighter teaching loads than at their less-ambitious sister schools. Young teachers are afraid that they will have fewer opportunities to advance in their professions at small colleges, and these schools have had to allay their fears by exhibiting more interest in the scholarly attainments of their faculty members.

This change has created a good deal of tension among untenured faculty members at small colleges. Expected to be excellent teachers, published scholars, and enthusiastic contributors to the life of the college and community, they fear that lack of success in any one of these areas might cause them not to receive tenure. Thus, it is extremely important for anyone coming out of graduate school and seeking employment at a small liberal arts college to require from that school a very clear policy statement regarding the relative weights of teaching, scholarship, and service in promotion and tenure decisions and an equally clear statement about what kind of support for scholarship the college supplies. Knowledge of such policies will help you to decide whether the small liberal arts college is the right place for you or whether it is asking from you commitments that do not suit your personality or your priorities.

But all this sounds too negative. Despite the struggle for time between teaching and scholarship, life at the small liberal arts college is frequently less stressful than that at the university, because there is less competition within each department. You will more than likely be able to teach courses within your area of specialization much sooner than at a university, because you will not be waiting for three other people in your field to retire. The likelihood is that you will be the only person in your special area, and for that reason you will be able to teach both advanced courses and seminars, often from the beginning of your career. The tenure situation is likely to be better for the same reason. A small college is not going to hire three young medievalists and then keep only one. If you are hired in a tenure-track position, you will usually find your colleagues in the department very supportive, because they would not have hired you in the first place if they did not believe in your potential, and you are not really competing with any of them.

You can also enrich your teaching life by a closeness to colleagues in other departments. At small liberal arts colleges, humanists are likely to be in the same building, frequently on the same hall. Political scientists, economists, and sociologists may be intermingled. The result is a healthy dialogue among disciplines that leads to a respect for and interest in interdisciplinary studies. A colleague of mine in the German department has an office with an English professor on one side of him, a Spanish professor on the other, and an anthropologist across the hall. The idea of liberal learning is fostered by communication among departments, not just within them. This same colleague, when asked what he teaches, frequently replies, not "German" but "students." That is a good answer.

Community Life

Let me turn, now, to some of the expectations that I have been alluding to under the heading of contributions to college and community life. The most important of these is advising of students, both formal and informal. Small liberal arts colleges are clearly student centered. At most schools faculty members are asked to serve as faculty advisers to both freshmen and sophomores and to upperclass majors. New faculty members are normally given a year or two to acclimate themselves, but advising duties start early and continue on a regular basis throughout the teacher's career. Advising is not a perfunctory matter. Students want time to talk, and they expect their advisers to know the curriculum and the faculty, not only their own fields but other areas as well. Advisers need to be familiar with the college's academic regulations, with special programs, and with the particular needs of individual students.

The facet of college life that small liberal arts colleges speak of most proudly is faculty-student relations. Thus the time faculty members spend with students extends far beyond the formal advising program. Faculty members are expected to keep regular office hours, and most colleges have an open-door policy; that is, faculty members should be accessible to students and available for consultation daily. In fact, the heart of the matter is that faculty members should genuinely like students and enjoy being around them. If you see time spent with students as an unavoidable but necessary interruption of your research time, then you don't belong at a small liberal arts college.

Faculty members are also frequently expected to entertain students in their homes at least once or twice a semester. Having advisees or classes visit is quite common and can sometimes become a source of friction when such entertaining is inconvenient for spouses and other family members. But relationships between students and faculty families can also be a tremendous source of pleasure for both parties. Students away from home for the first time are anxious for substitute families, complete with children and dogs, and faculty members often find their favorite babysitters in their classes. For single faculty members, relationships with students can be more complex. Because dating students is prohibited, single faculty members must be careful to avoid compromising situations, but within those limitations great opportunities exist for single faculty who wish to make college students their substitute family, much as teachers at Deerfield, Andover, Exeter, and other boarding schools do. Single faculty members frequently make greater contributions to student life because they are single and do not have the family responsibilities of their married colleagues.

The next most important area of college life is committee work. It's almost everyone's least favorite thing to do, but small colleges have small faculties, and that means more committee assignments per capita than at universities. The classroom is the professor's personal domain, so the committee is where she will have the most contact with other faculty members, and often it is here that her reputation as an important contributing member of the college community is advanced or diminished.

Faculty members can injure their reputations with their colleagues by missing committee meetings, by performing committee assignments poorly, and by failing to develop cordial relations with other faculty members on committees. Positive contributions to the work of committees and genuine interest in the welfare of the college as shown through such work can be important elements in the young teacher's success.

Closely related to committee work is departmental responsibility. Since most departments at small liberal arts colleges have only six to ten members, young professors have the opportunity to make an immediate impact on their departments by volunteering to share in departmental tasks as different as curricular evaluation and entertaining students. Although departmental duties are obviously not as important as writing a paper for the next regional meeting, junior members of the department who attend department-sponsored lectures and programs and volunteer to share the task of entertaining visitors to the college are more likely to win affection from colleagues than their less-active colleagues. Some might disagree with me, but I also believe that young professors who play a vigorous part in curricular planning and revision are more likely to be successful than are their reticent counterparts. The important thing is to care—both about the work of the department and the lives of your colleagues.

Finally, there is the wider issue of the community, especially the church. Most of America's small liberal arts colleges were founded by religious denominations, and for hundreds of years many of them had specific religious tests for tenured faculty members. Nearly all such tests have disappeared now, but it is still important for candidates for jobs at church-related colleges to ask what the religious requirements are. Some still have them. In the vast majority of these colleges, the religious requirement has been replaced with a statement of general concern about the professor's life outside the classroom. Teachers are supposed to be supportive members of the community in which the college is situated. That community may be defined in narrow terms as the college and in wider terms as the town. In the former case, for example, professors may be asked to participate in activities like Parents' Weekend, Alumni Weekend, and various special college celebrations. In the latter case, faculty members may be urged to be part of local activities like service clubs, the YMCA, the PTA, the church of one's choice, and the town government.

Teaching at a small liberal arts college is much more than a job; it is a way of life, a vocation. Most of these colleges feel, with some justification, that the ideals of liberal education should be supported in the lives of faculty and staff members who are there to instruct students not only in academic skills but in qualities of mind and heart and in humane values. If you think that what you do outside the classroom is nobody's business but your own, or if you plan to be away every weekend and every other Thursday doing research, then you had better seek a job at a large university. If you want to become the leading figure in your field and fly to London and Paris for conferences on a regular basis, you will also want to look elsewhere. But if you genuinely love teaching and being with college students, if you care about the values of community life, if you want to affect the way people live and think after they graduate from college, if you want to think of yourself first and foremost as a human being working with other human beings, then the small liberal arts college may be for you the very best teaching environment you can find.

Building a Future at "the Premiere Teaching University" in the Midwest

Roy Weaver

The renewed emphasis on teaching as an institutional priority should come as no surprise. Such emphasis has evolved from the historical development of the institution. Ball State University was founded as a state institution in 1918.

The Ball brothers, from a prominent Muncie industrial family, donated the campus and land of Muncie Normal Institute to the state. Through state action, the institution became a branch campus of what is today Indiana State University in Terre Haute, called the Eastern Division of the Indiana State Normal School. Recognizing the contributions of the Ball family, in 1922 the board of trustees changed the title of the institution to Ball State Teachers College. Seven years later, the Indiana General Assembly approved separation of the two campuses and gave the title of Ball State Teachers College to the Muncie campus. In 1965 the general assembly once again renamed the institution, this time dropping "Teachers College" and adding "University."

Historically, the mission of the institution focused on the preparation of teachers. Over the past 25 years, the institution has sought to expand its mission. Today, the university offers more than 120 undergraduate, 80 masters, and 20 doctoral degrees through seven colleges: Applied Sciences and Technology; Architecture and Planning; Business; Communication, Information, and Media; Fine Arts; Sciences and Humanities; and Teachers College. Approximately 18,000 graduate and undergraduate students are enrolled. The university has a current operating budget of $209 million and employs approximately 840 full-time faculty. Rapid change and development have marked the institution's recent past.

Demands on Teacher Scholars at
"the Premiere Teaching University"
in the Midwest

The expectations at a "premiere teaching institution" are like those of most other schools. The balance among these expectations differs. At Ball State, as the new undergraduate catalog attests, "research and service serve the needs of teaching." Faculty are viewed as "teacher-scholars." Teaching and research are inseparable. Faculty may improve teaching by conducting ongoing research related to the field or discipline taught. And, by sharing this information with others—students and peers—they may broaden their understanding of research, extend interest in research, sharpen their development of an area of expertise, and perhaps most importantly, model the concept of teacher-scholar. Last in the list of priorities, particularly for new faculty, is service. Service related to improving teaching or enhancing research is of greatest importance.

In terms of expectations Ball State has positioned itself somewhere between the small private liberal arts college and the major flagship institution. As in the liberal arts college, smaller classes, closer student-faculty relationships, and teaching excellence are priorities. Similar to the flagship institution, significant research and the use of technology are prized. The emphasis is largely on applied research, and even the most respected researchers, who may hold distinguished professorships, are engaged in ongoing teaching responsibilities.

The move from a teachers college to a university has altered institutional values. Qualitative judgments about faculty performance may differ markedly in some areas compared to a little over a decade ago. For example, at one time it may have been possible to obtain tenure or to get promoted by being an average teacher, by doing some writing, and by providing significant service activity. The writing could have been thoughts and opinions published without peer review rather than systematic research accepted for publication through a juried process. The service could have been primarily related to university and community service, not directly tied to service to one's profession. Extensive service, some good teaching, and very little or no substantive research and writing will no longer suffice.

With this context of changing institutional values the most often-asked questions are: "How effective a teacher must I be?" "How much research and writing must I do?" "How much service must I perform?"

How Effective a Teacher Must I Be?

During the process of interviewing for a faculty position, interviewees are expected to make a presentation. More often than not, the presentation involves teaching a class. In addition, interviewees are expected to make a presentation before faculty in the department in which they will hold rank. Such presentations are critical to persons who aspire to work at a "premiere teaching university."

Teaching is expected from everyone, including deans of colleges. Even the vice president for academic affairs teaches. From an institutional perspective, administrators are expected to model effective teaching and to provide leadership in faculty development. Spending time at least one semester a year in the classroom keeps administrators more sensitive to the pressures on faculty to maintain a high level of teaching effectiveness and to the needs of students.

Most colleges in the university require student evaluations of faculty instruction. Some, such as the Teachers College, require each faculty member to evaluate each course taught each semester. Striving for excellence in teaching is the goal, as opposed to being "average." Accordingly, faculty must demonstrate a high level of teaching. Student evaluations of courses are one way that documentation can be provided.

In order for such evaluation to be credible, an objective process must be used. The type of instrument—criterion or norm referenced—is not critical. Some departments use a departmentally produced instrument. Others use instruments that not only have data normed on Ball State faculty but on faculty from across the country as well. How the data are collected, tabulated, and reported is critical. The faculty member having a course evaluated should not be involved in the aforementioned three stages. Data should be collected and tabulated by someone other than the faculty member, most often done through the auspices of the department chairperson. Data should be reported to the faculty once a course has ended and grades have been submitted. Throughout the process of course evaluation, the identity of students should be protected. Data reported may be used for administrative decisions, such as determining merit increases, making course assignments, determining promotability, but the primary purpose of course evaluation is to improve instruction.

Faculty are encouraged to provide multiple sources of data for illustrating teaching effectiveness. Peer observations, course improvement activities, and self-assessment provide additional methods of describing teaching effectiveness. Having the department chairperson or a faculty colleague conduct a preobservation, observation, and postobservation process on a continual basis can be a valuable way to inform others of teaching competence as well as an objective, defensible data collection method. Changing course requirements, refining objectives, selecting more current readings, integrating video and computer technology into class instruction are some of the ways to demonstrate improvement in teaching. Finally, faculty members' reflection and future plans regarding courses taught not only can be instructive but also can provide additional information about efforts to improve teaching.

How Much Research and Writing Must I Do?

It is impossible to obtain tenure or promotion without doing some important research and writing. The word "important" is key and may be defined in several ways. How much of a contribution will it make to the field of research? What kind of credibility from other experts in the field? What kind of readership will it attain? To what extent will it help build a line of personal research upon which the faculty member can develop a reputation for expertise? Although it is impossible to give a definitive answer to the "how much" question, most new faculty remain unsettled without some advice.

The type of research, access to subjects, number of sites needed, availability of needed library resources, and other factors will affect how many studies can be accomplished in a year. In addition, the research competence of the faculty members along with their ability to manage time in a new job will contribute to how much can be done. The workload will also have an effect.

In my opinion, most new faculty members should seek to publish at least two solid pieces of research a year. In the first year, when you are making the transition to university life, such a goal may not be possible. However, in each succeeding year, such a goal ought to be sought. The publications should appear in highly regarded, juried outlets. Most disciplines and fields of study publish reputational rankings of journals which may serve as a useful guide to the aspiring teacher-scholar. Over the seven-year probationary period, faculty should seek to publish at least one important book.

Presentations of research at meetings of professional organizations are useful as well. However, they are never as important as a publication. The same criteria for documenting the importance of published research hold for research presentations. How was the presentation selected? What is the status of the organization sponsoring the meeting? How important is the research to the field? How many requests for the paper were received?

Other qualitative measures can be applied. One valuable measure, although somewhat difficult to obtain, is the extent of citation of the work. How often the research is listed in the bibliography or references of other publications is influential data. The independent, anonymous review of faculty research by experts in the field provides another influential qualitative data source.

Other publications and presentations, for example, that focus on theory, descriptions of practices, opinions about policy, or reviews of books count as well. However, they do not count as much as research and presentations that have undergone the scrutiny of peers and made it into print in leading journals or onto the presentation stage at major national conferences. How other publications get into print and their credibility in the discipline or field of study are even more important than with research-based publications and presentations.

How Much Service Must I Perform?

Service may be thought of broadly in terms of service to one's profession and service to the university, including one's college and department. Among the expectations, this one is, in some ways, as important as the others. From the standpoint of becoming known in the department, college, and university, understanding how the institution functions, or of establishing a network of ties with peers in the state, region, nation, or abroad, service is vital to success. Choosing among the various service options and identifying the purposes of participation are key.

Volunteering on a limited basis to serve on departmental committees related to academic issues is wise. Serving on the departmental social committee is less defensible, although perhaps more "tasteful." Marching in commencement is a duty. Attending all department meetings is an obligation. Setting other personal priorities related to departmental service is a right.

Agreeing to serve on one university-wide committee and participating in one university-sponsored program offer ways to become known quickly throughout the institution and ways to become more readily informed about the institution's workings. For example, serving on a creative teaching grants committee, which may meet twice a year to review grant proposals, affords an opportunity to meet and to interact with faculty from other colleges. In the process, faculty can become more attuned to what proposals are most likely to be accepted, in the event they wish to submit a proposal the following year.

Agreeing to attend off-campus recruiting efforts for colleges is another attractive alternative. Once or twice a year faculty may spend 24 to 72 hours in other cities with faculty and administrators from other colleges talking with prospective students and their parents. Again, this volunteer effort provides a way for new faculty to become known and get to know others. Away from campus, faculty and administrators tend to be more open about their perceptions about the institution and how it works—a learning experience to be viewed with caution. The point here is that although university, college, and departmental service is necessary and most often valuable, what faculty choose to do and why they choose to do it must be carefully considered.

Service to the profession is more important than any other service. Holding an office in a professional organization, reviewing manuscripts for a journal, serving as an executive secretary for an association, editing a newsletter, or assisting in the planning of a conference are more valuable activities from a qualitative perspective than most other forms of service. These efforts are aimed at building a network of support related to personal development as a professional and are more likely to lead to opportunities to participate in research symposia, externally funded projects, and joint authorship of published articles.

Securing external funds may be related to any of the institution's expectations—teaching, research or service. The amount of funds secured is less important than what can be accomplished with them. "Buying out" assigned time to reduce the teaching load, obtaining clerical support, equipment, materials, and travel dollars are essential. It is the output of the grant, not the input, that relates to success. For the new faculty member, making certain the grant will provide support which will lead to research and publication is essential. Any lesser purpose is questionable.

Providing Support for Expectations

Faculty are hired with the expectation that they will succeed. Accordingly, the university provides an array of programs aimed at helping faculty with teaching, research, and service. The most important aid is the assignment of a mentor. Every new faculty member is assigned one to enable him or her to avoid obstacles that faculty historically have faced as they made the transition to higher education. Learning how to use on-line library reference retrieval, fax mail, interactive television technology, computer systems and software; quickly understanding the theory, research, and practice underlying a course that must be taught; choosing teaching strategies that will work most effectively in a particular class setting; learning how to write a grant and get it cleared through university channels; clarifying what it takes to get tenure and to get promoted—all are issues for which a mentor can provide valuable counsel.

Beyond mentorship, there are other institutional support mechanisms. Some are related to the improvement of teaching, including creative teaching grants, travel support, and faculty development programs. Others are aimed at supporting research, including faculty research grants, travel support, and technological support. And some are related to supporting service. Most often these take the form of clerical support, travel funds, and assigned load credit for a service activity. Most institutional support programs are competitive. Some are earmarked specifically for new faculty. And all seek refreshing, innovative, productive proposals—a possible advantage to enthusiastic new faculty.

Finding Success

Each fall at the opening all-university meeting, faculty are recognized for outstanding achievement. An attractive, expensive plaque and a cash award are given for outstanding performance as a faculty member, junior faculty member, faculty academic adviser, and researcher and for creative endeavor, faculty service, and administrative service. Although it is an expectation that each new faculty member should succeed, it is an institutional dream that each should become outstanding. It's not a dream that all can fulfill. But with a clearer understanding of institutional expectations, it's a dream to which all can aspire.

Role Expectations for the New and Not-So-New Professors at Grambling State University

Lamore J. Carter

Role expectations for new professors differ greatly among institutions, and they should because institutions differ so greatly in mission, clientele, composition, and setting. However, there is much that is common in the expectations of new faculty at all colleges and universities. After all, a teacher is a teacher; therefore, subject-field competency and professional decorum are basic expectations. Beyond these qualities, there are special qualities sought in new faculty at an historically black institution such as Grambling State University because there are special needs of the clientele as viewed by the students, the faculty and administration, the parents, and the local and distant community.

The Institution

Grambling State University is an historically black institution in a very small and almost all-black town in rural north Louisiana. The university is the dominant social, political, educational, and economic force for black citizens in the region. Its students, 95 percent of whom are black, come from thirty-plus states. Eighty-five percent of the students are supported in part by some kind of financial aid; a large majority of them are first-generation college students in their families. Better than seven of every ten entering freshmen demonstrate significant unpreparedness in reading, writing, or mathematics; therefore, they must take developmental courses. This mixture of students of various socioeconomic levels from rural areas, small towns, and very large cities is composed of tremendous latent talent which only "a Grambling" can draw out. Because of this institutional composition, the university's mission and objectives, the nature and dynamics of the surrounding community, and the university administration's view of how the elements and dynamics of social, economic, cultural, and political forces impact the lives of blacks in America, the role of a new teacher is deemed as very special at Grambling State University.

The historically black institution has been under persistent attack since the first such institutions were created, and the argument is heard from several sources each year that there is no place for historically black colleges and universities (HBCUs) in America because of changes in laws which guarantee black students' access to all institutions. The truth with which black college officials and other responsible citizens must deal is that the HBCU, numbering approximately 100, graduate 40 percent of blacks who complete their degrees from over 3,500 colleges in America. The evidence shows clearly that HBCUs have made the critical difference in the education of blacks in America. It is this background of information that compels HBCU administrators to define the role of new faculty in terms of qualification (by training and experience) to advance the cause of black people and to enhance the survival of HBCUs.

Many black students desire and seek a predominance of same-race teachers/counselors because, therein, they believe, is a better chance of having teachers who not only know and understand their background and its relationship to day-to-day behavior but who have lived them; therefore they can draw upon common experience to embellish teaching and personal counseling. It is one thing for a black student to think maybe his teachers understand and another to know they understand "where he is coming from" in teaching and counseling.

Being a Role Model

One of the most pressing needs in the black community today, whether in a home, school, or college community, is for role models for black women and men. The need is greater for black men than black women, but there is a dire need for models for both sexes.

Young black men seemingly bent on acquiring a college education and moving to leadership positions in the workplace and community are becoming an endangered species in America, a result of poverty among blacks, black-on-black crime, an unfair criminal justice system, and lack of good/strong black male models. There are more black men in prison than in college, a fact which dramatizes the growing problem of cultivating and maintaining the black male pursuit of higher education.

Black students need a closer, longer, and en-masse look at role models with whom they can easily identify. The HBCU provides this with its predominance of black faculty and staff and good selection of faculty of other races. As students express these preferences and needs, HBCU officials are obligated to use them as criteria in hiring new faculty. In light of this need, there is a special expectation of new faculty at GSU that they be of sterling character and that they be easily and frequently visible on campus modeling the behavior expected of young people being educated for making a significant contribution to America. The strong black family, bent on getting a good education for its children, has been a major strength through the years. The already fragile and still worsening situation of the black family in America portends almost unfathomable consequences for blacks in another generation. Cognizant of this phenomenon, black colleges expect special help from new faculty.

Teacher Expectations of Students

The importance of teacher expectations of students' performance has been cited consistently. Some of the best trained and most scholarly professors in America would do a poor job of teaching at such an HBCU as Grambling because they would lack the inclination and/or ability to communicate well and consistently the necessary high achievement expectations to black students. This fact is the rationale for a special role expectation of new faculty hired at Grambling State University. This role expectation of new faculty for HBCUs must address the need of an intervention strategy that focuses on faculty expectations of black students as reflected in teaching behavior.

The relationship between the university and the town of Grambling and its surrounding community is such that the activities of each impact the other significantly, and the town and community, including the families and homes of faculty and staff, represent extensions of the university in terms of learningful opportunities. In light of the relationship of the university and town/community, a new faculty member is expected to reside in the predominantly black community, participate in community affairs, and interact regularly with students, other faculty, and staff in community activities.

Another problem acknowledged by black college faculty and administrators is the persistent pattern of low scores by black students on standardized tests such as the ACT and SAT. One response to this problem at Grambling State University is more frequent testing as a part of teaching and other special activities and programs designed to prepare black students for better performance on standardized tests. This special attention to test-taking skills is stressed in orientation sessions with new teachers.

Because faculty and administrators of HBCUs recognize that university life should prepare students for life after college, there is not only great stress placed on racial tolerance but on an active and successful effort to achieve increased racial/ethnic diversification of faculty, staff, and students via recruitment.

Predominantly black institutions such as Grambling State University make extraordinary efforts to use faculty and students of other ethnic groups and countries to teach students about the world at large and to counteract the belief that the staff wants to have an all-black university. It is recognized that not every person of any ethnic group can function daily without display of prejudice toward some other individual or group. Grambling State University sets a role expectation that teachers strive to minimize such behavior.

Summary

A new teacher at Grambling State University is asked to assume a role that requires the following actions:

1. Learn the history and goals of the university so as to incorporate in his/her teaching such facts as are needed and appropriate to build student pride in and instill student loyalty to the institution.
2. Find out how to teach and how to relate to students in and out of class by solicited advice of at least two of the most respected members of the department.
3. Discuss with department heads the nature and dynamics of instructional evaluation and ask for class visitation during the first semester.
4. Demonstrate a sensitivity to the complex needs of students and a willingness to devote extra time and effort to help the many marginal students whose significant talents may never develop without the extraordinary sensitivity and efforts of some professors. This sensitivity should be based on a knowledge of and appreciation for the black experience in the United States of America.

5. Sell himself/herself as a sincere and competent member of the faculty, eager to learn how to fit comfortably into the university family.

6. Seek learningful and contributing committee work and volunteer sponsorship or other helpful affiliation with student groups.

7. Achieve a visible and significant involvement in social civic affairs of the community.

8. Avail himself or herself of opportunities for professional development . . . faculty development opportunities.

9. Demonstrate a willingness to share/consider new ideas and educational practices.

10. Find a special niche as part of his/her work . . . do a service which no one else is doing or is not doing nearly as effectively. (Example: tutor the Hispanic group or sponsor a picnic each year for honor students in the department or join the student advocacy program.)

There is another reason to identify special role expectations of new faculty at Grambling State University. Many of our entering freshmen, because of what they were told by recruiters, friends, or parents, come to Grambling expecting to find a faculty fully capable and willing to reach out to them and relate to them in and out of class in such a manner as to bring forth the students' maximum effort. The dimensions of this expected reaching out defy complete description but extend even beyond the expectations enumerated here.

Women's Education at Women's Colleges: Responsibilities and Challenges for New Faculty Members

Mary E. Kitterman

The calendar of professional obligations for new faculty members at Stephens College sends a clear message regarding the institution's expectations of these new instructors for new faculty orientation occurs several days in advance of the all-faculty Fall Conference. A variety of special sessions, planned by the faculty's elected advising committee members, serve as both a social and professional introduction to the college's philosophy of education, its historical mission, and the curriculum as well as a source of information concerning the critical policies and procedures which inform the faculty's work with our students.

As a small private college, of course, we stress the centrality of the classroom teaching/learning experience and expect that a new faculty member has chosen to join our community because she or he wishes to become part of an educational environment which values small classes and fosters creative faculty-student dialogue both inside and outside of classrooms. However, in addition to specifying these expectations regarding the importance of scholarly competence and student-centered teaching for our college, the new faculty orientation also both articulates and models further crucial issues which are to be found at the heart of our enterprise, issues specific to our role as one of the nation's oldest women's colleges.

New faculty members are certainly not surprised by our determination to facilitate a nonsexist environment which supports women's intellectual and emotional development, but they may realize for the first time the pervasive manner in which these concerns permeate our curricular design as well as our cocurricular activities. In addition, new faculty members learn that our focus on women's educational needs has fostered a long series of innovative courses and programs based on research about women's changing roles in our society.

For the purposes of this brief essay the ramifications of these expectations are outlined in the following pages.

The Role of Women's Colleges in American Higher Education

The special role women's colleges play in American higher education must be recognized and clearly articulated by all who participate in our collegiate community. In an article published in *The Chronicle of Higher Education* (July 5, 1990), Dr. Mary S. Hartman, Dean of Douglass College of Rutgers, the State University of New Jersey, clarifies the unique contributions of colleges such as Stephens or Douglass that "place women students at the center of their educational mission" (p. A40). Dr. Hartman summarizes the data on the achievements of the graduates of women's colleges as compared with the achievements of college educated women in coeducational institutions.

> Their graduates are twice as likely as female graduates of coeducational institutions to earn doctoral degrees; their alumnae made up 42 per cent of the women members of the last Congress; they graduated 15 of 50 leading corporate women cited in an article in *Business Week*, even though they accounted for only 5 per cent of all college-educated women in the relevant age group (p. A40).

In addition, this essay underscores the responsibility women's colleges must assume as ". . . the very places where women together can more readily envision and then create alternative perspectives and programs to build a more livable and whole world—for women and men alike" (p. A40). Such comments clarify the essential role women's colleges play in enriching and enhancing the diversity of educational opportunities available in our system of higher education. Dr. Patsy H. Sampson, President of Stephens College, summarized this view.

> Just as with large public universities, private research universities, and traditional liberal arts colleges, women's colleges are not for everyone. But they are a wonderful educational choice that helps students build a strong future (Sampson, spring 1990, p. 4).

Curricular Concerns

The curriculum at a women's college must both reflect and create the current scholarship by and about women. Women's studies scholarship must also inform the pedagogical discussions in which faculty members engage. Studies such as *Women's Ways of Knowing* (Belenky, Clinchy, Goldberger, & Tarule, 1986) and *Finding Herself: Pathways to Identity Development in Women* (Josselson, 1990) are to be read by faculty and students alike, and special courses must be designed to provide opportunities for rigorous consideration of issues vital to women who will assume the challenges inherent in the emerging gender roles of the twenty-first century. At Stephens, for example, new faculty members must not only be able to incorporate the scholarship by and about women and ethnic minorities in all general education courses but should also be willing to serve as a member of a 15-member interdisciplinary team of instructors who teach our core course, "Issues That Shape the Human Experience." This course, required of all first-year students, focuses on "issues of race, class and gender to develop an understanding of what binds us as a community and what divides us as human beings" (FST 150 Syllabus). Units of study include analysis of the concepts of " education," "the family," "the self," and various social concerns such as poverty and the environment. A collaborative teaching model, which includes students who serve as peer teachers, places emphasis on critical thinking, small-group discussion, and "writing to learn." Thus, our new faculty members are expected to be interested in and effective in teaching both general education courses and interdisciplinary courses in addition to being competent scholars in the more traditional disciplinary mode.

Campus Climate

The environment of the college, both in the classroom and in cocurricular settings, must not only be free of the debilitating effects of gender bias but must also be above reproach with regard to sexual harassment issues. In an environment created to foster and sustain women's self-esteem, abuse of power or violation of trust on the part of a faculty member is particularly onerous, as such behavior would betray the essential nature of a community dedicated to women's intellectual and emotional development. As Bowen and Schuster assert in their study, *American Professors* (1986):

> In presenting themselves to students they [faculty members] become living representatives of what their particular colleges or universities stand for. Whether

intended or not, the character they display represents the values the institution is setting before its students (p. 16).

Agents of Change

Finally, new faculty members who teach at a women's college are expected to serve as catalytic change agents in the larger educational arena that extends beyond our own institution. A work titled *Educating the Majority* (Pearson, Shavlik, & Touchton, 1989) is composed of an exciting series of essays which focus on women's education; in an introductory comment, the editors write

> Now that women students constitute a numerical majority of all students, however, it is time that their issues be addressed. It makes no sense to continue to design education environments and experiences without a thorough and ongoing analysis of women students. As educators, parents, and concerned citizens, we need to know who our women students are and how colleges and universities can foster their full development and prepare them for full participation in society (p. 15).

At Stephens, as one would expect, we believe that faculty members engaged in teaching at a women's college should assume a leadership role in the analysis and articulation of the curricular and professional questions germane to this understanding of women's educational needs.

These concerns, then, determine the unique perspective from which Stephens College reviews applicants for faculty positions. In addition, these concerns are integrated into the criteria by which we evaluate the effectiveness of our faculty members: teaching, advising, research, and service must clearly reflect the College's mission and create an intellectual and moral climate which facilitates critical thinking regarding women's potential and also enhances women's ability to make responsible choices regarding themselves and their significant participation in the life of our democratic society.

References

Belenky, M. F., Clinchy, B. M., Goldberger, N. R., & Tarule, J. M. (1986). *Women's ways of knowing: The development of self, voice, and mind.* New York: Basic Books.

Bowen, H. R., & Schuster, J. H. (1986). *American professors: A national resource imperiled.* New York: Oxford University Press.

Hartman, M. S. (1990, July 5). Point of view: Mills students provided eloquent testimony to the value of women's colleges, *The Chronicle of Higher Education,* p. A40.

Josselson, R. (1990). *Finding herself: Pathways to identity development in women.* San Francisco: Jossey-Bass.

Pearson, C. S., Shavlik, D. L., & Touchton, J. G. (1989). *Educating the majority: Women challenge tradition in higher education.* New York: Macmillan.

Sampson, P. H. (1990, Spring). Message from the president. *Stephens,* p. 4.

Expectations for New Professors at Fresno Pacific College: A Religiously Oriented Institution

Norman Rempel

In this essay, I will reflect expectations for faculty which are likely to be found in the more than 75 members of one organization of church-related institutions, the Christian College Coalition. The coalition characterizes its members as "Christ-centered liberal arts colleges." Members are located in 29 states and Canada.

No doubt it is hazardous to attempt to characterize all institutions in the coalition. Some are large (some even rival public counterparts); many are small, some *very* small. Some promote limited curricular emphases, while others attempt to meet broad curricular needs. Financial resources vary widely. Facilities range from meager to expansive. One may find governance styles from autocratic to consensual.

Although there are great variations among coalition members, mutual commitments produce a good deal of homogeneity. And the principal point at which all faculty in these member institutions unite is found in terms of what is called "faith commitment." Member colleges agree that individuals who join the collegium will express personal faith in Jesus Christ. Precisely what this is understood to mean may vary somewhat, but without this basic commitment, further exploration of a prospective faculty member's credentials will not take place. These colleges have pledged themselves to work within an educational framework in which allegiance to Jesus Christ and all that that entails is considered absolutely foundational.

Fresno Pacific College

Fresno Pacific College, Fresno, California, has been a member of the Coalition since 1981. Not atypical of a number of the coalition schools, Fresno Pacific began as a Bible institute with the primary intent of educating students for Christian ministry. In those early years, the student body and faculty came largely from within the churches of the sponsoring denomination, the relatively small Mennonite Brethren Conference. What has emerged today would probably not have been envisioned by the institution's founders. Today, the college continues to provide undergraduate majors in Biblical and Religious Studies and Contemporary Christian Ministries but has enlarged its curriculum to include many other traditional liberal arts majors. Additionally, the college is widely known for its leadership in teacher education, offering work leading to both preliminary and advanced credentials and a Master of Arts in Education with various emphases. The past two decades have seen the growth of a large in-service program for K–12 educators in the Central Valley. The college is known regionally as a relatively small, personable alternative to local public postsecondary institutions.

College Characteristics

Perhaps one of the best ways for prospective faculty members to understand what they will be entering when they join the faculty at this type of institution is to describe some of the characteristics and emphases at my own college.

Concern with Mission

Fresno Pacific College wants to be known as an institution which "does not seek to duplicate the types of education which are available in public institutions nor does the college pattern itself after a specific model of church-related higher education" (College catalog, p. 8). A carefully crafted mission statement, "The Fresno Pacific College Idea," was forged as the institution emerged as a liberal arts college. This document speaks of the college as "an integral part of the mission of the church . . . providing preparation for service to church and society through vocational and professional development." The college views itself as "an extension of the educational mission of the Mennonite Brethren Church . . . integrating Christian faith and the liberal arts with career development." The concept of the college as a community is a central concept in the "Idea." Faculty are encouraged to view themselves as those members of the community who "participate in church and society as role models in relating Christian faith to matters of thought and action."

The concern for the role of mission statements as a reflection of an ideal for the community is evidenced by the recent development of separate mission statements for the Graduate and In-Service Divisions. Lively discussions relating to mission are frequent. Why should we exist? What are we trying to accomplish? How are we distinctive, and how do we want to be viewed in relation to our competitors? Does our actual practice match the ideals set forth in our stated mission? All of these questions are continuing matters of concern for faculty and administrators.

Concern with Roots

Although the college seeks to be forward looking, not unnecessarily tied to the concerns and emphases of the past, what is important to keep from the founding vision is also continually under discussion. Recently, at an all-day faculty retreat, questions were raised: What in the Mennonite Brethren "story" is important to retain, to continue to emphasize? To what extent should new faculty be expected to understand and articulate those emphases at the time of hire? How can faculty who do not share personal roots in the denomination be expected to carry on a legacy which is not their own? Does it matter? And, if it is determined that it doesn't matter all that much, will not the college lose its collective soul?

Concern with Denominational Affiliation

Fresno Pacific is not only affiliated with a denomination but is sponsored by it. The denominational budget provides a small portion of annual revenues. Churches encourage their young people to attend the college, and the college is remembered in the prayers of its members. A number of the college board members must be chosen from the denomination, and the president answers to and seeks guidance from that board. As is often the case, the relationship between the churches and the college is not always an easy one. Within the denomination, characterizations such as "too liberal," "too conservative," "too progressive," or "too tied to the past" perennially surface. As the college grows larger and the faculty and administration more heterogeneous, inevitably such tensions increase. Administrators are concerned to act in a manner which will give proper due to the college's churchly relationships while not being unnecessarily restricted by that tie.

Concern with Prayer

Concern for the holistic development of each member of the college community evidences itself in various ways. The faculty and administration meet once each week to share devotional thoughts and prayer requests. The needs of students and others in the college community are shared publicly. Each one is encouraged to pray and support each other toward fulfilling shared commitments.

Concern with Community

Consistent emphasis is placed upon thinking and acting as a "community," where each person is important, where the needs and concerns of each one are shared. Faculty, staff, and students are encouraged to attend the biweekly "College Hour" together, often eat lunch together, and attend many of the same extracurricular activities together. Throughout college life, "community" is stressed.

Perhaps a noteworthy indicator of the desire of the college to promote a sense of community rather than competitiveness is the college's decision to forego the use of a traditional academic rank structure. All appointed members of the teaching faculty are designated as professors, and all participate as equals in the life and the governance of the faculty. Conversational use of first names is encouraged at all levels.

Basic Hiring Criteria

What does Fresno Pacific look for when seeking new faculty? The following are indicated in the Faculty Handbook as minimal criteria for prospective faculty members:

Academic

Candidates are normally expected to hold the highest degree available in their field. In most cases, this will be the doctorate. Candidates will need to show evidence of success in teaching or significant promise of such.

Christian Commitment

"Faculty candidates are expected to be in agreement with the College's Theological Orientation, to have a personal commitment to Jesus Christ as God, Savior and Lord, to be active in the life of the church and to live a life consistent with their commitment to the Lordship of Christ" (Faculty Handbook). *Important is the ability to integrate the doctrines and ethical teachings of the Christian faith with an academic discipline.*

Church Identity

In keeping with the College's denominational sponsorship, preference is given to those who are already identified with a Mennonite Brethren Church or are from the larger Believer's Church movement.

Prospective faculty are brought to campus for an intensive round of interviews. Candidates appear before the full faculty to present one's "pilgrimage," an account of one's personal history, academic qualifications, professional experience, and Christian commitment. Faculty are polled, and the resultant vote is a major factor in the decision to extend a contract.

Newly appointed teaching faculty are hired on probation for a period of six years. Informal evaluations are conducted each of the first two years. Formal evaluations are conducted in the third and sixth years. Although the college does not have a formal tenure track, faculty members issued a favorable sixth-year report may be granted what is called "continuing" status. To achieve this status, a terminal degree in the faculty member's teaching field is normally required.

Expectations of Faculty

Teaching

In terms of the traditional faculty expectations in higher education—teaching, research, and community service—Christian liberal arts colleges generally place the greatest stress on teaching. Even though the latter two emphases have been receiving increased attention recently, quality teaching still receives top priority. A special view of teaching is stressed.

Teaching is important because there is truth to be passed on. This orientation is seen as a natural consequence of the Christian view of God and His world. A great deal of attention is paid to the notion that "all truth is God's truth." This is not the view that all truth is, strictly speaking, "theological," nor that the Christian educator is somehow less fallible, but that all understandings that are correct ultimately find their correspondence in the mind of God. Because God is viewed as the Ultimate Source of all that is, and is the Ultimate Knower of all that is accurate about reality, the educator who sees reality as God does is "thinking God's thoughts after Him."

All of this has implications for how faculty members view their profession. To be an educator in an institution with religious commitment means that truth is assumed to exist and that each faculty member will work to share truth as he or she has come to view it. Faculty members are expected to pursue truth within the context of the Christian world and life view, with the Bible as its basic foundation. This is not viewed as a limitation in the pursuit of truth but as providing the basic framework within which truth can be meaningfully sought.

Teaching is viewed as more than truth-telling—it must be matched by truth-living. Faculty are expected to take seriously the Biblical maxim "Be ye doers of the word, and not hearers only!" In a relatively small college, students soon pick out those whose walk is not consonant with their talk. Faculty with the greatest lasting impact on student lives usually have practiced what they have preached; their daily example has been a challenge.

Quality teaching goes beyond the classroom. At large research institutions a faculty member may gain a measure of recognition for one's quality and quantity of research, but at church-related liberal arts colleges, faculty are more often held in esteem for the attention they pay to nonclassroom teaching activities. Faculty are expected to be involved in the lives of students through counseling, leadership in spiritual development activities, quality academic advising, and attendance at student-oriented college events.

Service to Church and Community

Faculty are expected to be active members of a local church and to engage in community service activities. Many of these activities are related to the church: serving on a church board, teaching Sunday School, preaching, or providing expert consultation for denominational committees. Local churches and parachurch ministries look to the Christian college in the community as a valuable resource toward meeting their goals.

Faculty are also encouraged to participate in local and state efforts related to their areas of expertise. At Fresno Pacific, for example, faculty may serve as consultants to local school boards, be involved in community musical and theatrical productions, or host local and regional seminars and workshops in the field of teacher education.

Research, Writing, and Other Scholarly Activities

Faculty are encouraged to engage in research at Fresno Pacific, and the college can point with pride to the accomplishments of a number of its faculty. Several have published scholarly articles in refereed journals; others have published books and chapters of books. It is fair to say, though, that engagement in extensive research is not a requirement of continuance in good standing. Several on the faculty have contributed relatively little scholarly work recognized outside of the institution.

Faculty are expected to engage in professional development activities, which may take various forms other than research: formal study, reading, attendance at professional meetings, performances, exhibits of artistic work. The Faculty Development Fund may be used to assist faculty in their professional pursuits. The college provides opportunities for partially subsidized sabbatical and study leaves. Special emphasis is placed upon those activities which would lead to deeper theological awareness, especially in relation to the faculty member's academic discipline.

In addition to teaching, community service, and research, faculty are expected to enthusiastically engage in college governance activities. Numerous committee assignments are not uncommon in small colleges, and the faculty at Fresno Pacific are expected to willingly accept those assignments, attend sessions regularly, and carry out assignments faithfully.

Faculty sessions, in which faculty matters are considered, are viewed as specially important at Fresno Pacific. In the spirit of "community," consensus is sought only after considerable, good-spirited discussion. Faculty expression on issues is encouraged and taken seriously.

Advice to Prospective Faculty

What would be helpful for a prospective faculty member to know when approaching a possible position at a church-related college?

Do your homework before arriving for interviews. Admittedly, what one can learn about an institution before arriving is limited. Nevertheless, there is no substitute for spending the time to get a good feel for the distinctive character of the institution seeking your services.

Much can be gained from the usual sources: catalog, college newspaper, even the yearbook. The college catalog, for example, should contain the college's mission statement and a listing of objectives. These statements unfortunately do not always reflect the true nature of what goes on at the college, yet they are at the very least indications of what is considered ideal. Find out how recently these statements were revised; recently revised statements are more reliable.

The faculty handbook is an indispensable source of information for a prospective faculty member. Coverage typically includes: organizational and administrative structures, faculty personnel policies (i.e., faculty expectations, evaluation processes, academic freedom), salary and benefit schedules, and provisions for professional development. Again, the date of the most recent revision is important.

Religiously-affiliated institutions will typically have some form of a doctrinal statement or statement of faith. This statement is usually considered the basic statement of commitment; the ability to enthusiastically support its contents will be important in faculty selection. Often, however, one finds that much greater priority is given to some items, and that on some items a great deal of tolerance has evolved. When asked for reaction to this statement of faith, one must be candid, for should there be dispute later over whether one is out of step with the position of the college, the particulars of this document will no doubt be used as criteria.

Be sure that you identify with the college mission. Nothing is more likely to breed long-term problems than a poor match between the faculty member and the stated mission of the institution. Those who have invested a great deal to make the institution what it is when you arrive have a right to expect that you will make every effort to carry on the vision which gave impetus for the college's very existence. Coming to the institution with a hidden agenda is both dishonest and likely to lead to frustration.

This is not to say that mission statements are static. Generally, some modification is appropriate, even necessary, as internal and external factors are allowed to shape new priorities. New faculty bring fresh perspectives, and as occasions present themselves, those perspectives will help to move the institution in new directions. Change brought about in this manner is to be expected and encouraged, but the mission statement at the time of arrival is the starting point, and basic adherence should be viewed as an essential condition of employment.

Reconcile yourself to the basic institutional conditions as they exist at the time of employment. It is almost a given that the compensation *will be* too low; the facilities and benefits *will be* inadequate, and some students will bring definite inadequacies to the classroom. No doubt there will be many other immediately identifiable areas needing improvement. Most will already be recognized by those who have spent several years at the institution, and complaints from an "outsider" too early in one's tenure are rarely appreciated.

One of the most common complaints in religious private education is that salaries are too low. In many cases they probably are, although many institutions are working hard to rectify this situation. Historically, the justification for lower compensation has been framed in spiritual terms, namely, that the privilege to be able to "serve the Lord" carries its own eternal reward. Some of this legacy continues, and a prospective faculty member should not expect that salary levels are likely to increase rapidly even in the best of times. If the salary level offered is considerably lower than felt appropriate, it is best to look for other opportunities. In the excitement and activity of the first months, this problem might be temporarily forgotten, but it almost always eventually leads to discouragement, frustration, and even resentment.

Look forward to total involvement. The rewards of the professoriate are great: autonomy, satisfying collegial relationships, quality professional stimulation, and the exhilaration of challenging and learning from each successive group of students. Additionally, at Coalition colleges, the fulfillment of faculty responsibilities is viewed as part of the mission of the church and, therefore, takes on an eternal dimension. Whether a professor teaches theology, chairs the teacher education department, or coaches the women's volleyball team, each activity is considered to be involvement in "ministry," building "Christ's Kingdom." This view of the professoriate demands total involvement, to the point at which distinctions between one's professional and personal life seem artificial.

Perspectives on Values Needed for Teaching at the Two-Year College

David H. Bergquist

At the very beginning of the twentieth century, Charles W. Eliot referred to the essence of teaching as "the motive of joy through achievement." One hundred years later, one can argue that helping individuals achieve through higher learning still motivates individuals to become faculty members. Certainly, factors influencing the work of faculty have changed dramatically over a century. At the two-year institution, however, one factor remains the same: the centrality of teaching.

The Two-Year College

For the past 25 years, I have been employed at Becker College, a two-campus, two-year Massachusetts institution steeped in the teaching tradition. I have served for more than half of that time as academic dean, first of its Worcester campus and now of its Leicester campus. Forty-three full-time faculty and thirty regular adjunct faculty comprise its staff. For the past several years, I have served as chairperson of the Faculty Development Committee of The Colleges of the Worcester Consortium, a collaborative body of 15 colleges and universities, and I have been active in promoting events especially for new faculty. This experience and the management of academic affairs at my own college give me a unique perspective of what is needed for a new professor to be successful at a two-year college.

Becker College is not a community college in that it is privately governed by a board of trustees and receives no public money; it comes from the venerable nonprofit private junior college movement that predates

today's community college. Much, though, is similar about the junior college of my experience and the comprehensive community college. Both
offer academic programs that are focused on careers; both subscribe to
an open admissions process with entrance standards within easy reach of
most high school graduates; both appeal to a diversity of students; both
view the development of the student as vital to their role in assisting
students to achieve academic and personal growth, and both attract a
faculty that view teaching as central to their daily work. The only real
distinction between these two-year college types, in my view, is that the
private junior college normally offers a residential component although
many community colleges located in more remote areas now also provide
housing. Today, Becker College is moving away from this tradition with
an increasing emphasis on four-year career-oriented programmatic offerings, new since the mid-1990s; nevertheless, I am in a position to offer
observations on the importance of teaching within the two-year college
and the implications for individuals who seek faculty appointments there.

By its very nature, a two-year postsecondary degree-granting institution is an opportunities college—an aspiration college. Here, a student
can be successful although he or she may never have been academically
successful before; the whole institution is built around the possibility of
student success. Although the number of private nonprofit two-year colleges is shrinking, the comprehensive community college is growing faster
than any other segment of traditional higher education in the United States
as it seeks to provide education that is rooted in application and career
relevance. Historically, the community college sprang from the post-World
War II period to meet expanding educational needs within an increasingly
complex economy. Today, 47 percent of students enrolled in public undergraduate education are enrolled in two-year community colleges, and
this proportion is expected to increase. Of this enrollment, more than
one half are enrolled part time. Students range from traditional recent
high school graduates to nontraditional students, some of whom already
have attended college and may even have a degree. Many are first-generation students. So, today's two-year college setting provides opportunities
for rewarding faculty teaching careers.

Within this educational environment, what are the qualities needed for
success as a faculty member? I like to term these qualities "values" that
are held by individuals and which directly impact their daily work. Search
committees and academic deans are looking to identify these values in
their applicants. The primary function of the faculty is teaching, so the
values necessary for faculty success are "people values." Let me explain.

Belief in Student Potential

The first of these values is "belief in the potential of each individual to succeed." The two-year college has by tradition adopted a liberal approach to admissions. The definition of who is "educated" within our society has been greatly expanded by the two-year college, and thus the potentials, possibilities, and benefits of higher education have been brought within reach of anyone, regardless of socioeconomic status, who aspires to improve through higher education. The two-year college offers a wide array of individuals the opportunity to achieve; the two-year college welcomes these students. Faculty candidates must recognize this vital role of the two-year college, for it will impact the very dynamics of the classroom.

How then is this value identified? Search committees will ask applicants introspective questions that probe their beliefs. They need to determine a candidate's view of human potential, of the transforming possibilities of education in people's lives, of people's ability to succeed when given the opportunity, and of the role of the two-year college. Academic deans, in their separate interviews with candidates, will ask similar questions. Deans need to be satisfied that candidates have thought about the mission of a two-year college. Faculty must fully understand the importance of the two-year college as an "opportunities" college within contemporary American society.

Valuing Individuality

A second value that I have found of particular importance is "human individuality." Faculty candidates should recognize every student as unique and distinct. Even as factors within modern American culture, particularly the electronic media, strive to standardize individuals, the opposite is true by practice. As a society, we place great emphasis on the value of the individual; the two-year college reflects this value. Consequently, classes will be highly heterogeneous. Students within the classroom will range from traditional to nontraditional, full time to part time, native born to newly arrived immigrant, low income to high income, and differ in race and sexual identity. A very diverse population will be part of the classroom experience of today's two-year college faculty.

Faculty need tolerance for the wide diversity of students. In the interview process, candidates will need to address their belief in the value of each person. Candidates may be asked to cite examples from their own experience that support their views and to describe methodologies that they would employ in teaching a diverse group of students. Openness to student requests, flexibility in assignments, and the realization that learning occurs differently among students are fundamental approaches that support diversity. For example, faculty members must be sensitive to legitimate student requests for accommodations in testing and time needed to complete tasks. Faculty need to be prepared to offer alternative assignments that address the particular learning differences of a student while still meeting the learning outcomes established for the class. Today, two-year colleges offer academic support through centers that provide basic skills testing, tutorial services, remedial courses, study workshops, and the assistance of learning specialists. The Student Affairs office often complements these efforts by sponsoring events that support student differences across the institution.

Approachability

The third value the two-year college faculty member needs is "approachability." Approachability recognizes the importance of the daily interface with students. Some faculty will have an easier time with this than others. No matter what their own personality type, though, all faculty need to understand the importance of approachability within the two-year college setting. Professional expressions of interest in students, caring and concern for them, are extremely important. Remaining for a few minutes after class, keeping scheduled office hours, and issuing an open invitation to stop by the office at other times are ways faculty can demonstrate approachability. Other things faculty can do include being seen on campus outside of the classroom and in places students frequent. The traditional role of advisor, furthermore, provides an opportunity not only to impart sound academic counsel but also to meet with students outside of the classroom at critical times during the academic year.

Passion for Teaching

The passion for teaching within a discipline is the fourth value, one that is extremely important. Two-year colleges are teaching institutions; their mandate is to educate a broad spectrum of American society. To be effective, faculty need to be passionate about what they are teaching—excited about the theoretical concepts and practical applications alike and about the delivery of this content to students.

It has been my experience over the past several years that more and more faculty candidates possess the terminal degree within a discipline.

Although faculty with doctorates are welcome at the two-year institution, candidates must realize that they will be more consumers of scholarly research than producers. The application of disciplinary knowledge will be in teaching; little in the way of scholarly research is expected. Deans and members of search committees can get a sense of passion for teaching by the way candidates respond to questions of disciplinary interest. I have found that asking finalists to deliver a 20-minute presentation on a topic within their discipline is a highly effective way to discover their enthusiasm for teaching.

After the Appointment

Once the appointment is made and accepted, it is incumbent on all involved in the initial search and interview process to remain actively involved with the new faculty member. This involvement can be both personal and professional. Support needs to be made available to the new faculty members. If they need help, they should ask for it. Mentoring by senior faculty may be formal or informal, but it needs to be done. The dean and others in the administration need to be in frequent contact with the faculty to ensure an easy assimilation into the culture of the institution. Meetings with new faculty after three months and six months on the job are helpful, I have found. Informal conversations with a new faculty member over a cup of coffee or a sandwich can be both personal and effective. For their part, student search committee members may be helpful by maintaining contact and by offering assistance whenever appropriate.

Most institutions have mechanisms in place that provide support for new faculty, ranging from fully staffed offices to a designated individual who plans in-house workshops. Faculty development initiatives on campus or between collaborating colleges are increasingly common. I have found that workshops on advising and classroom assessment are especially helpful to new faculty. Often, faculty development events include new faculty receptions co-sponsored with a neighboring college or university. These events are very supportive of new faculty while establishing collegial relationships outside institutional walls.

Increasingly, two-year institutions offer sabbatical programs to faculty after an initial term of full-time service, usually five to seven years. Sabbaticals may vary from one to two semesters in length and are designed to enhance teaching. Sabbatical activities may include additional graduate study, travel, and work at other institutions. Special faculty development funds, furthermore, may offer faculty an opportunity to attend a national or international conference or workshop germane to their teaching. A reduction in a faculty member's teaching load is another way to support faculty in special initiatives.

New faculty, on the other hand, also have a responsibility to be actively involved in their acculturation into the college. Reaching out, networking, and introducing themselves are important. Volunteering to serve on a college committee or to advise a student club are excellent ways to become involved in the college community.

If institutions have a collective bargaining unit, the new faculty member will need to become familiar with the current contract, which will explicitly describe working conditions. Often, adjusting to this working culture can be confusing to a new faculty member, especially if he or she is unfamiliar with union terminology. Many times this confusion can be lessened through new faculty orientation hosted by the union or administration.

Faculty unionization at two-year colleges is not a new phenomenon; many have been unionized since the 1960s and 1970s. Consequently, at the college where a union exists, the relationship between the faculty and the administration is well established and understood. The collective bargaining agreements or contracts serve to define the working conditions and expectations for faculty and how the faculty members relate to the college administration. A process for resolving disputes between employer and employee normally is included within the contract and explains the rights and limitations of both parties. It has been my experience that when new contracts are negotiated, there is less acrimony over money than over language that may substantially impact working conditions. At any rate, disputes inevitably arise, especially when change is a factor. Sides quickly are chosen, but eventually reason prevails. Speedy implementation of a grievance process helps to diffuse anxiety and avoid protracted and unnecessary conflicts.

New faculty will find their first few years demanding and challenging. Class size may average 35 students, well above the class size advertised by liberal arts colleges. Teaching load may vary depending on whether the institution is public or private. At the very least, new faculty should expect to teach 12 credit hours per semester with two preparations; at the most, new faculty may teach 15 credit hours per semester with three and sometimes four preparations. Normally, there is extra compensation for extra work. Compensation levels at two-year colleges are competitive with public baccalaureate institutions. Faculty compensation at private two-year institutions is considerably less than at their public counterparts.

Evaluation of new faculty typically consists of student evaluations administered once a semester or year, classroom evaluation conducted annually by a qualified administrator, and other reviews focusing on course materials, student advising, and service. Promotion to a higher rank generally is based on the number of years at the college, level of professional credential, relevant professional development, and contribution to college or community through service. Many times, recommendations from key individuals within the institution are required. For faculty who serve the college for a set number of years, tenure may be available, but only after undergoing a thorough evaluation. At colleges that do not have tenure, faculty may be removed from probationary status and made nonprobationary. Promotion normally is overseen by a committee that formulates a recommendation to the dean or president.

Conclusion

In summary, the values of belief in student potential and human individuality, approachability, and passion for teaching are strong predictors, I believe, for success as a two-year college faculty member. Applicants should understand the unique history and mission of the two-year college (whether private nonprofit or community college), its place within our society, the diversity of its student body, and the internal structure that supports success as teaching faculty. Despite daily time demands, it is important for new faculty to take time to access the support mechanisms in place. Faculty development activities, furthermore, will only strengthen teaching performance and career satisfaction. Once employed, with the needed values and an understanding of what comprises a two-year college, a faculty member can be on the road to a productive and rewarding career.

Part II

STEP-BY-STEP ANALYSIS OF CAREER PATTERNS FOR FACULTY MEMBERS

Getting the Job: Anxiety and Aspirin

Jobs are rarely easy to secure. Usually, one must go to some lengths and trouble to locate an available position, and to secure it typically requires considerably more effort and planning. In this essay we offer some practical suggestions for people seeking their first professorial position.

What Sort of Applicant Are You?

One vital thing to consider is what sort of applicant you are. What are your talents and interests, and how will you present yourself to prospective employers? Applicants generally are of four types. The first type applies for all positions that are advertised, whether or not the position really matches his expertise. Put rather negatively, we might label this person the indiscriminate applicant. He figures that he can always make a convincing case that his expertise and experience really do match the job requirements. There might be some point to this strategy. Many times, jobs advertised will be somewhat ambiguous. Institutions purposely make the job description vague just so they can get some range of applicants to consider. A talented colleague is more important to them than having someone who exactly matches some job description. However, the gap between credentials and job requirements cannot be too great. Search committees are quick to identify indiscriminate applicants and do not rate them highly.

A second type of applicant generalizes her resume in the hope that she appears capable of fulfilling almost any role or position. This is the generalist at his or her best or worst. Unless a position really calls for a generalist's knowledge and experience, and that is pretty rare, search committees are unlikely to rate such applicants very highly.

The third applicant type is a graduate student or former graduate student at the college or university seeking to fill the vacancy. Hiring graduates leads to inbreeding and is often felt to decrease the quality of the institution. However, powerful faculty members may have sufficient clout to hire their "pets" on a permanent faculty line. This may cause some resentment among the rest of the faculty, and they may consider such new faculty members illegitimate. Professors of this background, even if qualified, will report that it took them many years to establish their independence and integrity with the faculty. Unless you really have strong support at your alma mater, this probably is not an approach you want to take.

The fourth type of applicant is the most common—the individual who has just received or is about to receive the doctorate who is seeking a position within her specialty or a position closely related to it. Often, this candidate faces stiff competition in the job market, but by the same token this is the path that is most likely to lead to a successful job search.

The Search Process: Four Focuses

Whatever the sort of applicant you are, the job search process has some fairly standard elements. We will group our suggestions into four areas of focus.

The first focus is upon the situation at the home institution. It is absolutely essential that you have a solid base of support from your major adviser and other professors at your home institution. For some candidates this presents no problem. For others, though, this involves mending fences. Not infrequently, the graduate student has had some difficulty with his major adviser. There is some ill-feeling built up over the dissertation, say, and as a result, egos may have been bruised. Therefore, it is important to do what one can to see that the relationships with the adviser and other faculty at the alma mater are corrected and brought up to a positive feeling. Nothing is so disastrous as to leave an unknown enemy in the rear when one is out job hunting. Not so many years ago, a young woman began to seek her first faculty position. There were an unusually high number of jobs open, but no institutions appeared interested in her. Her adviser asked the placement office to go over her file with him. A most demeaning "letter of recommendation" from the student's earlier days as a graduate student at another university was contained in the job file, and until that letter was removed, the candidate was not going to be considered seriously for any position.

A second focus in the process is to understand the various methods by which you can secure the professorial position. Know the various systems that operate and their relative effectiveness. One method for consideration is the college or university placement office. For the most part these merely provide leads and a service for mailing transcripts, resumes, and reference letters. You must be prepared to do the major share of the work.

One might title a second system the "Good Old Boys and Girls Club." If a candidate has a nationally known adviser, the mentor will have a series of contacts in other academic institutions which the candidate may draw upon. In conversations with other academics or at national meetings, the adviser may promote her doctoral students. Should a vacancy occur, the promoted candidate often will be given special consideration. A major adviser of national reputation will receive calls from deans, department chairpersons, or selection committee chairpersons to nominate individuals for a vacancy. If a graduate student has done his duty and worked in a positive manner with the major adviser (in short, paid his dues) the adviser may reward the doctoral candidate. Even if your advisor is not nationally known, he or she still can help you.

A third system, and one more often used in the past than at present, is often facetiously entitled the "Beauty Pageant." This marketing method requires attendance at a national meeting of an academic subject area or professional group. (Linda Haverty describes something like this in her essay that follows.) To such meetings universities bring both their faculty vacancies and aspiring candidates. A certain amount of horse trading goes on. Placement officers have resumes for their candidates on hand. Suites of rooms are reserved for conferencing. It is more or less a "beauty contest," but it is also merely the first look. Interest generated may lead to a campus visit and meetings with the full faculty at the institution.

A fourth system is that of national advertising. The *Chronicle of Higher Education* for years has been the chief vehicle for informing candidates about available positions. Other journals of lesser visibility and of a more specialized nature also supply information on available positions. Sometimes positions will be advertised electronically, through e-mail distribution lists or on the Web sites of professional associations. One must be aware that jobs advertised may indeed not be jobs available. A "wired-in" candidate may be waiting in the wings for the position, and the advertisement is merely fulfilling a legal obligation to notify academicians about the job.

A third focus in the process of getting a job is preparing for the interviews that are part of the visit to the campus. Once the invitation to visit is extended, one can be pretty sure that one is a contender. In an earlier period possibly half a dozen applicants would be called in to be looked over by the faculty. For a position at an Eastern university some years ago, eight applicants were brought to the campus to be assessed as to their research potential. None of the eight was offered the job. The university appeared to be merely shopping around. Those days are gone forever. It is far too expensive a process. On the other hand, unfortunately, it is possible that "extra" candidates are invited to campus merely because they belong to some underrepresented groups. This is intended to give the appearance of inclusiveness in the search, but the candidates may not be serious contenders.

There are a number of things you can do in order to interview well. Carefully study the geographic area. Know the place. Read a book or two on the history of the institution. Most institutions have Web pages that will tell you about the history of the institution, policies, programs, faculty, and so on. Know about the institutional structure. Download key faculty members' names and research interests if those are given. Always be prepared to break the silence that ensues when the faculty are tired or do not know what to ask you. They appreciate your awareness of who they are and what the institution is all about. The local geography, history, and political climate are always subjects of interest to them. Prepare for the series of interviews at the institution as carefully as you did for your doctoral orals.

Often, when candidates are invited to come for an interview, they will be asked if there are particular things they would like to do when they visit. Be ready with some ideas. For example, ask to tour the library to see the journals and other resources it has for your scholarship. Ask to be taken to the bookstore to see the texts your potential colleagues are using in their courses. Ask to talk to some students if that is not scheduled. Such things indicate you are serious about your work and really interested in knowing the institution.

Do not be shy about asking for relevant information. You certainly may ask about the rent or price of homes in the area or about primary and secondary schools. It is sometimes helpful to get a local newspaper in order to better understand the economic and academic climate of the community and institution. It is also quite legitimate and important to ask about promotion and tenure guidelines, salary, and benefits. Usually, a faculty member or administrator will volunteer such information without your asking.

If possible, arrive early for the interview, even if you have to check into a motel or hotel at your own expense. You will be fresh for the interview ordeal. It really can be an ordeal. One can never be too well rested for it.

Perhaps the most important events during the interviews are the candidate's formal or informal presentations on her scholarship and/or teaching. The candidate may be asked to teach a class or at least discuss her approach to teaching. Likely she will conduct a research seminar. Never try something totally new. Know where the humorous lines come. Know and plan for audience reaction. Try to do something that involves your audience. Neither students nor faculty like to be lectured. Some years ago, a candidate for a position at a large public university arrived and was well received. A class was made ready for his presentation. He went in. His audience's reaction was zero. The visit was, in effect, over. There would be no job offer. The candidate realized that immediately.

A lesson gained as a result of such incidents is that you should always inquire as to whether a presentation will be desired and what sort of presentation that should be. If you're asked to teach, check the nature of the class and ask for a syllabus for the course. For a research presentation, ask if there is some topic you should address. As much as you can, play it safe. An interview is a poor place to jump into material you know little about. Keep it on the light side. These presentations will be critical in your selection for the job. A slip here can cost you, and a bad slip can prove fatal.

During the course of the interviews you are almost certain to make connections with at least one faculty member who identifies with you and willingly becomes your advocate and inside informant. In private this person will tell you how many candidates have preceded you, what mistakes they each have made, what to watch out for, and what is in store for you should you actually be offered the job and accept it. The confidant may also tell you how you are being received by the rest of the faculty members. This is usually the moment of truth for you. Without this very candid discussion, you may fly blind throughout the rest of the interview process. However, you must very carefully evaluate what you are told by this volunteer informant. The information may be biased, misleading, or downright false. Sometimes such people are involved in departmental infighting and want to be sure you will be on their side. That is a bad spot to get yourself into. (We'll talk more about this in our essay on ethics.)

A fourth focus in the process concerns what happens after the interview. Do not expect or demand to know whether the job is yours prior to your departure. Play it cool. Appear detached. It may be that you really do need to know about your status because one or more offers already have been made to you. In that case, it is alright to ask, although the institution may not be able to give you a firm answer right then. You can ask that they let you know within a specific amount of time. But do not bluff here.

A brief thank-you note to the department chair and/or search committee chair is in order. Usually, it is the department secretaries who have worked hardest to schedule events for your visit. Thank them for their kindness and consideration. This is a mark of class on your part.

Thank senior faculty members for spending time with you. It is the senior faculty whose opinion is now critical in your selection. In your presentations, be scholarly but not argumentative with them. If they are powerful enough, senior faculty members can single-handedly veto your selection. All one has to say to the dean is that while you appear to be all right, in his or her opinion, the institution really can do better.

The dean or department chairperson usually cannot make you an offer at the conclusion of your visit. She must consult with the faculty and with the administration. She is likely to say that you will be hearing from them in a few days. A period of faculty-administration consultation must take place.

After you get back home, do not call and check out your status, unless of course there is a real need to know. You might receive a conference call involving several faculty members from the institution you have visited. Keep a record of relevant faculty members near your phone so that you can recall names, faces, and information about these people.

Of course, another important part of this postinterview process involves thinking about the merits and demerits of the job or jobs for which you have interviewed. That is a large issue in itself.

Getting the Job:
With a Little Bit of Luck . . .
and a Whole Lot of Forethought

Linda Haverty

The following pages chronicle my own particular job-market experience. I am a woman with an undergraduate degree from Barnard College and a Ph.D. in comparative literature from Harvard. Recently I landed a tenure-track position at Ohio State University. Though this essay is meant to provide helpful information as well as address problems, the reader should keep in mind the fact that the employment process varies considerably from individual to individual, depending not only upon experience, background, and qualifications but also, to an unsettlingly large degree, upon the luck of the draw. In my case, the very year I applied for jobs, Ohio State listed a position in Scandinavian and German. It happens that I specialized in German, Scandinavian, and American literature as a comparatist. Before the job list came out, I had assumed that there would be little chance of finding a position in which I would be able to teach in more than one of my fields; comparative positions are hard to come by, and most prefer someone who has done more work in French than I have. It is rare enough that a good tenure-track position in Scandinavian comes up—to have one appear at precisely that moment in Scandinavian and German defeats all odds. Further, the head of the search committee (i.e., the only Scandinavianist at OSU) was a woman who had taught me during my second year of graduate school while she was a Mellon Fellow at Harvard. So much for the luck of the draw.

Still, despite these odds, I was not inclined to make OSU my first choice. (Now we come to the factors of personal background and experience.) I was raised in Nebraska and had spent my adolescence plotting to live elsewhere. After four years of college in New York City and nine years of graduate school in Boston, an appointment at Ohio State looked a little too much like a return home to the vast windy spaces of the Great Plains, spaces punctuated only by an occasional silo or the golden arches. Also, after 13 years on the Ivy Coast, a large state institution with minimal entrance requirements, 55,000 students (primarily Ohioans in blue jeans and Buckeye sweatshirts), and rampant football mania frankly scared me. (The reader may begin to ascertain that my years in the East had left me brainwashed and effete.) Finally, my boyfriend, with whom I had moved in a few months before, was not eager to return to the Midwest. (He, too, is from Nebraska.)

So I fought the odds. I applied for 22 positions all told, primarily in German, but also in comparative literature. My research had focused on early twentieth-century literature, but I had done a good deal of teaching in nineteenth-century subjects as well, so I applied for "modern" jobs. ("Modern" can stretch from anywhere between the sixteenth to twenty-first centuries, depending upon whom one asks.) If the institution or location was particularly desirable, I applied for positions which advertised for applicants not specifically in my area of interest. I would suggest that job candidates apply for positions at their "dream" institutions, whether or not the position seems tailored to their experience. Obviously, if there is no way one either could or would teach a subject specified in the job description, it is probably best to forego application. But if one can imagine oneself teaching a course, why not? Job descriptions are often not an exact picture of what the institution wants.

A positive example to support this suggestion: I got an interview with a prestigious private Midwestern university, although their job listing indicated a need for an East German literature specialist. During the interview I discovered that they really wanted a twentieth-century generalist who could do a course in East German literature and who would do respectable scholarly research. A negative example: I breathlessly applied to an august Southern institution whose job description seemed to be a search warrant designed to find me. After a discouraging interview, I heard from a friend that they had decided to hire an eighteenth-century specialist.

Another obvious factor determining my application pool was geography. Although the Midwest was not entirely eliminated, the position and/or institution had to be very attractive to compel me to apply to go there. My boyfriend expressed strong objections to Texas, most of the South, and any extremely rural area. Again, if the position or institution were appealing, his objections were overturned, which brings me to a very difficult subject: the question of relationship vs. job. Although I think that this problem has been characterized as a woman's issue in the past, it is more accurate to say that both male and female academics will be confronted with it at some point and that traditional notions of gender will play a role. Whose career is more important? Which is more important, staying competitive in the profession or keeping a relationship? Is a commuting relationship a possibility? Does it cast doubts upon a man's masculinity to move for a woman? Does it cast aspersions upon a woman's strength and dependence to move (or not move) for a man? Until one has actually gone through this process, it is nearly impossible to predict one's decisions. I can only say that in my own case, because we were not married and had no plans to be married, we decided that I should apply for the jobs I wanted, leaving his considerations aside. (This of course was very abstract; I found myself incapable of leaving him out of the decisions I made, but at least he didn't pressure me to plan for both of us.)

We left the question of whether he would move with me open until I had taken a job . . . and at that point, he decided that he would not accompany me to Ohio. This was a difficult moment, but I was surprised to find that I was determined to go forward with my choice, feeling that I couldn't compromise my career for a relationship that seemed uncertain. I moved out alone and was quite miserable, except that I was (almost) sure that I had done the right thing. In fact, after a summer of separation, he decided that perhaps Ohio was not intolerable, and he joined me here. I was most fortunate in the fact that he is not an academic himself but has a lifestyle that allowed him the freedom to move at will. This is not true in all cases. Unless we see the promised rising demand for Ph.D.s in the near future, I'm afraid that couples will continue to agonize over the job market and changing gender roles. If nothing else, it forces us to think hard about the things that matter most to us.

As my list of applications burgeoned, my adviser began to caution me: "You wouldn't be happy there." "There" was a small school in which the German Department consisted of one or two people occupied almost entirely with language teaching. Such an institution would afford no opportunity to teach theoretical or advanced literature courses. There would be no graduate school and no Comparative Literature Department into which I could branch out. These positions were most appropriate for language pedagogues, and though I had taught language and expected to continue doing so, my adviser was right; my main focus was literature. In the first flush of excitement and anxiety about competition for jobs, I almost forgot to consider what I would be willing to do.

I applied for temporary positions only if they were at institutions of some merit, with a possibility of interesting courses and colleagues. It was understood both by these institutions and by me that if a tenure-track position was offered by practically anyone else, the tenure-track position would be my first choice. My advisor had cautioned me that no matter how attractive the temporary position, one rarely achieves recognition as a full-fledged colleague, and it might even be better to continue with a temporary position at Harvard than to pull up stakes again only a year later.

This winnowing-out process went on during the months of October and November as I scoured our Modern Language Association (MLA) listings and the job announcements that arrived almost daily in the Comparative Literature and German departments. By late November, I had sent out letters to 22 institutions. Because I was applying to a wide range of positions, I created two "template" letters (one for German and one for Comparative Literature), altering them as required for different jobs. Both letters assured the search committees that I would be finished by June. I gave the title of my dissertation, identified my advisor, and delivered a short summary of the dissertation, referring the reader to the enclosed single-page summary. A second paragraph outlined my teaching experience (which, in the course of nine years, had been extensive) and projected my prospective research and teaching interests. A final paragraph offered to forward my dossier (if it had not already been requested) and expressed my willingness to meet with the committee for an interview at the MLA national convention in December.

The organization of the curriculum vitae was more difficult. I was quickly able to comprehend that CV's are almost as peculiar to their owners as fingerprints—there is no standard form. I also found that for every person I asked for advice on the writing of the CV, a new suggestion would be made that overturned earlier suggestions. Of most help were my dissertation adviser and a staff member at Harvard's placement office. On their advice, I included not only the names of courses but also the names of the professors for whom I had taught. This proved a good idea, as some of these names were familiar to my interviewers. I also wrote a section headed "Works in Progress," in which I listed articles submitted for publication and conference papers. A "Teaching Interests" category allowed me to try to convince my interviewers that I was interested in teaching the courses for which they needed coverage, but I also used it to inform them of new directions I might like to take.

The final item of that first mailing was the single-page dissertation summary. This proved to be the most important document of all in terms of the first interview. While many interviewers may not have the time or patience to plow through a 30-page writing sample, most will latch onto a short summary with gusto. I tried to open mine with the most provocative aspect of my dissertation in the hope that this would open a discussion. In almost every case, it did. In several of the interviews, one of the interviewers read from the summary, and I saw that notes had been made in the margins. This summary was in no way an exhaustive review of my argument and examples; I tried to touch upon the issues covered in each chapter and give an overall motivation for the topic. The rest could be discussed in the interview.

Many applicants include self-addressed, stamped postcards as part of their first inquiry; I did this only when it was requested by the institution. I found, however, that my anxiety about the job search gave rise to an unusual pattern of behavior: extreme organization. I created a binder in which I placed copies of all the descriptions of jobs for which I had applied, recording the date on which I had sent out my first application materials, the dates of any ensuing responses, and the contents of all telephone calls. A copy of my letter and CV followed the description, and all of their correspondence to me was included as it arrived. This binder gave me something to do during the waiting period—it also gave me a sense of control over a situation in which I actually had very little.

At this point, requests for dossiers began to come in. If I had been canny about assembling a dossier, I would have started collecting letters from recommenders in the years leading up to the job search. As it was, I was fortunate that the people who could most ably recommend me were still in residence. In the summer before the job search, I began to nudge the professors for whom I had taught. I sent them the recommendation forms from Harvard's dossier service, along with a letter reminding them of the work we had done together, emphasizing details of my contribution that might have been forgotten. (For instance, "I believe you visited my class during our lively discussion of *The Turn of the Screw*," or "I did a guest lecture for you on ethnicity and autobiography.") Refreshing the recommender's memory as to dates and subjects is vital, but additional detail can make for a lively and convincing letter, in which it seems the recommender actually knows (and perhaps even likes) you. A quick run-down of the kinds of positions for which you are applying is also helpful. My adviser asked me for the job descriptions of the positions for which I had applied and went over each of them carefully with me. She had me remind her of all the coursework and teaching I had done for her, and we discussed my research and teaching interests. The reader may have by now realized that I was blessed with an unusually attentive adviser; she could hardly have been more thorough and helpful.

Although the selection of an adviser does have a great deal to do with the aforementioned luck of the draw, one doesn't have to advocate the pin-the-tail-on-the-donkey method. I cannot claim that I was foresightful enough to calculate my later needs when I entered graduate school; 20/20 hindsight tells me that I wanted a person of stature, who would not only be rigorous in her demands on me, but who would also be well-known in the profession as a rigorous teacher. My adviser had been around long enough to serve on hiring committees herself and was, therefore, able to proffer experienced advice. She was active in the profession, attending conferences and writing articles; thus people knew her, and she knew them.

Once the dossiers had been sent out, requests for interviews at the December convention (and rejections) began coming in. Rejection letters ranged from the painfully abrupt (scrawled on a postcard) to the eloquently empathetic. The first two weeks of December saw a flurry of telephone calls and letters, and rejections continued to trickle in as late as spring of the following year. When the dust settled, I was invited to seven interviews at the convention, two of which were for temporary positions. Most of the search committees contacted me by telephone to schedule the interviews.

As soon as I received notice of my interviews, I betook myself to the library and scanned the microfiche copies of the course catalogues for the institutions in question. I noted the names of faculty members and the courses offered. How large was the student body? What kinds of backgrounds did they have (cultural, educational, geographical, etc.) How many of those students majored in German or Comparative Literature? How many faculty members shared the load of teaching? Did everyone seem to be teaching language as well as literature, or was the language teaching left to graduate students? Would my ideas for courses fit into the program? I recorded as much information as I could glean and went on to the library computer, where I checked the names of faculty from the various schools. What had they written? What sorts of questions were likely to interest them? What sort of ideological pitfalls was I likely to encounter? And so on.

Our chairman, Judith Ryan, did some interview coaching that proved valuable. She urged job applicants to frame and reframe the thesis of the dissertation, expressing it first as a page, then as a paragraph, then as a single sentence. As we practiced on one another, we became more and more adept at focusing on the core of our argument. She also suggested that we develop syllabi for courses we would like to teach and have them ready to show our interviewers. Simply reviewing the names of texts one might like to include on such a syllabus helped to eliminate black holes in the interview. One of my interviewers, in fact, asked me to develop a syllabus on the spot for one of his department's "big courses"—a survey of world mythology. I would, therefore, suggest that a job applicant both develop a "dream course" and develop a course that would fit into the institution's present listings. My retrospective impression is that I fell down in this area during my interviews; the course I suggested was too arcane and had nothing to do with either my dissertation or standard departmental courses. It would have been better to gear my "dream" to their reality.

The MLA convention, held in New Orleans in my job-search year, occurs just after Christmas and attracts a cast of thousands. My boyfriend and I arrived from Nebraska's bitter cold to the Crescent City's air-conditioned comfort on the 27th of December, and both of us promptly fell victim to an exceptionally nasty Merry Christmas virus. Somehow I dragged myself through six interviews on the 28th. Five of these took place in hotel rooms or suites, and one was held in the rather frightening interview "salon," in which perhaps a hundred tables had been set up for as many search committees, who interviewed their applicants in open view (and hearing) of all. Numbered placards on each table were apparently meant to produce an impression of safe anonymity but did little to allay my feelings of nakedness. I realize that the "salon" approach probably caters to the economic strictures of various departments, but surely there must be a more humane solution.

On the 28th, three of the interviews (including the "salon") were held by a solitary man; on that day only my interview with Smith College was conducted by a group of men and women. The seventh interview, on the 29th of December, was with a genial group of men and one woman who said precisely nothing throughout the conversation, despite my attempts to address her directly, catch her eye, or otherwise engage her. The other interviewers had forgotten to mention that she was a graduate student representative, brought along to observe. I was unsettled by the experience, wondering how this apparently kind, articulate, and sensitive group of men had managed to muzzle their female colleague. I didn't learn the facts of the case until well after the convention.

The interview process, in other words, made me aware of my gender in ways I had not anticipated. No one asked the taboo questions about marriage, age, and pregnancy about which I had been warned. No one made sexist jests or inappropriate comments about my personal appearance. Everyone was, in a word, gentlemanly (at least as far as my gender was concerned). Still, almost every situation found me in a hotel room with one or more men. My academic life, I realized, had been rather misleading up to that point. At Barnard, the German Department was comprised of two women. Active, vital women made up half of Harvard's German Department. Suddenly in the interview situation, I was confronted with something I had always known in the abstract: most Germanists are men. (Ironically, my present department at Ohio State is also unusual in its proportion of tenured female faculty members.) I am not discomfited by men, nor do I necessarily protest that the institutions in question should have sent women (in at least two cases, they didn't have any to send); I am just mentioning this to indicate a condition of the interview situation that does have a psychological impact on female applicants. Also, people, couldn't we find a more appropriate venue for interviews than hotel rooms?

The majority of the interviews were far less threatening than I had anticipated. The interviewers seemed less interested in taking my ideas to task than in simply getting a look at me. In almost all cases, however, the first question regarded the completion of my dissertation. If I had been unable to look the interviewers straight in the eye and say, "It will be done in June, sir," the situation might have seemed more threatening.

After the question about my time frame, the interviewers focused on the aspects of my dissertation that had caught their eye, usually drawn from the one-page summary. They would describe the position they were offering and ask for my notions of how I might teach the necessary courses. This often demanded detail, i.e., names of books and authors, how I would organize the course, what sort of assignments I would make, etc. I was asked to outline an introduction to theory course, the mythology course mentioned above, and a course in postmodern literature. Interviewers often inquired about my "Teaching Interests" rubric, and there I was required to make stabs at creating courses as well. Larger research institutions asked me to elaborate on my immediate plans for writing and research. Two interviewers did their best to convince me that I would be desperately unhappy at their institutions, and a third group inadvertently convinced me of this.

This last-mentioned interview should perhaps be described in more detail. I was ushered into the standard hotel room just as my predecessor, blushing furiously, was ushered out. The man who welcomed me (Interviewer "A") was large and hearty, with a big handshake. His companions were thoroughly unlike him: "B" was tall, lanky, and looked a bit worn; "C" was small and natty and kept looking nervously at his watch. As it turned out, he had an appointment scheduled for half-way through the interview. "A" addressed me with a sparkle in his eye; my summary had fascinated him with its assertions:

- Did I really think that the genre I discussed had its beginnings in the eighteenth century?
- Well, I hadn't precisely said that, I was talking about a particular species of that genre . . . .
- Yes, but didn't I know of any examples from the seventeenth century?
- Actually, I haven't done all that much work in the seventeenth century, but I do know of a Swedish author . . . .
- No, a German work. Couldn't I think of a German work from the seventeenth century? A particular one?
- Well, no, if he put it that way, I probably couldn't.
- "B" rolled his eyes. "Can we go on," he asked. "A" didn't glance in his direction. "C" perched nervously on the edge of his seat. I heard him mutter, "Harass away, harass away," just under his breath.
- Well, let's just see. What forms of literature were being written during the seventeenth century?
- Uh . . . (I try to apply this question to my limited experience of seventeenth-century literature and the nature of my topic . . .) Diary novels? Epistolary forms? (Those are more common in the eighteenth, though . . .) Uh . . . .
- Yes, and what else?
- Well . . . (shot in the dark) lyric?
- Yes, yes! What about lyricists? Whose work do you know?
- From the seventeenth century? Well, Gryphius? (I watch his face. Zero.) Weckherlin? Opitz? (Now I've named the best-known ones, nearly my whole stock . . . and still no glimmer from "A.")
- What about . . . (he named a writer whose name even now escapes me. "B" stretched out in his chair and gazed at the ceiling.) You know his work "Blahderblahmisch," of course? Count that as the first German work of your genre. (As I have never heard of the work, I have little to say on that score. Still, I have enough sense of self to attempt a rally.)
- Well, if we're counting lyric poetry, don't you think we might discuss medieval works, such as Walther von der Vogelweide's? (Not being a medievalist, I was simply going on the dimly remembered comments of a professor. But "C" suddenly shot up in his chair with interest.)
- That's right! Walter von der Vogelweide! Very good observation! (He was beaming . . . clearly a medievalist. "A" wheeled on him.)

- Absolutely not! Vogelweide's work has never been established as a specimen of this genre! "Blahderblahmisch" is the earliest possible candidate! This heated exchange took up the next ten minutes of the interview. Finally, "C" had to depart at top speed for his next meeting. "B" turned to me with a little sigh and said:
- Why don't we talk about Chapter Four of your dissertation? I was fascinated with it when I read your summary.

After another five minutes or so, I was dismissed, blushing furiously, and my successor was ushered in. Later, one of the Harvard professors present at the convention told me that "A" had described the interview as "brilliant."

This long account of a much longer interview is not intended to fan the flames of anxiety, but to show how ridiculous the actual transpiration of one's fears can be. I had dreaded being asked such a question, but when it actually faced me, I felt very calm. I knew that I was not in possession of the desired fact, that no amount of cajoling could extract "Blahderblahmisch" from me, and that I had never represented myself as an expert in the seventeenth century. Further, the other interviewers did not approve of this form of interrogation. And finally, it became clear to me that this position was perhaps not as attractive as it had first appeared in the job list. I began to think that the convention might be an excellent opportunity for *me* to get a look at *them*.

The final part of the interview usually focused on precisely this point; that is, my questions for them. I asked about the size of the classes, the number of majors, which language class discussions were conducted in, research time and resources, whether I would teach graduate students (if there were any), etc. Then we shook hands, and they told me about their schedule for notifying applicants (if they didn't tell me, I asked them). In two cases I received requests for writing samples later that evening, so apparently some of the ranking took place immediately after the initial interview.

It was upon my return to Cambridge that the truly trying portion of the job search began: helpless waiting. This traumatic period of silence was broken by my on-campus interview at Ohio State; they had not interviewed me at the convention, but the chairman had called me on December 8 to arrange an on-campus interview. I assume that because there were so few qualified applicants for the position, it was possible for the university to invite all of them to campus. I traveled to Columbus on January 19.

From the moment I was picked up at the airport that Thursday night to my departure the following Sunday morning, it was clear that this was an experience of another order. Everyone in the large department was welcoming and gracious; I was made to feel in the strongest terms that my presence was desired. My schedule was crammed with breakfast, coffee, luncheon, dinner, and cocktail engagements, during which I met most of my future colleagues, deans, members of the Comparative Studies Department, and graduate students. Most of these meetings were informal, though a few were official and informative. I was bombarded with details of the university's excellent benefits program, its commitment to giving time and money for research, the reasonable teaching load, and the democratic nature of department administration. Negative aspects were harder to come by; graduate students were the best sources for those, not surprisingly. Some admitted that library funding was low and collections limited; a few complained that the student body was apathetic and below average in preparation, and it was clear to all of us that I might find moving back to the Midwest undesirable. However, after a few days of such treatment, Ohio began to gain in appeal.

I was required to teach a Swedish class, which made me rather nervous, because I had neither taught nor spoken the language on a regular basis for a couple of years. I was observed by two faculty members, one of whom spoke Swedish. I was happy to find that the students were not apathetic but alert and responsive, and it helped to make them stand up and be active during the class. It also helped that my colleague had sent me a copy of the textbook and an outline of the class's progress.

Later that afternoon, I gave a lecture for the faculty and graduate students. This was a portion of my dissertation, shortened to the time allotted for the lecture. I recommend highly that an applicant give a lecture that has already served as a conference paper. It is so difficult to gauge the amount of time a lecture will take if one has never given it before, and often the responses given at a conference can provide hints for revision or discussion. If you are unable to give the paper at a conference, at least enlist some friends to listen to you beforehand (preferably academic friends from your discipline).

On Saturday, my colleague-to-be gave me a little tour of Columbus homes and neighborhoods, bringing along a copy of real estate and apartment ads for my information. She showed me my potential colleagues' homes and explained the character of the various neighborhoods. One of Columbus's major advantages is the cost of housing; an academic is able to own or rent a nice home in a pleasant and convenient neighborhood here without having to forego all of life's pleasures. This is not true of Eastern cities unless the academic's life partner happens to hold an M.B.A. or its financial equivalent. If an applicant has an on-campus interview, he/she should take the time to conduct such a tour, with apartment ads in hand. The real value of the offered salary cannot be calculated without such information.

At the very end of my visit, the department chair sat down to talk with me about tenure and promotion and salary. I was pleasantly surprised by most of the information, and the salary was on the high end of the offers I had seen or heard about. Taking into consideration that Ohio is significantly less expensive than, say, California, it seemed a very solid offer. She indicated that I would hear from them within the next couple of weeks. For my part, I let her know that I was still waiting to hear from several schools. In fact, I knew that an offer from Ohio State would have to cancel out most of the schools in question, but there were two, especially, about which I still held out hope. Besides, there was the heavy matter of my relationship to consider, and I suspected that my boyfriend would balk at Ohio.

I returned home that Sunday to find a letter from one of the two most desirables. My interviewer stated simply that I was still under serious consideration and that I should contact him if anything developed. He had informed me earlier that his university was notoriously slow in making decisions, mostly because of bureaucratic snarls in the administration. I had a feeling even then that trouble might develop, and indeed it did. On Tuesday morning, the chairman at Ohio State called to inform me that the department had voted to make me an offer. I was both elated and stymied. It was wonderful to have an offer, but it would be more wonderful to be able to choose. She gave me two weeks to give my answer, and I promised that I would. Then I called up the interviewer who had sent me the letter.

This interviewer seemed genuinely discouraged that I had been made an early offer. Still, he couldn't urge me not to take it. He listened thoughtfully to my description of the job and told me that (a) he could by no means even bring me to campus within two weeks, so (b) he certainly could not guarantee a job, and (c) Ohio State seemed an excellent opportunity for me. He wasn't sure that I wouldn't do better there. He recommended that I take it. I am grateful to this man for his careful consideration and honest assessment of my position, but at the time I felt disappointed to lose a shot at a very good school in a city that would have held considerable appeal for both my boyfriend and myself. My call to the other "most desirable" yielded an almost audible sigh of relief from their side—I had not made their campus interview list and the search chair had felt considerable guilt about calling me. He gave me many verbal pats on the back and signed off. The rest of my prospects could not compare with the offer Ohio State had made. I called them to withdraw my candidacy, and by Friday I had called Ohio State to accept.

Perhaps if I were made of different stuff, I might have tried to bargain for more time from Ohio in order to keep my spot at the other school. But despite all of my adolescent rejection of the Midwest, I could feel the strong attraction of the position and the people in Ohio. Now that I have been here for a quarter, I am grateful for the luck of the draw. The attention and concern of my colleagues has continued past the courtship phase, and I am treated like a full-fledged member of the department. This is quite different from the treatment of junior faculty members I observed at Harvard and other Ivy institutions. Efforts have been made to give me time for research, and my opinion on administrative matters seems to be valued despite my lack of experience. My students range from below average to very bright in terms of performance, but the majority of them evince intellectual curiosity and the Midwestern openness and friendliness I grew up with. With the research time allowance and relatively light teaching load here, I might be able to write a couple of books and think about heading back East. Or, on the other hand, I might prefer to stay, given the chance. In either case, now I have to write a couple of books.

The Complexities of the Job Search Multiplied by Two

Constance J. Pollard and Richard R. Pollard

As that graduation date draws nearer, most of us are disgruntled by what we feel is perhaps the last major obstacle before embarking upon our careers. We have just spent the last few years in graduate school facing every conceivable obstacle, jumping every hurdle in our paths, and leaping through every obligatory bureaucratic hoop (as well as many that may not have been necessary). We have dotted every "i" and filed every "pink slip" required for the completion of our degrees. We are not about to be deterred by that last barrier—that of acquiring employment in our chosen fields.

At this juncture in our lives, we begin our search for that "perfect" position, at the "perfect" institution, and in the "perfect" location. Although most of us realize this may be unattainable, there is always that little glimmer of hope that fortune will smile upon us, that a suitable position will be available, and that the search committee will have the foresight and intelligence to realize that we are the ideal candidates.

This is the usual case for new graduates; however, our situation was rather unique as we were a husband and wife with two young children, who were scheduled to graduate at the same time. In essence, we were looking for two "perfect" jobs. However, we were realistic and realized that we would have to be a little less selective and arrange our priorities (after all, how often had mother fortune leapt from wherever she hides and smiled upon us during graduate school?).

This essay describes our job search in higher education, the hurdles and pitfalls we encountered, as well as the results. When we entered our doctoral programs, we had made a decision to complete the entire program and leave only with degrees in hand. Our observation was that too many doctoral candidates acquire an ABD status and then have difficulty becoming motivated enough to complete the degree. Because our graduation was scheduled for August, after the Christmas holidays seemed an appropriate time to begin our actual job search. Not only is it a natural break in the school year with departments beginning to plan for the summer and fall sessions, but it was also a good excuse for us to enjoy the season break before leaping into the real world.

The job search for any candidate is an involved process which requires a great deal of time and energy. The old adage that two heads are better than one cannot be applied here; two people, each with their own careers, had to jointly decide what was acceptable and what was not acceptable for employment.

The first step, the determination of acceptable employment criteria, was a joint process; of course, as one might expect, decisions were not reached without much discussion (husbands and wives seldom argue— they discuss the issues). Basically, we identified criteria regarding what constitutes an acceptable position at an acceptable institution. The list we generated was a ruler with which we could gauge the acceptability of a position based on our lifestyles and expectations.

Early in the job-search process, we were quite hopeful that our expectations could be met and that both of us would be able to acquire acceptable positions. In fact, a major priority was that there be a job for each of us as we had just spent the previous two years completing the requirements for Ph.D.s and were excited about continuing work in our areas of expertise. Another obvious factor that entered into this desire was that a family can live better on two salaries than on one.

The criteria for an acceptable higher education institution involved consideration of the geographic location, philosophical orientation, reputation, and stability. Our major and overriding concern was whether the area in which the institution was located would be a good place in which to raise children—a place with educational and cultural opportunities and without a high crime rate. Also, we preferred an area within striking distance of outdoor recreational areas. This criterion could virtually have eliminated any large metropolitan areas for consideration; however, we had not ruled out the possibility of moving to a city. Such a decision could be possible if other criteria could be met.

We were from the western part of the United States and preferred to return to that section of the country; however, we decided that we would not limit our search geographically. The attainment of two jobs might make such a limitation impossible.

The philosophical orientation of the institution in which we accepted employment was also an important consideration. Our preference was for an institution that was both research and student oriented, an institution which provided support for research efforts but also emphasized teaching. This eliminated many state colleges and all community colleges from our list of possibilities.

Another concern was that of the reputation of the institution; our search was for an institution that was noted for its academic excellence. This was especially important in the event we wanted to make a future move in higher education. A move from such an institution would not be a hindrance but would rather enhance our opportunities.

Our final institutional criterion involved the stability of the institution. In our examination of universities, we had discovered that, in many cases, there was much internal stress within departments and universities. We wanted a university in which there were no major shake-ups taking place and with no great turnover of university administrators and faculty. Another factor that entered into determining stability was the number of higher education institutions within a state and the financial strength of that state to support those institutions. Many institutions were experiencing budget cuts and staff layoffs. Our choice would be to locate an institution that was relatively stable and could support long-term positions.

In evaluating criteria involving the acceptability of a particular position within an institution, we identified the following considerations: the attainment of tenure-track positions, type of classes to be taught, number of classes to be taught, research opportunities, the faculty, and salary.

Although tenure-track positions would be desirable, they were not our major concern. We realized that it would be difficult for both of us to attain tenure-track positions at the same institution at the same time; however, we also were cognizant of the fact that temporary positions do have the possibility of becoming permanent, or a tenure line may become available at a later date.

Although we have qualifications to fill many different positions, we preferred employment in our current areas of interest and expertise. Both of us desired teaching positions, but we were willing to make adjustments if necessary. One of us might consider an administrative position or teaching in an area in which we had specialized on the bachelor's or master's level. The opportunity to teach a variety of classes on the graduate and undergraduate levels would be a real bonus and influence our decision to accept employment. Our preference would also be for classes held on a semester and not a quarter basis; moreover, the teaching load should be limited to three classes a semester to allow sufficient time for our research efforts.

The research opportunities available were also an important consideration. What kind of support would there be for research—financial assistance, clerical assistance, library facilities, collaborative possibilities, and the recognition that new faculty need time to initiate research projects? The more research support that was available, the more attractive the position would be.

Our desire to locate a faculty with which we would be compatible was an essential criterion. Our expectations were for a faculty similar to that with which we had been working for the past two years. The faculty should be friendly, open, dynamic, supportive, energetic and willing to work collaboratively (should we have added "able to walk on water" to the list?). We did not want to become involved with a faculty in which internal strife existed to a great extent.

Money—you knew we would get to that concern sooner or later; however, it was at the bottom of our list (let's keep this information confidential). Yes, we did want to be paid adequately; but if both of us could acquire positions, we would be willing to take less. If only one of us could acquire a position, we wanted substantially more.

The identification of these employment criteria was the first step in the job search process. Although each individual's or couple's needs and concerns are different, it is important to realize a necessity for identifying factors and concerns, prioritizing them, and then finding the solution. Now, we had a dearer picture of the "perfect" jobs and had a foundation from which to work. The employment criteria we had identified also served as a basis for devising questions to ask at the interview.

Our next step was to revise our resumes to reflect our qualifications and achievements and be consistent with the standards expected in higher education. Our most current resumes were derived from the business world, so a complete rewrite was in order. Members of our faculty supplied us with copies of their CVs vitae, which we used to construct a template for ours.

What are search committees looking for in candidates and how can one project the right image? Information for each CV was grouped into the following categories: education, teaching experience, business experience, professional organization membership, professional growth (included attendance at conferences), research and writing activities (publications, accepted for publication, submitted for publication, current research activities, and proposals), committees, presentations, and references. Assembling all the information and writing the CVs took longer than we expected; also, we were continually updating them as the semester progressed to reflect our current research projects, conventions, publications, and presentations. The final products (at least for the current week) were effective, and we were ready to jump into the water. We might add that by the time we jumped in, the water was muddy—have you ever tried to keep a CV current?

Having completed these preliminary steps, we compiled a list of institutions which met most of the criteria we had identified and sent letters early in January to the department chairs outlining our qualifications and informing them of our interest in their university. We made it clear that we were a "package deal" and included copies of our CVs. Our belief was that even if they did not currently have or know of openings, we had at least made contact in the event that a position(s) would become available. One of our advisers mentioned that more than likely this would be a waste of time but that graduate students are underworked and the time involved would at least keep us off the streets and out of trouble. Unfortunately, he was right—as usual. Some of the department chairs did respond, but we did not get any real job leads.

Would we recommend this strategy to other graduates? Yes! It provided us with an opportunity to approach these people at a convention we later attended with an excellent ice breaker; the prior, limited contact by letter allowed us a means of introducing ourselves and of opening a conversation with individuals in our fields at the convention.

At this time we were also reviewing the *Chronicle of Higher Education* (the employment bible in higher education), journals that were prominent in our fields, and any other literature that might advertise openings of interest. These sources disclosed a multitude of positions, but we were very selective in whom we contacted. Many of the advertised vacancies did not meet our criteria, and we knew that even if the positions were offered we would not be satisfied. Perhaps one could make the statement that, "Beggars can't be choosers"; but, it was still very early in our job search, and we hadn't achieved the status of "beggar" yet. However, we don't want our readers to become disappointed because toward the end of the job search we believe that all of us come very close to or achieve this undesirable status whether it be through actual circumstances or pure unadulterated panic.

Throughout the job search process our advisers and other members of the faculty continued to inform us there was no need to worry. They assured us that there were still many good positions out there that hadn't even been advertised. They emphasized the opinion that we should not take one position but should wait for two positions. Also, they reminded us that we were exceptionally well qualified and very diversified in our capabilities. These conversations were very reassuring (at least until we had left their offices and had taken five minutes to ponder our situation).

Our next step was to attend a national convention which encompassed both of our fields of study. This provided us with an opportunity to meet with individuals in our areas of expertise. At this convention, we learned of several openings through bulletin board postings as well as word of mouth. We also became eternally grateful to our advisers and department chair (a further reminder of the importance of an excellent faculty). These individuals, having established networks in their fields, located several possible positions, spoke with department chairs and selection committee members, and even went so far as to begin negotiations for two positions. At this convention, our department chair learned of a possible job for Connie at a northwestern university. A telephone call revealed a real interest and a possibility that "shifting" could occur, providing a position for Rick as well. We sent copies of our CVs (and crossed our fingers).

After the convention, we became more serious and less selective about finding positions. Now, we initiated inquiries into positions which we had earlier considered less than ideal. The problem was that there would be only one position available. At this point, one of us (the one who best fit the job description) would make a phone call to the department chair or member of the search committee to discuss the potential opening. We found this practice invaluable as a means of determining our interest in the university and the possibility of a position for the other spouse. Names of individuals to contact in the other spouse's department were obtained, and we were able to eliminate undesirable positions, saving a lot of time and aggravation in the application process. In essence, it was a means of acquiring a feel for the position, university, department, faculty, etc.

A question that may be asked is how we could determine through one phone call all this information. One example: at one southwestern university, different philosophies were discussed. The head of the search committee said it was imperative that the new faculty member be in agreement with his philosophy as their department was in the process of changing their philosophy. The new faculty member would provide the swing vote. "No, thank you!" A new untenured faculty member caught in the middle of a philosophical dispute was definitely not what we wanted to be.

Another situation was a position available in a northern state—during the telephone conversation, the department chair continually degraded one of our faculty members of national prominence. The gentleman was not interested in discussing his program but was more concerned with degrading our university and faculty. It was very interesting to us that even though neither one of us applied for the position, we received a letter of rejection stating that a qualified candidate was not found, and an interim instructor had been appointed.

Other information derived from these conversations was that in many cases the advertised openings were not always what they appeared to be. In some cases, many of the advertised qualifications were incomplete or not detailed enough to actually explain what the selection committee wanted. Information could be obtained about teaching load and research expectations. The telephone calls served to fill in the blanks and assist us in determining the suitability of the job and institution.

Again, the primary (seemingly insurmountable) obstacle we encountered in the job-search process was that only one position was available. Two universities had dual openings, but unfortunately, one of the universities did not meet enough of the employment criteria we had identified.

The other university that had openings which might suit both of us was one that members of our faculty had contacted at the national convention we attended. This was a major land-grant, research university with an excellent faculty. We called the department chair, and he appeared to be a person with whom we would enjoy working. The only drawback was that the university was located in a large metropolitan area in the southern portion of the country. However, we decided that if the opportunity arose, the positives definitely outweighed the negative considerations. Members of our faculty were in close contact with the department chair at this university, and we felt we had an excellent chance of being considered. Imagine our disappointment when we were informed that funding had been cut, and only one position would be available.

As our job search continued, we discovered an interesting phenomenon—a university position would be advertised for which one of us was qualified, and then at a later time an opening would be advertised at the same university for the other spouse (after the call for applications for the first position had been closed). Because these universities did not meet our employment criteria—with only one position available—we had not applied. With this in mind, our recommendation to serious job-searching couples is to apply even when only one position is advertised. If a position is offered, it can always be declined. Also, if the university is very interested, there is always a possibility that a position can be negotiated for the remaining spouse.

That was our hope when a position at a western university was advertised for which Rick was well qualified. After a phone conversation with the department chair, he sent out the required documents, feeling very confident that he would at least be asked for an interview. Sure enough— the letter arrived announcing that he was a finalist, that his references were going to be contacted, and requesting that he fill out the enclosed data applicant card stipulating the usual Affirmative Action information. To our surprise, a letter arrived ten days later stating that a "young" doctoral candidate had been hired. Rick talked to his references only to discover that no one had contacted them. The letter made it appear that the criterion that landed the job was that the candidate was "young"— Rick, however, is in the over-forty age bracket. As you can imagine, this was quite a blow to a candidate who knows he is qualified for the position. Rick called the Affirmative Action Office on campus and discussed the letters. The reaction was, "You've got them. It appears, from the letters, that age might have been a determining factor." What recourse did he have? He could begin an action against the western university, the result of which might be a job or monetary compensation. Before initiating a suit of this nature, one must consider the consequences. Was it really age discrimination or inadequate handling of communication by the university? Would he be blackballed at other universities on the state or national level? Would one want to work for that department? We decided not to sue.

As the semester progressed, our concern about locating positions heightened, but before we reached a level of total panic, we still had a couple of conventions to attend. It was at one of these that our situation finally began to take a turn in the right direction. A "professional opportunities" service was provided at this national convention to present an opportunity for employers and candidates to meet, discuss openings, and schedule interviews. Connie interviewed with selection committees from around the country; each time they expressed interest in her but knew of no openings for Rick. One midwestern university told of a husband and wife who were looking for jobs in the same fields that we were; it looked unlikely that they would both be offered jobs as they were experiencing the same problems as we were.

However, Connie met with a faculty member from the University of Idaho (the northwestern university she had contacted earlier) and was informed that she was in final contention for the position and would be contacted very shortly for an interview. Of course, this came as a total surprise to us as she had not heard from the selection committee and the cutoff date for the position was two months prior. When she asked what position would be available for Rick, she was told, "There are possibilities, but let's see about you first." Although it was encouraging, there was only one position available.

Connie was asked to interview at the University of Idaho. Although each of us had been interviewed at conventions, this was the first time one of us was invited to visit the university. Armed with a list of questions, she interviewed with the dean, assistant dean, selection committee, faculty, and department chair. During the interviews she emphasized our concern about only having one position. She informed the interviewers that if there was no chance of a position for her spouse in the near future, she would be forced to leave. They understood our concern and felt that because there were two other higher education institutions within a short distance (Washington State University and Lewis and Clark State College) and that "shifting" is always occurring, there would eventually be something available for both of us. The department chair voiced concern that Connie might quit if Rick did locate a better position during the year. She assured him that this would not occur, but Rick could not drop out of the higher education scene indefinitely. Because of this and other conversations, Connie did not believe she would be offered the job.

Upon returning from her interview and reviewing our options, we decided it was time to re-circle the wagons and began applying to some of the institutions which from our perspective were less than ideal. It was the early part of May, and we had no real serious prospects. There were still a number of positions available, and we began getting our information ready for mass mailings to these institutions. We had proceeded to apply at a couple of these institutions when Connie received a call from the University of Idaho offering her the position.

She informed them that the only negative to the job offer was that there was no position for Rick. We needed time to think it over. Again, mention was made that things were continually shifting and with Rick's qualifications, something would eventually become available. The department chair informed Connie that she was the unanimous choice of the department and asked her to respond as soon as possible as they would be offering it to another candidate if she refused. Connie asked for a week to consider, and the department chair agreed.

During this week, we discussed and reviewed our options. We knew that one of us could always acquire a position when the time came, but we also knew that the position may not be as ideal as the present one. The university was the major research institution in the state; the location was ideal, and Connie felt she would be compatible with the faculty.

After deliberating for several days, Rick contacted the department chair and the dean of the college and discussed his concern about not having a position. They both acknowledged that concern and indicated that they would do everything possible to assist in locating a position. They assured Rick at the time that situations at the university continually changed and because he did have such a diversified background and excellent qualifications eventually something would become available. They indicated that there is always a need for instructors for classes on a part-time basis and that there might be an opening for a student-teaching supervisor. Of course, there was also the potential for a job at one of the neighboring institutions—Washington State University or Lewis and Clark State College. Moreover, the department chair indicated that Rick could use the university as a base in which to continue his research projects.

After conversing with the dean and department chair, we again continued our discussion on whether we would be making the right move if Connie accepted the position. The one overwhelming negative was there was no position available for Rick. However, there were many items in the positive column such as (a) we would be fortunate enough to be located at one of the universities which we had initially targeted for employment; (b) the faculty appeared to be one with which Connie would enjoy working; (c) there were two major universities in which Rick could do postdoctoral work; (d) there were job possibilities for Rick at one of the institutions of higher education; (e) it would be an excellent place to live in the event a position did become available for Rick or until we could locate two positions that met our needs; (f) the University of Idaho met the majority of our employment selection criteria; and (g) one salary was better than none. Our decision—Connie should accept the position.

After accepting the position, we continued to stay current with the job market listings. As always happens, there were openings at two other universities in which we were interested. The major consolation was that there was still only one position available. Our predicament would have been the same, but in a reverse situation, with Rick being employed and Connie not employed. However, we did contact one of the universities, which informed us it expected two openings next year for which we are well qualified.

Upon arriving at the University of Idaho, Rick was offered a part-time job teaching a couple of courses and working with an internship program. Although he is well qualified for the position, we do feel that a special effort has been made to accommodate us. No promises for a tenure-track position have been made, but we are hopeful that one will become available by the beginning of the next academic year.

If it becomes apparent that there is no possibility for a full-time position, we will continue our job search. At least we are now able to take our time in locating "two perfect positions."

Accepting the Job: The Die Is Cast

If one has been fortunate in having a number of interviews or campus visits, with luck, the day will arrive when a call or letter comes offering a faculty position. If you need time to think about the offer or if you have other interviews, ask for some time before you give the institution your decision. Institutions usually are willing to allow you some time, especially if they are anxious to get you. It's reasonable to ask for a week or even two. You might need to negotiate the length of time; even institutions that want you cannot wait forever.

Some Things to Ponder

Obviously, there is a lot to think about as you decide whether to accept or reject an offer. We will discuss just a few basic things.

If you have the nerve, you can attempt to bargain for things like a higher salary or particular teaching responsibilities. Most deans and department chairs have some flexibility with regard to such requests. Most beginners do not realize this and are so delighted to receive the call that they accept without considering other possibilities. In any event, before you accept a position, be sure the terms of the contract are made clear to you.

Before accepting the job become as well acquainted as possible with the new institution and the local community. Get a copy of the community's Sunday newspaper if possible. The Sunday paper contains all the rental and real estate ads. It will provide insight into the community and the university or college's place in it if one reads it carefully. It will give clues about the cultural growth and interests of the area. The level of cultural sophistication or provincialism will be quickly revealed in the newspaper. Many communities have Web sites you can peruse for useful information.

Housing is a big concern for those considering a move. To buy or to rent, that is the question. The answer again "just depends." However, one should be forewarned that faculty members at the new institution, the chairperson, and deans frequently have friends who deal in real estate. They may well push the new faculty member into purchasing. The same can be said with respect to rentals. Be cautious. Remember, as a new person in a new community, you are vulnerable. Possibly, the best advice that can be given is to buy time. Rent something for a year or two until you can size up the situation in terms of property values, schools for your children, opportunities for recreation, and so on.

One of the most important bits of knowledge that one needs early on the job or even prior to going to it is whether there are internal troubles or divisions within the department, what those troubles are, and who is on the differing sides of the issues. One can never fully know from the interview the troubles that may exist at the institution. Often, no one tells you, but slowly the troubles will emerge. One legitimate question to ask is how many of the faculty supported you. Was the faculty unanimous in its support? If not, just how divided was the vote? Not only is it important for you to know if people opposed your hiring, this information might give you some sense of the cohesiveness of the faculty.

Married couples often face unique problems in accepting a new academic position. (See the essay by Constance and Richard Pollard.) It is not unusual for both partners to be academicians. They have a problem in finding two positions at the same institution or at least in the same general locale. If the institution is sufficiently interested in one of them, it may on occasion find a place for the other; however, often there will be something of a stigma attached to the second partner. It becomes a package deal with the parts not always being equally desirable to the institution. There are exceptions, but they are fairly rare. The administration frequently must bring pressure on a college dean to provide a place for the second academician. Therefore, moves by such a couple must be carefully considered. The path will not be easy. Salaries for these "twofers" may be quite different. This is also true of rank or title. Probably, there are going to be fewer career moves. Once the couple locates in what is considered by both to be an adequate-to-good situation, they often remain there. If such partners are in the same or closely related academic areas, it is possible for them to publish together and receive the deserved credit; however, it must not appear that one is carrying the other in research or publications. Some years ago at a midwestern university two married professors published material together. Their text carried both their names and indicated equal distribution of scholarly efforts. However, the faculty did not believe that the work was equally done nor that recognition should be equally shared.

Frequently, the faculty member's partner is not an academic. The partner still may have trouble finding employment that is satisfying.

As life styles change, it is not infrequent today to find unmarried academicians living together or in other nontraditional arrangements. Institutions have long ago learned not to interfere with such arrangements or even question them. Evaluations are done on the job, not off. There may be exceptions at schools with religious orientations; however, public institutions do not dabble in such matters unless the relationship creates obvious problems that affect the faculty member's job performance. At the same time, though, unmarried couples might face a particular disadvantage. Benefits available to a faculty member's spouse—benefits such as health insurance and life insurance—may be denied to a faculty member's partner if they are not married.

This shows that couples should be extremely aware of the population base of the community. The larger and more diverse the community, the greater the chances of finding acceptance and suitable employment. In some instances, the college or university is one of the larger if not the largest employer in the area. The new faculty member's partner may seek employment at the university in a capacity other than teaching. At very large institutions, this probably creates little conflict. However, if the partner is employed as a receptionist, secretary, or office worker in a capacity that places him or her in close proximity with the faculty member, such an arrangement may create difficulties. Smaller institutions frequently abound in such arrangements. And in many instances there is no strain. However, the potential does exist for problems. Other faculty members may not be as willing to openly discuss issues that may concern one of the partners if the other is present. Suspicions of the rest of the faculty are often aroused irrespective of the fairness of such suspicions. Such an arrangement can be a two-edged sword.

Many institutions of higher education have cooperative arrangements when it comes to educating the children of faculty members. They will take care of tuition and possibly other basic financial needs of children of faculty members. If one has or is planning to have children and one enjoys the environment of such often smaller but excellent educational communities, it is not a bad idea to take positions at them. Such institutions usually place a very high priority on faculty stability. The pay is less than at other schools, but they may have fringe benefits, such as education for children and spouses, that may make up for a lower salary.

The Unthinkable—No Job

What do you do if the unthinkable happens—you do not get a job offer or you get only an offer you do not really wish to accept? Consensus suggests that it is extremely unwise to drop out of academia and still hope to make a comeback. The missing time must be accounted for. There are few resurrections from professional death. Going to work in construction, the hardware company, or in the shoe department may put bread on the table, but doing so for any extended time will jeopardize your academic career.

Of course, one option (if you have it) is to take the job offered, even if it is a poor one. You can always keep your eyes open and apply for other jobs. There are dangers in changing positions too often, but sometimes one just has to move.

However, you would not have that option if you get no job offer. Fortunately, you do have choices: You might take a temporary appointment. (See the essay by Jay Rojewski.) Institutions sometimes offer one- or two-year temporary appointments, perhaps because the holder of the position is on leave, and they need someone to take over teaching duties. You should not count on such jobs turning into a regular position. The regular faculty member may return, in which case you are out. On the other hand, sometimes the regular faculty member does not return. She or he might have been offered a position at the institution where she or he has been a visiting scholar, say. Or maybe the temporary position was created because there had been an unsuccessful search; the position was not filled, but someone was needed to cover the teaching duties. In such a case, you are not automatically "in," but you might have some advantage just because you are known. But, again, be cautious. A temporary position is a way to be in academia, which is good, but it easily can become a dead end.

Another, more desirable, alternative is a postdoctoral fellowship. Typically, these are quite competitive, but it is a prestigious and fruitful way to spend a couple years. Such fellowships can make you attractive when you are ready to try again for a faculty position.

A third path is to take a position on "soft money." Soft-money jobs are of limited duration and typically are under the supervision and direction of a professor who has secured a substantial grant. The work may or may not be especially interesting, but it is a way to stay active in higher education and might enable you to make contacts. Much depends on the sort of work the director allows you to do. For instance, if you are a coauthor on some publications that will count more than if you just wash test tubes.

A fourth option, which likely is about the last thing a new graduate wants to think about, is continuing one's education, perhaps even starting a new doctoral program. But if part of the problem in finding a job is that there is a glut of graduates in the field, one option is to get a degree in a field in which there is no such glut. A second degree, or at least further study, might also make you more competitive in your first field, especially if your additional study has some clear relevance to that field.

A fifth possibility may be to "hang on" at the institution where you graduated. For example, in colleges or schools of education, student teacher supervisors are always needed. Some arts and sciences departments must staff large introductory undergraduate courses. Sometimes they will hire their graduates as instructors. The pay and prestige are not high, but one can survive. And survival is the name of the game at this stage. If you want a job in higher education, you need to find some way to keep your hand in.

Lastly, there are a wide variety of jobs in government and other areas that can preserve one's academic credentials until a more desirable position is offered. State departments of education frequently employ a wide variety of degree holders to handle the public school system's programs, evaluations, and so on. Although such positions are not the best, at least if you are aiming for a faculty position, they should not be sneered at. A few years ago, a young man holding a doctorate in a social science area and finding no available teaching position discovered that the medical college of the state university had some education-related positions open. He took one and made a career out of audiovisual education in the training of physicians. He became the expert in this field within the medical school. Social work and the court systems often employ people with doctoral degrees in one area or another. They need the experts and often pay quite well for them. Some of these positions can actually enhance the credentials of the candidate for a later faculty position and provide an experiential base for later lectures.

The Decisions, Dilemmas, and Opportunities Involved in Accepting a Non-Tenure Track Appointment

Jay W. Rojewski

I have an opportunity here to describe experiences and situations I've encountered while looking for and accepting my first faculty position in higher education. Recently, I accepted a position at the University of Illinois as a visiting assistant professor in the Department of Vocational and Technical Education but not without my share of anxiety and concern about my future in academia.

In this essay, I pay particular attention to my decision to accept a non-tenure line appointment and focus on some of the unique situations which I have encountered in the process. Although my journey cannot be duplicated and should not be generalized, it is my sincere hope that what follows may provide food for thought to those who find themselves in similar circumstances. If my insight appears naive and idealistic or perhaps even crude and simple in comparison with that of those more experienced, I offer my apology.

I received an undergraduate degree in psychology from a small private liberal arts college in the Midwest and subsequently entered the workforce of a nonprofit vocational rehabilitation facility. Later, I enrolled in courses at the University of Nebraska-Lincoln on a full-time basis and was hired as a graduate research assistant in the Department of Vocational and Adult Education. I served in this position until my graduation with a Ph.D. in vocational special education.

To some degree, I am still caught up in the excitement of realizing a long-held dream. Yet, my excitement is tempered by the sobering awareness that I must now go out into the real world and demonstrate that I can teach and conduct research of the quality expected from faculty at the postsecondary level.

The job application and interview process are really the first steps on that long road of demonstrating one's ability and gradually being accepted into the faculty ranks of higher education. Scheduled to graduate in May, in the latter half of the preceding year, I started to scour the *Chronicle of Higher Education* for positions which met my qualifications and expectations for that first job. Of course, I began my quest with the "ideal" job clearly in view: a tenure-track, assistant-professor-level position at a land-grant institution. Initially, my resolve to apply for only those positions which fit this ideal was so strong that I seriously contemplated completing a year of postdoctoral study rather than take a position which did not meet my guidelines. It didn't take very long, however, for me to realize that there was not a great demand for faculty of vocational special needs education. In fact, there were no positions listed specifically for personnel in vocational special education during this time period. So with my adviser's assistance, I began to look and apply for positions in special education and general vocational education which seemed to tap some of my strengths (i.e., an emphasis in vocational and transition programming, characteristics of students with special needs, general issues in vocational education, etc.). All told, I applied for 15 different positions, mostly with land-grant or research-oriented institutions representing varying degrees of suitability to my background and preparation.

Then, in early December, I received a copy of a job announcement at the American Vocational Association's annual convention. The University of Illinois job announcement described a visiting assistant professor position and the federally funded leadership development program of which it was a part. The project involved training and preparing secondary educators to work with and develop programs for students with special needs. The announcement stipulated that the availability of the position was contingent on receipt of requested federal funding. Quite frankly, my first reaction to the announcement was little more than a passing glance—after all it was a non-tenure-track position funded by soft money. A grant-funded project? No thanks. It's definitely not what I was looking for! And it really didn't matter at this point that the personnel qualifications and job requirements matched my background and preparation almost perfectly. I placed the job announcement in my "dead file" (along with a list of the institutions I had applied to, letters of rejection received, and my CV) and put it out of my mind. After looking for my ideal position for another two months, I decided to apply for the Illinois position in mid-February;

the pangs of anxiety and apprehension about not locating many available positions were a big motivator. Having people tell me, "Oh, it's still early, don't worry" did not ease my discomfort! About two weeks after the application deadline, I received a call from the department chair asking me about my availability for a job interview.

In retrospect, I went to the interview not as well prepared as I probably should have been to go through the rigorous process, but, after all, I wasn't that sure I was interested in being a temporary faculty member. I kept thinking that, at the very least, it wouldn't be a total loss; this would be good practice for job interviews which were sure to come. As the day of the interview progressed, I felt myself becoming more excited, even anxious, about the seemingly unlimited opportunity which the university offered. Increasingly, I found myself wanting to impress those who might become my colleagues.

The interview process itself was a grueling yet extremely informative experience. I didn't notice it so much during the day, but as I boarded my flight home, I realized I was completely exhausted. During the day-long interview process, I met with a number of different people including members of the search committee, a representative from the dean's office, and most of the departmental faculty members. I also had an opportunity to have lunch with several departmental graduate students. In fact, I had requested an opportunity to visit with graduate students prior to the interview. Although initially I was quite eager to meet with these students, my feelings began to change as the time to meet with them approached. I found myself becoming more and more apprehensive. I began to imagine these whiz kids ripping me to shreds, searching out and finding well-hidden limitations. My intent was not to use these students as a way of finding out the real dirt about the department but rather to determine the caliber of students—were these the kind of students I would want to teach and advise? As it turned out, the three students I had lunch with were quite bright, energetic, and genuine. I really enjoyed the time spent with them. All in all, a good decision, I think.

Having no prior experience, I had imagined that a visiting appointment was synonymous with detachment from and lack of integration with the department. After all, this appointment was only temporary. Surely, the best one could hope for from a visiting appointment was an invitation to the weekly faculty meeting. This wasn't a real faculty appointment—right? Wrong. I found that the visiting faculty actually made significant contributions to the department. The involvement of current visiting faculty was viewed as integral to the continued success of the department in all phases. A visiting faculty member sat on the search committee to hire me! I left with an awakened sense of anticipation . . . maybe I needed to rethink my hasty decision to write off this job so quickly.

I returned home from the interview tired and still not certain about the desirability of the position. But, by this point, I was beginning to think about accepting the job if it were offered. The more I thought about it, the more confident I felt that the position would be a good first job, especially when viewed from the perspective of my desired future career path.

Several days after my return home, I received a call from another school to which I had applied. Was I interested in the position and would I come to their campus for an interview? My initial reaction was a resounding yes! After all, this school was a major land-grant institution in the Southeast, and the appointment was a tenure-track assistant professor position—ideal! What was not ideal was that the courses I would be required to teach were not in my specific areas of interest but were much more of a general nature than I had hoped for.

An offer for the Illinois position was extended to me several weeks after the interview. A dilemma arose—do I opt for a non-tenure track position in order to teach in my areas of interest, or do I pursue an opportunity for a tenure-line appointment which would require a shift in my teaching and research interests? My decision did not come easily. I was excited about receiving the opportunity to interview for a tenure-track position, but in the end, I chose to teach in areas in which my interests and skills were greatest. I accepted the Illinois offer contingent on official notification of the grant award which was expected on or before the first of June. Finally, I could let out a sigh of relief; the decisions were over and my professional career was about to begin . . . well, almost.

As June approached, everything was set for our move—the moving van was rented and our belongings were packed. The only problem was that notification of funding for all new projects in this particular grant competition was delayed in Washington, D.C., for two weeks. Panic! I was scheduled to begin teaching a summer course in less than two weeks, but couldn't afford to move everything without knowing my employment status after completing the summer course (the midyear funding cycle and scheduling of project activities allowed me to teach one summer course under the previously funded project prior to funding for the project I was hired to direct).

So, instead of moving to our new home, we moved the majority of our possessions into storage, literally stuffed our small car with as many clothes and reference books as it would hold, and set out for Illinois on a temporary basis. We lived out of suitcases for the next several weeks, hopeful but uncertain of our future. During the delay, I became increasingly aware that it was possible I could be unemployed if the project was not funded. I was able to arrange a job interview at another land-grant institution during this turbulent period, but in the end notification of federal funding for the project was received, and I officially committed to Illinois.

When I initially received the Illinois offer, I asked for and received a week to think about my decision. During this week, I agonized about making the right decision—examining a number of factors and issues pertinent to the decision and to the long-term ramifications represented. For example, why accept a temporary position as a visiting assistant professor; worse yet, why accept one dependent on soft money and established as a non-tenure track appointment? This is a valid question, especially in light of the fact that when I left the rehabilitation facility to complete my doctorate, I swore that I would never, ever, again put myself in a position where I would be dependent on the funding of a grant proposal for my professional livelihood. Even though I have enjoyed a fair degree of success with grant-funded programs and other soft-money projects, I experienced enough insecurity, stress, and sleepless nights during my tenure as a grant writer and project supervisor to last me a lifetime. Never again, right? Wrong. . . .

I guess the bottom line in a lot of this can be summed up with one word—opportunity. A land-grant, research-oriented institution can provide many opportunities to advance one's professional research and also places its faculty in a position which allows exposure to professionals who are considered at the top of their respective fields. In addition, this particular institution has been considered to be among the best in the country and, as a result, has a good deal of status and prestige. Recently, the department was highly rated in a national study, and its research and teaching efforts on students with special needs have been consistently recognized for their national impact. This national recognition, in turn, has fostered continual development of numerous research and teaching opportunities in vocational special needs education (my areas of expertise) over the past several years. The chance to work in this type of environment rarely happens more than once in a lifetime and often doesn't happen at all.

For me, the position was (and is) a desirable one; it is not a lesser position because it is a visiting appointment. Some of the main reasons that it is desirable are the responsibilities and expectations inherent with the appointment. I will be allowed to teach and advise graduate students in my interest areas immediately whereas other positions of interest to me often combined undergraduate and graduate responsibilities. The soft money also allows me to hire a graduate assistant, something I probably would not have had for at least a year or two at other institutions. By working on one specific project, I believe that I can make an immediate impact and, at the same time, gain valuable experience. The position provides me with an immediate direction for both my teaching and research, something I would have had to wait for in other positions. Because this project has been operating for several funding cycles, it has an established and proven track record. I will be able to benefit from the success, momentum, and exposure it has already achieved.

Obviously, tenure-line positions will become available over the next several years at similar institutions for which I will be able to apply. This appointment only enhances my opportunities to be a serious candidate for these positions. I have decided to invest time now as a non-tenure line faculty member to both prove myself and become integrated into the complex system of higher education.

A number of people gave their advice and suggestions to me during the decision-making process; but three exceptional people really stand out. I feel fortunate to have had opportunities to work with the highest caliber of professionals at the University of Nebraska. My adviser and my assistantship supervisor (who is also the departmental chair) both gave me more than a reasonable amount of their time. They listened patiently to my concerns and helped to sort out areas of confusion and doubt. Yet, they also made it clear that, in the end, the decision had to be mine. Their extraordinary patience and concern for my future well-being will always be appreciated.

A friend, now retired from a long and distinguished career in higher education, provided me with wise counsel. She likened the job search and acceptance process to that of buying a house. When I asked her for advice on the wisdom of accepting a non-tenured, grant-funded position, she stated that "When you are in the market to purchase a home, there are three things you must consider: location, location, location!" She did not elaborate; however, her point was well taken.

Accepting this visiting appointment provides me a way of starting my career at a premier institution. I perceive it as a foot in the door, an opportunity to work with the highest caliber of professionals—a springboard to the rest of my career. As a rookie, it could conceivably take me ten years or more to work my way up from a smaller teaching-oriented college to a research-oriented institution comparable to Illinois and many other land-grant research institutions. And several different people pointed out that it is much easier to go from a school with the stature and reputation of Illinois to a smaller, teaching-oriented university than the other way around. Taking my current interests and long-term goals into consideration, I would much rather have this option than face an uphill battle. (I do not mean to downplay or diminish those who work at teaching-oriented institutions. However, in order to meet my long-term career goals, which include research as well as teaching, I must seek employment at an institution which will allow me opportunities and encourage me to conduct research.)

Some readers may point out the fact that I had few, if any, real choices in this situation, making my discussion moot. Even so, the close fit between the job description and requirements and my background and training would have weighed considerably in my final decision.

A number of additional factors, other than those mentioned, also influenced my decision to accept a higher-risk visiting appointment. My situation allowed me flexibility which others may not have. Because my wife and I don't have any children at the present time, I think we had more flexibility in being able to accept a visiting appointment. At present, we are not as concerned about moving or settling down as we would be with a family. Another factor was that the salary of the position was comparable to that which I had anticipated as a tenure-line faculty member. A third factor for this particular position was the geographic location, which presented, in my opinion, the best of both worlds. Being born and raised in the Midwest, the draw of familiar territory (a university community of fewer than 100,000 people with similar cultural values and norms) was appealing. On the other hand, it should prove to be exciting to have three large metropolitan areas within a couple of hours drive from our new home in central Illinois.

So, does a visiting appointment still bother me? Quite frankly, at times and to some degree it does. Does the fact that my position is on a nontenure line concern me? Yes, I would much prefer to be on a tenure-track line. Does the uncertainty of a soft-money position cause me some hesitation? Of course. Yet, despite these concerns, I still feel the job is a good move for me in the long term. Increasingly, I find myself excited about what I will be doing within the job and less concerned about my title. For now, it is an ideal compromise—a very solid first step.

Conceivably, I could maintain this position for two or three years and then, I hope, secure a tenure-track position at another research-oriented institution. As a number of people have pointed out to me, I am still relatively young in terms of my entire potential career in higher education. As such, I can afford to take two or three years in a non-tenured position in exchange for the experience gained, the potential networks developed, and opportunities for involvement in many exciting national projects. I tend to agree.

In this essay, I have attempted to provide some insight into my thoughts and feelings about making a decision concerning my first job out of graduate school. I don't think it possible to generalize from my experiences and say it is a typical or even a representative model. However, portions of my experience can be examined in terms of the issues and concerns which others may also encounter. I have talked about the blue and orange of the University of Illinois with zest but think that the scenario and my thoughts about it would be appropriate for most research-oriented institutions.

How do I feel about this decision? My feelings are an odd and amorphous mixture of anxiety and excitement, fear and eagerness, concern over my ability to succeed and confidence that I can. For now, my career is headed in the right direction, but the wisdom of my decision can only be determined years from now when the clarity and certainty of hindsight can put all of this into perspective. Until then. . . .

Author's Note

The author would like to acknowledge Michael T. Miller for his assistance and support during the past year and for his helpful comments on this essay.

Benefits

Gregory P. Clayton

When you are deciding on a position with a college or university, one important element is the benefits package offered to the faculty. The benefits package can easily amount to 20 percent to 25 percent of your total compensation package, and generally this additional compensation is not considered taxable income. Because the monetary value is great, what should you look for, what questions should you ask, and how should you make your decision? In the following pages I will try to address the major benefit categories such as health insurance, dental insurance, life insurance, disability benefits, and retirement plans. Other plans, such as for eye care and coverage for job-related legal expenses, will not be covered.

Some Basic Questions

In your discussion with a college or university, some general concepts that you should understand and questions you should ask are: What are the eligibility requirements for the benefits package? Do you have to be employed for a certain number of days or months before you can participate in the plan? Do you have to be in a full-time or a permanent position to participate in the plan? Are there required coverages, or can you take any plan you want? What about the premiums that will be deducted from your paycheck? Are they on a before- or after-tax basis? Some colleges and universities offer a benefit package that allows the faculty member's deductions to be on a before-tax basis. From the faculty member's standpoint, this is an ideal situation in that the net pay will be higher because less taxes are being withheld. If the college and university contributes to Social Security, the deductions will also reduce your Social Security wages, which will have a small effect on your Social Security retirement benefit and must be considered. Generally the tax savings outweigh any disadvantages in regard to your Social Security benefit. Many colleges and universities are offering flexible benefit programs. Under these types of programs, faculty members are given so many credits or dollars to spend on the benefit package and then make choices about what benefits they need. If faculty members do not spend all the credits or dollars allotted, they are then added back to their checks as taxable cash. If the cost of the selected benefits is greater than the credits, then a deduction is made from the faculty members' paychecks, usually on a pretax basis. The advantage is not having to take a benefit in order to get the college or university's contribution, thus giving the faculty more flexibility. Also, under these plans, there may be options for spending accounts or reimbursement accounts which allow you to prepay certain medical or child-care expenses on a pretax basis. These accounts have certain restrictions but can be of great advantage to the faculty member.

Health Benefits

Most faculty members think first of health benefits. In this area there are many choices and many considerations. Several initial questions should be asked before a plan is selected. The first is when does the coverage go into effect? The faculty member needs to know the eligibility requirements: Do you have to be half-time or greater? Do you have to be in a permanent position to be eligible to participate in the benefit programs of the college or university? Is the university contribution to the plan reduced if you are not full-time? Another important point is, are there any pre-existing conditions, limitations, or waiting periods? Some health plans have a waiting period before they will cover any pre-existing conditions. (A preexisting condition is one that you were treated for or were taking medication for prior to the start of coverage.) This period may take the form of a number of months exclusion or a dollar-amount limitation. If he or she has any health problems the faculty member must be aware of the restrictions the different plans have. There may be a delayed starting date, for example, you might have to be employed several months before the coverage goes into effect and the college or university's contribution to the plan starts. After the general entry requirements have been discussed, then you would need to decide what type of health plan you want. Most colleges and universities will offer at least two types of health plans.

The first type is generally a traditional insurance contract. This plan may have a deductible which is an amount you pay before any medical bills would be paid. The deductible extends over a period of time, such as a calendar year or policy year. Then after the deductible, the plan will pay a percentage of the medical expenses, such as 80 percent. Generally under these plans, there is a stop loss, which refers to the out-of-pocket expense you incur on the remaining 20 percent after the plan pays 80 percent. This stop loss is very important because it limits your liability in the event of a serious illness which involves large medical bills. Under this type of health plan, there are no restrictions on who you use as a physician or where you receive the service. But these plans may have requirements such as required second opinion on surgeries, precertification before a hospital stay, and review of the length of hospital stays. These plans will provide worldwide coverage.

The other type of health plan offered is a Health Maintenance Organization (HMO), a managed health plan. The plan generally uses only certain providers and thereby can better control medical cost. Under this program 100 percent of medical expenses are generally covered, but there are restrictions on whom you see as a physician.

There are two types of HMOs. The most common is the Independent Practice Model (IPM). Under this type of arrangement the HMO will contract with local physicians who have a private practice to provide care for their members. The members then select which physician they wish to see. In most plans each family member could choose a different physician. The physician chosen would provide all the medical care for that person. If a specialist is needed, the primary-care physician would provide a referral to one of the contracting specialists. Hospitalization would be provided in area hospitals that the HMO has contracts with. The other type of HMO is a closed panel, in which the physicians are employees of the HMO. Again, you would choose one of the physicians to provide your care. This person would then make referrals to specialists when necessary. Generally, there are restrictions on providers used, and out-of-area service is limited. But with an HMO, you do receive additional services such as preventive medical services. Also most HMOs use a monthly charge for a 30-day supply of prescription drugs. Under the HMOs there are no claim forms or other types of paper work to receive payment for services because the HMOs provide the service.

Another plan that you may be offered is a Preferred Provider Organization (PPO). This plan is somewhat of a mix between an insurance contract and the HMO. If you use certain providers the insurance will pay a higher amount. Instead of 80 percent, for example, the plan would pay 90 percent. If certain providers are used, no deductible would be assessed.

If you choose to use a physician who was not a Preferred Provider, then the insurance would pay in the traditional manner.

In choosing the plan that is best for you and your family, you need to look at how much risk you are comfortable accepting. If your family is healthy and you rarely use medical services, perhaps a lower option plan with a lower cost might be best. If you and your family have a tendency to use medical services often, then a plan that provides greater coverage may be best, because even if the premium is higher, the overall cost would be less. Look at the premium charged and the coverage and the risk you are willing to take when deciding which plan is best for you. Look at the restrictions. Does having to use a certain physician cause you a problem? If so, then an HMO may not be for you. Does paying a deductible cause a financial hardship? Then full coverage with a higher monthly premium may be the best approach. In addition, always review the exclusions of the plans being offered. Also look at features such as precertification before a hospital stay, second opinion for surgeries, and other cost-containment features that may require action on your part. A final consideration, does the college or university ever offer you a chance to change health carriers? Most schools do, but this can be a very important consideration.

Life Insurance

Life insurance is another important benefit that colleges and universities offer their faculty members. Generally, a base amount is provided by the school. This may be as a factor of salary such as two times salary, or it may be a flat dollar amount of coverage for the faculty member. The life insurance most often offered is group term life. With group term life insurance, you are buying protection only as compared to whole-life or universal life, which has a savings component. The life insurance offered by the school usually will have no waiting periods or restrictions. The college or university also may offer the faculty member the option of purchasing additional term insurance with no restrictions such as evidence of insurability. You also may be offered an additional coverage called Accidental Death and Dismemberment, which pays only in the event of an accident. Some schools will have a plan that covers people only when they are on university business; others will have a blanket policy that covers the faculty member 24 hours a day.

In choosing life insurance, you should consider your needs. As a rule of thumb, a person should have life insurance equal to six times her or his salary, but this can vary depending on the number of dependents and one's current financial situation. In making a decision on how much life insurance you should have, you need to look at other policies you own and death benefits from retirement plans and current investments. Also, consider how much you should carry with an employer group plan. Group term life is very economical, but should you leave the institution, the coverage would have to be converted to an individual plan. Normally, policies are converted to a whole-life or universal plan at your current age, which makes them a lot more expensive than the group term policy. This may be one reason not to have all your life insurance with your employer. Some colleges and universities will offer the option to buy individual life plans through payroll deduction. These are usually a universal life plan or a whole-life plan. These are attractive in the sense that if you leave your present employment you continue on with these coverages by paying the premium directly. Another plus is that the underwriting standards are not as strict, and coverage up to a certain face amount is guaranteed.

One consideration is the age-old argument on whether to buy term insurance and invest the difference or buy whole-life or universal that has a savings component. A younger faculty member will need more life insurance because of family, mortgage, and so on, but can least afford the savings component in whole-life or universal life. Here term insurance is the most effective because one can purchase the amount of coverage needed. In these cases, the college or university will offer some type of tax-deferred annuity or deferred compensation plan, and the faculty member can save on a tax-sheltered basis. This is true for faculty in all situations. Therefore, term insurance may be more advantageous.

Long-Term Disability

One benefit that is critically important is a long-term disability (LTD) income plan. This type of coverage replaces your income in the event you are disabled and unable to work. On these plans, review the definition of "disability." Many plans will use, for the initial years, a more liberal definition such as being unable to perform the main duties of your present job. Another plan may consider you disabled if you are unable to do jobs that your education or background would suit. Some plans will use a combination: In the first two years, your job is the basis, but after that, the broader definition is used. The length of the waiting period before benefits begin is another factor that must be considered. Many plans use six months as a waiting period. Generally the shorter the waiting period, the higher the premium. Related to this is the way that the school continues your salary during this waiting period. Is sick leave used or some type of short-term disability plan? Does the plan have a coordination of benefits provision? If so, the amount you would receive would be reduced by benefits received from Social Security and/or Workers Compensation. This is a common feature because it keeps premium costs low and still provides an adequate benefit. The next point is how much of your income does the plan replace? Most plans use 60 percent of salary as a basis, some plans will use 66.66 percent of salary. Make sure this is an adequate amount for your situation. Also see if there is a maximum benefit; this only affects the higher-paid individual, but can be important. If there is a maximum and your salary exceeds it, then you are not going to receive an adequate benefit and may have to supplement the plan. You also need to look at what salary is used to determine the benefit. Is it your budgeted salary? If you teach summer sessions, too, using a budgeted salary may not replace your actual annual income. Some schools will use as salary either the budgeted amount or your last year W-2 salary, whichever is greater. This way your summer session income is included. Another question to ask is does the plan have a cost-of-living increase during disability payments? Most plans use a 3 percent cost-of-living increase while you are receiving benefits. This is a very important feature because without it, your income would shrink as the cost of living increased. Does the plan make any provisions for partial disability? This would be important if you could not return to full-time work, but you could do part-time work. In this case, some plans will continue a partial benefit. One feature that should not be overlooked is whether the disability plan continues the contribution to your pension while you are receiving the income benefit. Many LTD plans do have a provision that pays your contribution and the school's contribution to your pension plan. Some schools may use another basis to continue the pension contribution or service credit. This important provision assures that when the LTD plan ends, you will have a funded pension plan to draw on plus Social Security, if applicable, and personal savings. This will assure a secure retirement.

Retirement Plan

The last major benefit is the college or university's retirement plan. This is a benefit that many younger faculty members do not consider very carefully even though it is one of the most important benefits. Younger faculty might think they have plenty of time to consider retirement, but time goes by quickly. There are two major types of retirement plans—they are a defined benefit plan and a defined contribution plan. Under a defined benefit plan, the benefit is based on a formula such as 50 percent of the average of the highest five years of salary with 25 years of service. The contribution to this type of plan is based on an actuarial assumption, and the school's contribution would be funded according to this projection. This type of plan is seen in many state teacher retirement systems. The other type of plan is a defined contribution plan in which the benefit is unknown but the contribution is defined, such as 5 percent by the employee and 10 percent by the employer. Then at retirement time, the money contributed by the employee and the employer plus interest and dividends is taken to buy a retirement benefit which provides an income. In many colleges and universities the Teachers Insurance and Annuity Association and College Retirement Equity Fund (TIAA/CREF) is one funding vehicle for a defined contribution plan.

Several factors should be looked at no matter which plan is offered. The first is the entry requirements. Do you have to be a certain age and have so many years of service with that school in order to participate in the retirement plan? The sooner you are able to join the plan, the better because your retirement benefit will generally be larger. What are the vesting schedules? In other words, when do you get the school's contribution to your plan? Some schools insist upon five years of employment before you can receive a portion of the employer's contribution and ten years before you are 100 percent vested. Other plans may vest immediately or in a shorter time period. This can be very important if for some reason you would decide to leave that school and go to another college or university. If the plan had a vesting schedule and you did not work long enough, you may only receive your portion of the contributions and lose the school's contribution.

In a defined contribution plan, you may have a choice of investment options. You can obtain some diversity by investing in, say, bonds in one fund, stocks in another and possibly real estate in another. By having some choice in where the money is invested, you may be able to receive an increased return and, thereby, receive a greater retirement benefit.

Does the retirement plan allow you to make tax-deferred contributions to the plan? This is a very effective way to save money in that you put in money and do not pay taxes on the contributions or the interest earned until you receive a benefit from the plan. Also most schools will offer employees opportunities to tax defer greater amounts than the required contribution to the basic retirement plan. This ability to defer is a great way to reduce your current tax liability and provide a more tax-efficient savings plan.

Is the school covered by Social Security, or is there a state system? Most schools are covered by Social Security, which requires a contribution by you and the employer. This will then provide a retirement benefit and other benefits in the event of disability and death. Some schools may pay part of your share to Social Security which helps improve your salary situation.

Institutional Contributions

The last point to review with regard to retirement plans is the amount of contributions the school makes on your behalf. Comparing two defined contribution plans is relatively simple in that you can look at the percent of contribution between the two schools, but comparing a defined contribution plan to a defined benefit is more difficult. Here you will need to look at the formula and also what the school has put in over the past years. Also you will need to ask if the plan has any unfunded liability. This amount of contribution can have a significant effect on your total compensation package. Another question to ask is whether the school contributes overall salaries including such things as summer school, or does the school only pay its contribution on the nine-month salary? This question is relevant for both the defined contribution and the defined benefits plan. Does this extra salary count in the formula for benefits in the defined benefit plan?

This essay has been a general discussion of questions that should be asked and items to be reviewed in your benefit package. In the interview process, it may be appropriate to talk to the college or university's benefits manager to get additional information about specific questions. I have not covered all benefits that might be offered but reviewed the plans that almost all schools will offer. Tuition programs, eye-care plans, and sabbatical leaves are still other benefits to consider.

Making the Transition:
Demands and Decisions
of the First Months on the Job

So now you have a job. Now what? How do you make the transition? What do you do when you show up at your new office for the first time? How do you stick it out, and what manner do you take on to survive? The first year is a particularly important and stressful period as one makes the transition from graduate student to professor and begins to confront the demands and decisions of one's vocation. Hence, in this essay, we focus on the first months on the job, on some of the particular challenges, and how one might begin to deal with them. Some issues are unique to the first year; others occupy professors throughout their careers. Even in this latter case, though, these problems have a particular spin in the context of the transition period.

First, it should be noted that the first year *is* a time of transition. Of course, all graduate students get some taste of "professoring" if only from watching professors do it and from engaging in the business of research, writing, and creating. And some students get an even bigger taste in that they teach some classes and have even more intensive research experiences than usual. But even for people in this latter group, when moving from student to professor one is confronted by the need to see oneself rather differently. All of a sudden you are an authority. You are, in fact, possibly *the* authority, at least at your institution. It is now you who will make all of the decisions about what will be taught and how it will be taught. For the brand-new faculty member it may be hard to picture oneself in this new situation. You must achieve a new mental set.

First of all, we should confront a feeling that new professors often get. Far from trying to figure out ways to work into the institution, they think they need to find ways to get out! They have the feeling that they've made a big mistake in taking the position.

"I've Made a Mistake!!"

It is fairly common for new professors to anticipate a time when they can let down. They want a time to relax and get to know the family again or to enjoy the comforts and affluence not affordable to doctoral students. They tend to see the worst as being over. They have passed the test and defended the dissertation. And the honeymoon, the live-happily-ever-after scenario, just "must" be so. It isn't.

Contrary to the expectations of many new professors, there may even be an anti-honeymoon. It is not uncommon for the beginning faculty member to experience a sense of sharp disappointment with the position. One has only been able to interview with the faculty members for a short while prior to agreeing to take the position. One has been forced to make up one's mind based on about a day and a half of observations and discussions. In this brief period and limited set of interviews, one is likely to want to believe he or she has selected the perfect place to practice the profession. But then one finds out the place is not perfect.

Plus, typically, the pressure is on from day one. When one becomes a professor, one is expected to be able to perform at a level similar to senior colleagues, and, to some extent, new professors want to be considered fully equal with the senior faculty. Physicians and lawyers are expected to perform on a professional level the minute they walk onto the job. Professors, too, must be able to practice immediately and in all legitimate areas of the domain. Few excuses are acceptable.

Now that you are on the job and may have discovered that it, indeed, is not perfect, remember there is no turning back, at least not immediately. You have rejected all other offers; and they are most likely no longer available. In fact, you probably cannot, if you are wise, even leave after the first year without risking your academic complexion and future prospects. Institutions of higher learning tend to frown on "leapfroggers." You are where you are probably going to be for the next two to three years at least.

What do you do if you do find yourself thinking you've made a mistake? Before you do anything rash, take some time to think through your situation. Try to take an objective look at the demands being placed on you. But think, too, about the help and support you might get. The transition is bound to be tough, but it might not really be as bad as it first appears.

Juggling Personal and Professional Concerns

One focus of stress is the demands the job places on your personal life. Think carefully about what those job demands are. In accepting the job you should have understood these demands and should be prepared to live with them. But, given the heat of the job search and the possible fuzziness of those demands, it is fairly rare that one has determined in great detail how to deal with all those demands. You now need to carefully discern and prioritize your personal interests, ambitions, concerns, and needs. Basic conflicts or at least tensions may exist between your own interests and institutional demands. What is it to be? Academic work? What sort of academic work? Do you want to be a star in your field? What about your family? How important is your social life?

Perhaps the best advice is to concentrate on the job and the academic requirements mandated by the job during the first months. Focus on the job even at the cost of neglecting or shortchanging your other interests. The job must come first. It has long been said "academia is a very jealous lover." As our essayists in Part I make quite clear, colleges and universities want a commitment. Perhaps you will have to spend more time away from family than you would wish. But one does one's family little good if the job is neglected and the appointment terminated. And if you do decide to move on, you want to be able to show you were doing a good job and are not being forced out. Finally, by focusing on the job, you'll have a better idea just what the job is demanding of you, and so you can act with real knowledge of your situation and its benefits and costs.

Of course, gauging institutional demands is not always easy. Such demands are stated in some form or other, certainly, for example in the institution's mission statement and your employment contract. However, these stated demands may not match actual demands, or it may not be clear how you are expected to fulfill those stated demands. So here's a very basic principle to follow as you try to make your way through the transition period: Actions speak louder than words. To get a handle on the realities of your situation, attempt to discern which professors are most respected at the institution and study what they do. Use them as models. Try to ascertain their ways of understanding and dealing with institutional demands. How do they interact with colleagues? How many publications do they have? How do they order their priorities? We are not saying that you should simply imitate senior colleagues, but their paths to success can give you some helpful insights.

Facing the Demands of Teaching,
Scholarship, and Service

One thing to consider is how you might prioritize the holy trinity of the institution: teaching, scholarship, and service. If your time is limited, as it is bound to be, be smart about budgeting it. Some institutions make their priorities quite clear. Others claim to value all three elements nearly equally. Where there is ambiguity, perhaps a good rule of thumb is to rank the categories this way (from least pressing to most important): service, research, teaching.

Generally, one can afford to devote little or no time to service at the beginning of a career. After all, you are not well known in the academic or larger community. Often, new faculty are hesitant to say "no" when invited to perform service activities. But by and large, if people ask you to do things, and you can't accommodate them, they are ready to understand your situation. Fellow faculty members and administrators are more ready to forgive neglect in this area than in others.

Next in importance is scholarship. At institutions where scholarship is an expectation, you must give attention to it from day one. However, colleagues expect that it may take some time before you can show results. For example, grants, if they are required and must be applied for, show faculty colleagues that research is being planned but that it takes time to get it rolling. Or you may need some form of support such as computers or research assistants. All faculty members know that it takes time to acquire this support. Therefore, they will permit you some time to get set up and get down to the business of research. But even so, you can expect to be warned almost on a daily basis about the importance of research work.

Your most immediate priority on the job is teaching. Whether you are teaching on the undergraduate level, the graduate level, or on both, the quality of your teaching is crucial in gaining recognition and favor at the institution. For new faculty members it is a potential Achilles heel. True, teaching often does not count in the weighty manner that research does in the promotion and tenure process, but through the grapevine or by the more formal communications systems existent at every college and university, everyone will shortly become aware of the quality of your teaching. The senior faculty members are very aware of the good or bad vibrations emanating from the students who attend your classes. The administrators will not be far behind in learning about the quality of your teaching. Students talk a great deal. It is nearly impossible to cover up poor teaching. Poor research can be destroyed, and few will know about it. Not so for the public performance that teaching entails. On the other hand, reports of good teaching on the part of the new faculty member make the entire faculty feel their recruitment process was successful. Although it is difficult to document exactly the qualities of good teaching and obtain data to this effect, the faculty need use no such methods to confirm good or bad teaching anyway. Your colleagues merely have to whisper in the hall that so-and-so, a new faculty member, is having considerable difficulties in his or her teaching to permanently impair the new professor's reputation at the institution.

Relationships with People

Another quite important part of the transition is establishing relationships with the people around you. This can be a chore. It's part of the job to establish relationships with the people with whom you work. But good interpersonal relationships can be a source of support, too. Below we will say a bit about relationships with particular sorts of people, but first we will note four general possibilities for relationships.

The first of these involves the "confidant." This is the person to whom you tell all. He or she helps to relieve the stress. You let off steam with them. They help to give you balance during trying times. They can, without penalty or offense, tell you to cool it, to defer your action, or to buy time before acting. They serve, and rightly so, as a sort of balance wheel for you. The relationship is almost always mutually beneficial if it is genuine. For someone feeling down, a confidant can be a real boost. However, remember that it is better not to have a confidant than to have a disloyal one or one who cannot keep the confidences you share with them. Be careful!

A second somewhat more distant relationship can be labeled "camaraderie." Here, professional aspects of the job are discussed with a colleague in a less intimate way. These colleagues become an intellectual sounding board. A certain degree of trust is needed here, too, but a comrade differs significantly from the confidant in that the relationship does not go beyond the professional level. You cannot get at your deepest feelings with a comrade; indeed, with a comrade it is a violation to get too personal. Still, a comrade can be helpful in helping you sort through issues.

A third sort of relationship is the social relationship. Here one has a companion with whom one may participate in athletic activities, do some partying, play cards or the horses, go to the theater, and so forth, yet with whom one does not share the confidences one does with one's confidant. And this differs from camaraderie in that in many instances the companion is not in college or university work and may know little or care little about the work of academia. He or she may be quite refreshing in that he or she is completely turned off by academic conversation. For faculty down on their job, it can be helpful to be reminded that there is life outside the academy.

Finally, there is, of course, the possibility of a really intimate relationship. For a new faculty member without a spouse or other intimate partner, life in a new, stressful environment can be tough. So you fall in love with one of your colleagues. Stranger things have happened. Love isn't the sort of thing one can control. But do be cautious. Obviously, love has significant benefits. But intimate relationships with people with whom you are connected professionally, say, faculty colleagues or students, present major ethical and professional issues. (We talk a bit more about these in our essay on ethics.)

We have glossed over the issue of who these "colleagues" are. Clearly, it makes a great difference whether the colleague is a faculty member, a staff person, or a student. For example, it is one thing to have an intimate relationship with a faculty member and quite another to have one with an undergraduate student. It is one thing to confide in a faculty colleague about your displeasure with a departmental policy and quite another to bring a student into that. We do not say the issue is uncomplicated. We know professors who have married one of their undergraduate students, and both spouses have had a happy life together. Sometimes students can be some of the best confidants, as they possess none of the jealousies that faculty colleagues might harbor. We do say, though, that in all cases, you should consider your relationships with care for your sake and for others' sake.

For example, the beginning faculty member should be careful about establishing a relationship with a confidant during the first year. True, one may feel desperately the need to do so. However, as a beginner one does not know the power or relationships of the faculty. Trust can be badly misplaced with dire results for the new professor. You simply do not have sufficient knowledge of who talks to whom and about what. You do not yet know the political infrastructure of the faculty and administration.

A second bit of advice is that the same person should not fill all three roles of confidant, comrade, and social companion. If such a relationship exists, beginning faculty members or even senior ones may find that their world begins to narrow. They become very dependent on this single person, and this in itself may create considerable stress for all involved. Of course you will prefer some of your colleagues to others, but avoid cutting yourself off from any of your colleagues.

Next we will say a bit about a few special groups of people.

Relationships with Staff

One important relationship, but one that often is overlooked, is between the beginner and the support system. By this we mean the secretarial staff, the people in word processing, library staff, or those in the audiovisual department. Remember, the secretaries know just about everything. They can spot your errors in all the letters or research you have them type. They hear students talk. They may have been employed in the office for some years. They are probably well educated and understand the standards of academic competence expected at the institution. Indeed, they may designate themselves to be the "keepers of the faith" and see themselves as guardians of the integrity of the institution. Consequently, they may view the beginner's work as a travesty. On the other hand, they may see it as being of excellent quality. They know when you bug out in the afternoon. Do not, for a moment, discount their intelligence. Remember this in your dealings with those who may on occasion be considered your subordinates: They may be just as bright as you are, and in many instances, they are far more experienced in the ways of the institution at which you are currently employed. They can readily spot winners and losers among the new faculty members.

Illustrative of this is an incident that occurred some years ago in which a new professor arrived at the university in a most forceful mood. He appeared to perceive his relationship with the secretarial staff as being akin to that of the lord of the manor to the peasants. He ordered them about even though they were in most instances in no way attached to his own department. In very short order, all secretaries, whether they knew him or not, were fully armed to deal with him. Staff can be some of your greatest supporters. Treat them well.

Relationships with Students

Facing students for the first time can be very intimidating, especially if you have not had the chance to teach during your graduate program. We say more about students later, but here we will say a few things.

To begin with the upbeat, it is possible that when you show up in the classroom, the students will regard you as a reward and a treat. They are apt to believe that a "new deal" is in the making. Your newness may create excitement on the part of the students. You are, irrespective of your age, the new kid on the block and will likely be viewed very differently and more positively than the older faculty members. The experienced faculty member may have drifted into something of a routine performance. The students will likely be more excited and interested in your presentation that is still evolving and is still in the experimental stage. The newer and possibly younger faculty member quite frankly is apt to be more in tune with the students currently occupying seats in the classroom. Your vocabulary is up to date. The new faculty member is more culturally adapted to the age group and to the period of time. You may not have the seniority or the clout, but you do have very real power in that you know more about the students themselves than do the senior faculty members; you are, in addition, probably closer to their age.

Of course, students can be frustrating. Often they do not share your enthusiasm for the material, but they can also give you some of your greatest rewards. Fifteen students might call you a jerk, but the one who thinks you're great can more than make up for that. Try to stay focused on the positive.

New professors typically make two different sorts of mistakes with students. On the one hand, some new (and not so new) faculty treat students as an enemy. On the other hand, other faculty treat students as buddies. Clearly, students will pick up on and resent the first attitude, but our experience is that students, at least a sizable portion, resent the latter attitude, too. They may not all want to learn, but neither do they want to think you're just wasting their time. Be pleasant and respectful, but get down to business.

Relevant to this, one advantage you are likely to possess is that you have graduated from an institution that is somewhat superior in its academic ranking to the one where you have been hired. You have studied and learned subject content at an institution that is nearer the cutting edge of theory. As a result, your command of subject content might be superior to that of the older colleagues on the faculty.

But this brings us to relationships with faculty colleagues, and in some ways, that is the most important group for you to think about. Compared to the other two groups we just discussed, this group has the greatest power over you—the greatest power to help you but also the greatest power to make things difficult.

Relationships with Faculty Colleagues

Clearly, it is wise for the beginning professor to get on good terms with faculty colleagues. If you have found favor with them and have extended yourself to make them like and appreciate you and your work, they will likely forgive you if you should happen to "blow it" with respect to some duty or task. Getting along with colleagues is simply purchasing a type of insurance policy. Try to be collegial. There is no reason not to be and many reasons to be. You cannot possibly predict when you will get into a tight spot or be on the hot spot. In such instances, nothing can help so much as colleagues voluntarily coming to your aid.

Diplomacy is of the utmost importance in dealing with the senior faculty. The beginner must show leadership in the subject content area, but he or she must also be respectful to the senior faculty. One must defer to the senior faculty at appropriate moments. Diplomacy is always viewed in a favorable light, even when the senior faculty member knows that probably you are in the right.

Of course, one situation that many have experienced is the discovery that they are, in a very real sense, too smart for the rest of the faculty. And this is not a facetious remark. Frequently, the faculty is older, and in truth, out of date with respect to the knowledge being generated within the academic specialization. They have simply not kept up with it. They may be heavily inbred philosophically in that they all adhere to the same school of thought, one that may differ radically from your own.

Furthermore, one may discover that the faculty elders have set standards for promotion and tenure for the new faculty members that they themselves did not have to meet or to endure. It was a different system in their time. They now insist that you not only jump the low hurdles but the high ones as well. This can generate a good deal of resentment among newer faculty.

One may also discover that some number of the older faculty are intent on doing only one thing: successfully reaching retirement age. By urging you on they can say they are setting high standards for departmental productivity, but you are the designated producer. If you are able to produce, they can proclaim themselves winners. By focusing on you, they manage to take attention off themselves.

Another worst-case scenario is one in which the faculty tends to hold a philosophic position that is extremely different from your own. For example, the faculty may, as is increasingly possible at some institutions, hold attitudes critical of traditional curriculum and teaching methods.

They may feel the culture and knowledge of Western Europe should be de-emphasized, and literature and thought of a different type substituted. If you are a traditionalist, you may be in deep trouble and find the situation extremely stressful. The reverse may also be true if you are the lone dissenter among faculty members who are dyed-in-the-wool conservatives and traditionalists. If the faculty members cover the spectrum in their philosophic dispositions, the situation probably produces little conflict. They have learned to live with each other or even enjoy the differences. But when you are the odd person out, you can be in a very difficult spot. You may be assured that you are not going to convert the rest of the faculty to your point of view. Philosophically they are going to oppose you. That need not be a problem. Good faculty revel in philosophical argumentation and encourage it. However, it is a fact that philosophical differences may lead colleagues to evaluate your work unfavorably. They simply do not believe in it. If this is the situation you face, you might have to consider leaving. Keep your head down, and do what you can to build up a strong CV. There will probably be others on the faculty and administration who will realize your dilemma and help you in this effort, who will be ready to give you good references. We are not saying you should be a coward, but we see little virtue in being a fool, either.

Some faculty members have a sixth sense or special set of abilities that can prove very valuable. Some would refer to it as possessing political antennae. Others may refer to it as good instincts or awareness. These individuals are able to anticipate events, providing them with insights and the power of prophecy. They are able to analyze situations and personnel to their advantage. They know when to jump and when not to jump. They may anticipate that others will throw themselves onto the barbed wire and that they may then proceed on their way uninjured. They, to a degree, have survival techniques many others do not possess. One academic philosopher suggested that such individuals tend to view the academic environment as basically hostile, and they are able to maneuver themselves over all crises or around such crises due to their early warning systems. They keep a low profile when it is to their advantage to be in that position. It is suggested by some that such instincts or survival kits are the necessary equipment of those who would rise out of the ranks of the faculty into the positions of college and university presidents and chancellors.

If you do find yourself running into trouble with colleagues—and even if you don't—one of the most important questions you can ask yourself and others very early on is "Why did this institution hire me and not someone else?" Reflections on this question and the consequent answers you receive should help to reveal what people are expecting of you. Normally, the faculty and administration will have selected you on the strength of your CV, apparent abilities to get along with and adjust to the present faculty, potential for productivity, relationship to a prominent scholar at your graduate institution, and/or involvement in a particular school of academic thought in your area of specialization. These are the positive aspects related to your selection.

However, two incidents show that hidden problems can exist. Some few years ago, the faculty in a department and the dean at a state university were in complete disagreement with regard to hiring a young person for a vacant position as assistant professor. It was a tenure-line appointment. The person had interviewed at the institution; however, he did not realize that, even prior to his application, a conflict existed over the appointment. The dean and faculty were on a collision course. The faculty within the department unanimously voted not to hire the person. It was near the end of the semester. The faculty shortly disappeared for summer vacations or became concerned with summer school teaching. The dean, despite the faculty vote, proceeded to hire the individual. When the new professor appeared at the college that fall, he was still unaware of the faculty and administrative split. The faculty simply refused to accept the appointment, which made the person's life very difficult.

A second case did not involve beginning faculty members but is another illustration of hidden dynamics faculty can be caught in. Two professors had not actually applied for positions at a state university but had been recommended for the positions by others who were well respected in their academic areas. Unknown to the two professors, there had been considerable dispute between the dean of the college and their chairperson. The dean felt that the chairperson, a person of considerable power on the faculty, had over the previous half dozen years hired faculty members who had turned out to be losers. The dean wanted no more of this.

So the two new faculty members were brought on board without the chairperson's backing. Upon arriving at the campus, the new faculty members faced a humiliating situation. The dean and his cohort promptly forgot the new faculty members and did not consider that they needed to be looked after. The defeated chairperson consciously or unconsciously got his revenge, but it was revenge on the unknowing new faculty members. He promptly told them there was no office space available for them and sent them to look for desks in a large unkempt room in which graduate students occasionally occupied desks. They were warned by the chairperson not to take desks already occupied by graduate students and that it would be unwise to take the desk where the lone telephone was located. There were some 20 desks in the room. Both professors later commented that they would have turned around then and there and gone back to their prior schools, had the positions still been available.

In short, conflicts may have nothing to do with one's academic credentials. In our examples, the faculty may well have been quite qualified, but people objected to the process through which they were appointed. In such instances, unless the greatest diplomatic skills are used, the productivity of the new professor is jeopardized. New professors may naturally be puzzled for a long time as to what the problem is if their appointment was tainted by infighting

Still another situation sometimes confronted by the first-year faculty member and one in which it is not so easy to point the accusing finger occurs when the new professor is the only one in the department or institution in his or her academic area. He or she is highly specialized and knows the field; however, the department or college is budgeted for only one such person and is extremely unlikely ever to hire a second. Thus, the incumbent may be literally starved for intellectual stimulation and companionship. No others exist in his or her proximity who are interested in this specific area of expertise. This scholar has been placed in intellectual solitary confinement. Such a person might still gain a confidant, but there is something about having an intellectual soul-mate that a mere confidant cannot provide.

In graduate school, these individuals have associated with numbers of faculty members or fellow graduate students who are working with some intensity in the same academic domain. If the graduate school is a good one, the area of concern is likely to have reached the cutting edge in thought and theory. Now as the only such appointment at the college or university, a stressful situation arises. A problem is created with respect to research productivity and intellectual stimulation. It may come as a very unwelcome cultural shock to realize the possibility of loneliness associated with being the only faculty member in a certain area of endeavor. However, perhaps what this means is not that one must leave the institution but rather look for colleagues elsewhere. Computer technology and fax machines make it possible to network nationally and even internationally.

How to Respond to Difficulties?

We fear we have little to say about how new professors should respond to difficulties in the transition period. Certainly we would advise that one not be rash. Think carefully. Things might not be as bad as they seem. Or they may get better with time. Look for support from colleagues. Rarely will there be no one to lend a hand.

At the same time, we have to acknowledge another real possibility: the demands of the job really are intolerable; the professorship is not for you. What do you do then?

Probably, your investment in higher education, in terms of time and money and emotion, has been significant, to say the least. It may appear far too late to pull back, but perhaps there are individuals for whom the best advice is to cut their losses and get out. Certainly, there are other areas besides academia in which their investment in education can pay off for them.

On the other hand, we say again that one needs to remember that the first years are particularly stressful and that with patience and grit one may be able to weather the storm. In addition, as we have seen, there is considerable variety among institutions of higher education. Just because things do not work out at one place does not mean that one cannot be successful somewhere else where there is a better match between institutional demands and one's personal interests and strengths.

Lastly, we emphasize once again that one need not face the stress of the job alone. There may be formal and/or informal ways to get help and support. Some colleges and universities maintain a professional staff to help faculty with their personal problems, and where they do not, such help may be available in the private sector.

We wish to be careful not to depict too gloomy a picture. The first months and years are particularly difficult and stressful, but rarely do problems reach crisis proportions. Along with the problems come very rewarding experiences. And though the demands and decisions new professors face are serious matters, usually they can be handled.

We close out this essay by offering some more thoughts about what beginning professors can do to deal with some fairly common and specific concerns. Some of these concerns are rather directly job related. We do a bit to address them here but consider them in more depth in later chapters. Other concerns are less directly related to job demands, and although we do not spend a great deal of time with them, they are legitimate concerns and we wish to offer at least a few thoughts about them.

Concern Number One: How Do I Manage My Time to Greater Effect?

First, remember that you are not a factory worker or in an industrial corporation. Don't feel that it is essential to maintain an 8:00 A.M. to 5:00 P.M. schedule. Some people work best at night, others, early in the morning. Some want a couple of hours of relaxation at midday and then return to the office later. Figure out the schedule that works best for you.

Do not in the least feel it is necessary to follow someone else's program or schedule. It may not be right for you. As a professor, you are a professional. If you like to work at night and sleep until noon, fine. Make your own hours and arrange them to facilitate your greatest productivity. Don't worry about what the neighbors say. However, it is important to have a schedule and to advertise it so that people know you are working. Generally, your research will go better if you have regular times for it and if you set aside blocks of time for it. Each block should be composed of some three to four hours at least. In addition, there are three times that must be rigidly observed by the first-year professor: (1) the time when you meet your classes; (2) the time when you are scheduled to hold office hours, during which students or others can conference with you; and (3) the time designated for committee meetings, faculty meetings, and scheduled appointments.

Concern Number Two: How Do I Get Started on My Research Program?

Although not all institutions encourage it, consider using your dissertation to generate an article or two or even a book. These projects may require little or no major reworking. Furthermore, there is likely to be an entire range of research topics contained in the dissertation that were touched upon but not explored in depth. Examine these and develop them for refereed articles. These require some work, but at least you are working from a research base that you have already developed. The point is don't try to plow new ground your first year. It frequently happens that one is so sick of the dissertation that one wants to put it on the shelf forever. Don't.

Study the research market by perusing the journals in your area. Plan a research agenda, and plan to stick to it. Don't go jumping all over the area in search of topics. Focus as best you can. If others in your department or college know of your research interests and such interests are well publicized, you may find faculty members who wish to collaborate with you.

Do not hesitate to do some research addressed to committee reports or concerns of the college. Ideas generated by these minor, internal studies can be utilized for publications and can also generate interest on the part of faculty colleagues. Some faculty members use this sort of thing as bait to lure others with similar interests into working with them on larger research topics.

Continue to network with your former graduate student colleagues. While they may be at other institutions, publications generated by two or three such individuals may find a readier market than those initiated and carried out at a single school. Present-day communications systems facilitate the exchange of ideas. Different faculty in different places and working under different conditions may stimulate each other and encourage more original ideas.

In your first year or two, do not attempt to publish only in the more prestigious journals. Try for good, though perhaps not top-flight, journals. You have a better chance of getting your articles accepted if you write for those journals.

Lastly, journals often issue invitations for articles that deal with specific topics relevant to your research plan. These solicited pieces of research are important to the editors of the journal. Keep your eyes open for these announcements.

Concern Number Three: How Do I Keep Up with the Scholarly Developments in My Field?

Consider subscribing to one or possibly two journals that are major outlets for the sort of research you do; it's helpful to have these handy. However, journals usually are rather expensive. The university or college library may carry the important journals; however, given the increasing costs of publications and restricted library budgets, this may not be the case. See your college or departmental representative on the library committee and ask him or her to request subscriptions to the preferred journals in your area. Library committees usually defer to those who make requests. Be insistent, if need be. If you feel you have time, explore setting up a departmental library at which the faculty and graduate students can have easy access to the journals of relevance. More and more, materials are available electronically, so that's a resource to explore.

Set aside one day a week to read in your academic field. Snow, sleet, or dark of night must not deter you from doing your serious reading. Time management is very important here. Failure to read in the field is probably the single most important reason that the faculty members become outdated. Indeed, should you interview with another institution three or four years into your current job, an awareness of the newer developments and your part in them serve as invaluable material with which to impress the prospective hiring institution. In addition, it should be remembered that book reviews and responses to published papers are good ways to get some publications.

One well-known professor in the social sciences set a schedule for himself that many admired but few copied. It is highly recommended by the authors. The faculty member made it a point to spend one day every week in the university library. He made a list of the most important journals in his academic field. He made notes on what he read when he found the information to be of importance. He then kept a file of the notes and always appeared to be abreast of developments in his field. He was never out of date.

Begin to network almost immediately upon arrival at your first position with academicians and others from across the United States or overseas. Personal correspondence may prove invaluable when it comes to collecting suitable credentials to present to promotion and tenure committees. But don't be afraid to be selective. For example, some meetings of associations and professional groups will prove valuable in furthering your knowledge of the field whereas others will not. Study the announcements of professional meetings to see if they appear to be of value to you.

Concern Number Four: How Do I Find a Place to Do Quiet Thinking, Research, and Studying?

The answers to this question will vary considerably whether you are married or single and whether children are involved; whether you do research in a laboratory, in the field, or in the office. If a spouse or small children make it virtually impossible to isolate yourself at home, you may explore the possibilities of obtaining space to study in the library. Campus libraries almost always provide workspace for faculty members. Find out about it and use it on a regular basis. It may be that you must return to your office at nights, weekends, or during vacations to get office work done. If you must use your office, think about using a technique that may be referred to as "door discipline." If the faculty member's door is wide open, this means a colleague or others may feel free to walk in. If the door is barely open, this may be interpreted to mean that unless the visitor's business is urgent and of utmost importance, don't bother her. If the door is fully closed, the signal is issued that unless the place is in imminent danger of being destroyed by fire, riot, or tornado, leave her alone. Surprisingly, it will be only a short time until all who might wish to enter can read these signs.

Concern Number Five: How Do I Recruit Students to My Courses and Popularize Them?

As we said above, being the new kid on the block has its advantages. The downside is that you likely will have to build up your student clientele, just as a physician builds a new practice. Your presentations are likely to be your best advertisements. It does not take long for the faculty member's reputation as a fascinating lecturer or discussant to spread across campus. You can do it almost as easily by giving high grades for anything and everything done in the class. Don't do that. Such grading policies will be seen immediately by your colleagues and administrators as unprofessional.

Speak on campus to the students on any and all occasions when invited to do so. Student groups are always seeking to find those who will come to the housing units and give talks. Many will walk up to you after an excellent presentation and ask what courses you teach. Enrollments can be increased this way.

Cultivate the faculty members or others who do student advising. They can throw students in your direction without any great effort.

Concern Number Six: How Do I Deal with the Parking Problem?

Indeed, this may appear to be a trivial concern. And perhaps it is. However, deans, chancellors, and presidents will confirm that it is one that they receive many calls about and one that infuriates the faculty. Faculty, student, and administrative committees have worked valiantly for years in an attempt to find an egalitarian solution to the problem. Thus far, they have largely failed. Where competition prevails with regard to parking space, the law of the jungle is the law of the land. The best advice that can be given here is to purchase, at whatever the cost, not only a parking permit, but a parking space. Many colleges and universities today rent parking space to the faculty. Spaces may range in cost from a titular sum to several hundred dollars per year. The spaces that are nearest the office complexes are, naturally, also more expensive than those at some distance or so far away that one has to use a shuttle service to get to and from the lot.

Spend the money on the nearest and hence best space. It will be well worth it. The space will be reserved for your vehicle. You will, hence, be more likely to arrive at your office in a pleasant mood. You have not had to compete for the limited space available.

Permanent and convenient parking space means you can return to the office day or night (though perhaps not on football Saturdays) and expect to immediately begin your work without irritations that frequently occur in the almost always overcrowded and oversold parking areas where a simple parking permit merely admits you to the competition.

Concern Number Seven: How Do I
Find Good and Affordable Housing?

This often becomes a crucial concern for new faculty members. Most colleges and universities today provide faculty housing. True, the apartments are often small; however, they are priced very reasonably. Many such institutions, do, however, place some restrictions on how long one can remain in such housing. Several permit the new faculty member and his or her family to remain only two years after which they must locate their own housing in the community. Others permit the faculty to rent on a semipermanent basis.

The best advice for everyone who is a stranger in a strange land is to rent for the first year. Do not rush into the purchase of a house as tempting as it might be to have a place to call your own. You do not know property values or where the good schools for your children are.

Concern Number Eight: How Do I Manage
My Finances and Stabilize My Income?

Don't expect to live in the same manner and in the same lifestyle as the senior faculty members. They have been at the job for a long time and have built up substantial salaries.

Don't try to get weekend jobs such as selling clothing or selling cars. This is very bad for your professional reputation. It literally destroys your professional image. Recognize the fact that your income is limited, and you must live within the boundaries set by that salary. If the bill collectors come calling at the college or university for you, you can bet everyone will know about it quickly.

There are some good and legitimate means of earning extra cash. First, make sure you have an opportunity to teach summer classes. This extra salary has been used for many years to educate professors' children in college or to provide the luxuries for the household. Second, many institutions offer correspondence courses. One may grade the students in these programs and earn substantial additions to the base salary. Third, many institutions of higher education run speakers bureaus. If you are a talented speaker, you will get invitations to speak. Fourth, money can be earned from book royalties although rarely does one get rich from those. Fifth, one can be a paid consultant to some group or for some project outside the university. Finally, there may be some legitimate ways to earn money that are not job related, say, through craft projects you make and sell.

Just remember that the job needs to come first. Book royalties are nice, but don't neglect your teaching. Similarly with consulting. In fact, colleges and universities have rules about how much consulting faculty are permitted to do. Be sure you know what those rules are.

Concern Number Nine: Can I Involve Myself in Causes, Crusades, and Political Activism?

Universities are often places of controversy and lively discussion. Today, they are likely to be politically oriented. Some faculty members view their role as very much including political activities. It would take the wisdom of Solomon to advise the beginning faculty member on political activities and on becoming an activist for social causes. However, there are certain limits to which one can go in these causes, and the new professor should be aware of them.

(1) Is the activity or the degree of activity clearly unlawful? Some years ago at a large university, a new faculty member deeply committed to the plight of the Central Americans in El Salvador's civil war became a leader of the movement to bring refugees from this conflict into the United States. It was clearly an illegal action. She spoke excellent Spanish and helped to bring the illegal aliens across the border. In fact, she sometimes drove them herself. Further, she was involved in hiding them out. The F.B.I. arrived at the university and began to make inquiries. Clearly, she was placing herself at a high risk. If you are willing to involve yourself in what is currently defined as illegal behavior—which your conscience may compel you to do—then you must also be willing to take the high risk. Realize that the institution of higher education may not look kindly upon such activities.

(2) Does the activity detract from and diminish the new faculty member's academic productivity and credibility in the classroom, in research, or other professional duty? In short, does the activity hinder you from carrying out your obligations as a faculty member? If so, then again you may be placing students or colleagues at risk. You may be at risk.

(3) Does the activity preclude the faculty member's treating all students or colleagues fairly irrespective of their political or social beliefs and behaviors? A faculty member who taught a course in women's poetry frankly announced at the first class meeting that no men were wanted in the class and any who remained would find it uncomfortable to do so. Such a policy raises serious ethical questions.

(4) One should be aware of the state's possible restrictions with respect to political activities for governmental employees. Of course, this holds only for those faculty members at state-supported institutions, and few states now have such restrictions; however, they may exist where you are.

(5) If one is inclined to become involved in social or political causes, be sure to understand the cause and others involved in it. It is wise to know the leaders of the causes, their commitments, and whether they have obtained legal counsel with respect to their activities or whether they maintain legal counsel for the benefit of their membership. Guard as best you can against being manipulated by others who may not have as deep an interest in the cause as you do. Some may view the social or political cause merely as a means of advancing themselves. Buy some time, if possible, to carefully study the cause and to ascertain its relationship to other social or political factors. Become schooled in it. Emotional involvement is fine; however, emotional involvement backed by knowledge and expertise is even better. After all, you are a scholar.

(6) Be cautious in carrying your cause into undergraduate classrooms. Graduate students are fairly sophisticated and will give you the benefit of the doubt with respect to your beliefs provided they (a) have a bearing on the material being taught, (b) relate to and are part of the advertised curriculum, (c) are revisionist theories that contradict accepted doctrine, and (d) are used as examples of thesis and antithesis and act to demonstrate aspects of basic theory. But be leery of introducing your political conclusions or social thought into classroom situations that are clearly inappropriate.

Observation suggests that those faculty members who feel deeply with respect to political or social causes must be extremely careful about shifting to the role of preacher or evangelist without fully realizing it.

Concern Number Ten: How Can I Best Ensure That I Will Become a Successful Faculty Member?

This is the million-dollar question. It would seem that successful faculty members have one underlying characteristic—focus. The new faculty member who can achieve a high degree of focus in the workplace almost always is the one who is in the fast lane in academia. Such people are going someplace, and it will not take long for them to get there.

For the new faculty member, there are many pressures within the institution that can pull one in multiple directions. If you permit institutional pressures to define your role as professor, you are apt to find it a very diffuse one. Politely but firmly determine your own goals and career pattern. Begin to do this immediately upon arriving. Failure to do this probably means you are going to become a generalist. After a few years you may grow tired of being a storekeeper, but you will probably find that it is too late to revolt. Your colleagues and the administration will not take you seriously. You will find they continue to pull and push you about. There-fore, the minute you are out of the starting gate, make your aims clear to yourself and others.

Focus is most easily achieved through knowing your goals and using effective time management. These goals should be cohesive and coher-ent. Your research within your academic field should aim to be close to the cutting edge of theoretical development. Set a timetable for achieve-ment and stick to it as best you can. Know what you want to achieve and know why you want to achieve it.

Far from resenting your efforts to achieve focus, the faculty will, albeit at some distance, express their admiration. Many will insist that they, too, would do the same except for institutional demands they cannot shed. Nonsense. Many such individuals may be so diffuse in their professional activities because they, consciously or unconsciously, wish to avoid be-coming first-rate scholars and academicians. They take the easier path. They have managed to escape the freedom to choose and let others decide their fate. They may be better liked and more popular because they are pliant; however, they are far less admired and less likely to be able to move as associate or full professors to top-flight institutions.

The flip side of focus is detachment. Taking breaks from work can actually make you more productive. Plan to get away from the job on a regular basis. Join a good sports club or athletic group. You will find that regular exercise will relax you. You will make new friends of your age group; your temper will be improved considerably, and you might just possibly get into good physical shape. During graduate school days, you probably said, "As soon as this is over I'll begin to exercise again. But, I don't have the time just now." Well, now is the time. And there is no better way to meet people and make friends in the new community than working out with them. You may find at the end of the hour or two of vigorous exercise that you cannot remember exactly what it was that was so upsetting.

Take some time for family and friends. If you paint, play music, or are involved in any other hobbies, you should make some time for them and, in so doing, get away from your professional work. Many communities have orchestras, choral groups, community playhouses, and so on. If you are talented, it, of course, helps.

Don't overreact to the job. When you become angry and frustrated, get away from the office. What you don't say, you do not have to apolo-gize for. If you must take a fighting stand, do so. However, be selective in your conflicts. Be sure they are worthwhile causes. If you fight every day on every issue, you will burn yourself out, and you will find that you have decreased the number of your friends and supporters.

Make sure a substantial number of your associates are people outside of the university. Do not concentrate your friendships in academia. You can blow off steam much easier with people who are completely outside of the institution.

Remember, one should view the job realistically. It never was, and never will be, as good as you hoped nor as bad as you feared. You may have built up false expectations and are now sharply disappointed. Take another look at your expectations and the costs and benefits that higher education holds for you.

On Becoming a Professor: Identity and Responsibility in the Student-to-Professor Transition

Linda J. Koenig

The following essay, in which I present some thoughts and observations about my transition from student trainee to assistant professor, is based on my experience as a new assistant professor of psychology at Emory University in Atlanta, Georgia. As a professor of clinical psychology, my experiences may not be representative of all, or even most, first-year professors in other disciplines or even the other social sciences. In addition, I am certain that any individual's experiences will vary as a function of his or her unique personality and characteristics. However, in looking back over the year, I tried to identify some general issues that might characterize this particular professional transition regardless of academic discipline. From the variety of things that happened that year, I have chosen to focus on changes in two areas—personal definition and professional responsibility—that have been both important and challenging to me.

The personal challenges associated with assistant professorhood actually started months before I arrived in Atlanta. As everyone knows, the academic search process is an arduous one. In the course of two and a half months, I went on 12 interviews, gave 16 talks, and ate more airplane meals than I care to remember; it was both physically and emotionally taxing. This was not, however, the most difficult part of the process. For me, the most difficult part was making a decision about which job to take. I don't say this to boast about the fact that I had multiple job offers, because I believe that part of my success was a function of being in the right place at the right time. Nevertheless, having a choice of this nature presented a dilemma. Those people who knew me then can testify that I changed overnight from "Linda Koenig: Successful Job Candidate" to "Linda Koenig: Basket Case." I found myself emotionally distressed and unable to make a decision. I even cried at times. Time was passing, and I felt that deadlines would be upon me before I knew what to do. For the first time in many years, I was faced with a real choice about the direction of my life. For the first time in a long time, I was making a decision not about a temporary relocation but, rather, about where I might be spending most of my adulthood. For the first time in my life, I allowed myself to think about the personal needs which I had put on hold in order to pursue the very best training. And, as may be typical of women who contemplate academic careers, for the first time in my life, I honestly confronted the question of whether I was really good enough to make it in a high-powered institution; perhaps I'd be more successful in a less competitive environment. All of these questions faced me as I struggled to identify the importance of each of my needs and to integrate them in a way that would make me most happy.

Thank goodness there were deadlines, and mine came. I made a decision, *and the decision made me.* I say this, because I now believe that that decision played an important role in my self-definition. It was the last act of my student self as well as the first act of my professor self. It helped me to clarify my identity by giving me the words to define myself. I was a person who wanted to live in a large urban environment. I was a person whose religious identity was important enough to want to be in a place where there was a Jewish community. I was a person who could tolerate living far, far from my family even though in an ideal world I'd like to live closer. And most importantly, I was a person who wanted a chance to have a successful academic career. I wanted more than just an academic job; I wanted a job that would give me a shot at the big time.

All of these things represented just the beginning of my developing professor self. When I entered my job, this self was just a fledgling notion. I had goals to direct me and role models on which to pattern myself, but I had very little experience on which to base this particular self. By the end of the first year, however, my professor self had grown quite strong. Every work-related decision I made—evaluating students, supervising clinical trainees, directing the course of my research program, or just speaking at faculty meetings—provided experiences around which it could take shape. Every introduction in which I was asked what I did caused me to say it out loud. At first, I was uneasy announcing, "I am a psychology professor at Emory." Men seemed intimidated. (Some even began telling me their personal problems!) Most people said: "You don't look old enough to be a professor!" But gradually, I became more comfortable saying it as if simply repeating it over and over gave it a reality it hadn't had before. I stopped caring about how people responded (and I think the job gave me a few gray hairs, so that I aged into the title). Nevertheless, regardless of what others thought, it was me; after all, I had a host of experiences to back it up. It is in thinking about these experiences that I've come to believe that an important part of this crucial time is developing one's general (and discipline-specific) academic identity. In the transition from student to assistant professor, we make a quantum leap in professional status, from an underling position that's usually associated with little responsibility to one which commands respect and high regard in our society. People start responding to us differently. I think it takes a while for self-identity to catch up with position.

Along with this change in identity and status comes an increase in power and responsibility. There are a number of ways in which new professors exercise power over students. The most obvious is probably in the classroom, and if you're not aware of the power you wield over something important (i.e., students' grades), the students will probably remind you of it. At least mine did. My first undergraduate course was a very large one. Students who did poorly on the tests stormed to my office to tell me the tests were unfair, that too much material was covered, and that the problem must be mine since they had done so much better in other professors' classes. Some cried in my office. Many let me know in no uncertain terms that my grading scale was harder than that of the typical psychology class. In this they may have been right. I tried hard to accommodate them by listening to their concerns, personally reviewing their tests with them, and providing information on multiple-choice test-taking strategies that might help them next time. What it took me a while to learn was that the more I tried to help certain students, the more I felt that I could never do enough. Some students just weren't happy unless I changed their grades. I had a lot of power because I had something they wanted. Other professors told me that students will push if they feel they can get something out of you, and that young female professors appear most vulnerable and so get pushed the hardest. I have since tried to appear more confident about and committed to my decisions. In addition, I have made some changes in my class in order to strike a better balance between the way I structure my tests and the grading norms in my institution. This has helped as well. Finally, I am slowly coming to accept the fact that I can't make all students happy. This has been hard because I want to be liked.

Nevertheless, I sometimes have to think of myself as a broker of a highly valued commodity. I try to set the "price" of grades at fair market value because I know that if I don't, they'll have no value at all.

A second place where new faculty wield power is in the admissions process. As a member of the clinical psychology admissions committee, I played a role in altering the criteria by which we rank and select graduate candidates. More importantly, as prospective graduate students paraded through my office on their interviews, I again became aware that I was making important decisions about other people's lives. Clinical psychology is an incredibly competitive field; we have several hundred applicants for six slots in our program. Out of necessity, students try to be impressive, and it is the faculty they are trying to impress. As prospective candidates talked about wanting to come and work with me, I realized that *I* had now become the gatekeeper. This hit close to home because I still recalled how difficult it had been to get into graduate school and how hard it was to receive my own rejection letters.

I had a similar experience during my second year as a member of a search committee for a new faculty member in my program. I had only recently been a candidate myself, and I must admit, I felt at first as if I were reading confidential material that I was not supposed to see. After all, these were recommendation letters for people who were my contemporaries. Moreover, I felt quite intimidated as I read each and every letter stating that this was indeed the best student ever to grace the lab of this professor. If this were the case, what was I doing here? Why would they have hired me when they could have had any one of these wonderful people? Of course, I had never read this type of recommendation letter before, and I didn't know how glowing they typically are. Luckily, I half-jokingly voiced my insecurities to one of my senior colleagues, and was surprised to hear him say, "Linda, they said all the same things about you!" They did? Well, so much for believing the press.

As the faculty candidates came through, all of them met with me individually. Everyone wanted to know what it was like to be a new faculty member here. This was also a dilemma. Although I am very happy here, no place is perfect. I wanted to be as honest as I could when they asked me questions like, "What's the worst thing about being here?" After all, I had sought this type of information myself. At the same time, I had a stake in whether our first choice-candidate would accept, and I wanted to emphasize the positive aspects! Once again, I became aware that no matter how similar I was to the candidates in age or position, I was on one side of the fence and they were on the other. These differences notwithstanding, I felt so close to the candidates' situation that each time someone began their job talk, a little part of me cringed inside. I prayed that the talk would go well, because I could still feel how devastating a mistake or an error would be. Still, I have to admit that the view from the audience was much better than the view from the podium. I stated in one introduction that it brought me great pleasure to be introducing the job candidate. Indeed it did—introducing the candidate is infinitely more pleasurable than *being* the candidate.

Power and responsibility go hand in hand, and one of the things that made last year feel qualitatively different from graduate school was the nature and type of responsibility required. The first responsibility that most new professors have is probably the teaching of undergraduates. If you haven't taught before, you learn quickly that your minimum obligation is to put together a syllabus and show up every day with a lecture in hand. You no longer have the luxury of believing that if you aren't feeling well or you oversleep, no one will really miss you. I am reminded of a dream I had as a graduate student just before I taught my first independent class. My knowledge and preparation notwithstanding, I dreamed that I was hopelessly lost as I took one bus after the other struggling to find my way to the university. I did finally get there, five minutes before this three-hour seminar was to end. There sat all of my students, waiting patiently at their desks with hands folded, still anticipating the arrival of the teacher. Needless to say, this (luckily) never actually happened, and perhaps my Freudian friends might offer me another interpretation for this dream. For me, however, it has always served as a reminder that my first concern about teaching was not whether I'd be good; it was whether I could pull it off. Because I had taught mostly small courses as a graduate student, the major change for me was getting used to the large-lecture format. It's a bit like being an entertainer. Too large for personal interactions or discussion, this type of class seems to require one to be somewhat entertaining if students are expected to stay involved for 75 minutes. I am now searching for a few good jokes.

Teaching graduate students evoked a different kind of concern. I thought about the fact that these students were just as bright as I was and not much younger (indeed, some of them were older). I was now responsible for educating the future members of my field. To bolster my confidence, I reminded myself that I knew things that they had not yet learned. At the same time, I recalled an observation made by an experienced professor addressing the incoming class of graduate teaching assistants at Northwestern University where I trained. He told us that although students may be as intellectually bright as their teachers, a teacher's advantage is that he or she *knows* more. However, he noted that it is not comforting when you realize that the better you do your job, the more you wear away your advantage. This may be true, but once you have " worn away your advantage," your job is done. I have also realized that the graduate students I've taught over the last two years have all been eager to learn, and none has ever been hostilely challenging. And even if that is not the case for you, you can relax because by nature, the experience of being inexperienced is time limited.

The responsibility of training graduate students has been a challenging one. Having them in class is one thing; being their research supervisor is another. Although at some institutions first-year faculty members do not direct graduate research, I was not prohibited from doing so and was lucky to have been assigned an extremely bright and motivated student. She arrived at Emory all eager and ready to go; I was busy unpacking my books and worrying about where my next lecture was coming from. Although I was as anxious as she was to get my research program going, I was operating under survival mode, just trying to adjust and meet my daily obligations. We had some ups and downs in the beginning, as we struggled to identify a project that would combine both of our interests and then make the community contacts necessary to carry it out. Ultimately, we worked out both a project and a method of working together. Through that experience, I came to realize that as graduate students, we learn how to be teachers, and we learn how to be researchers. I learned very little about how to direct and supervise graduate students. Being responsible for the development of someone else's career is a big responsibility, particularly when you are struggling to get your own career off the ground. I don't mean to imply that this was a bad experience. On the contrary, I have realized that working with graduate students is my favorite part of the job. However, it is one for which graduate school does not usually train us. In a recent interview, a prospective graduate student asked me to identify my philosophy and methods for training graduate students. Philosophy? Method? Heck, I had just been flying by the seat of my pants. I hadn't had *time* yet to develop a philosophy. This is something I've been working out through trial and error.

It is also possible that different fields will have unique obligations that will represent an increased level of responsibility when compared to that required in graduate school. As a member of the clinical psychology program, part of my teaching activities involves the training and supervision of graduate students who are seeing therapy clients through our clinic.

Although I had engaged in clinical activities before and during graduate school, the ultimate (and legal) responsibility for a client's care rested with the supervisor. During training, I received sometimes as much as an hour of supervision for every hour spent with a client. As a first-year faculty member, I still had the benefit of some minimal supervision from my colleagues, but the primary responsibility for the direction of treatment was now mine. I thought a lot about things that could go wrong, and I prayed that I would make the right decisions if a crisis situation arose. After all, the consequences of a poor judgment call here were much greater than if I didn't show for a lecture or misgraded an exam. This was the type of responsibility that they do try to prepare you for in school, but I don't think I knew what it felt like until I experienced it. I breathed a sigh of relief when the semester ended, and all my student's clients were alive and well. Of course, nothing happened that I couldn't handle. I now realize that it wasn't due to luck (or my prayers); it was because I was trained to know what to do to avert or to handle a crisis. Somehow, the process of graduate training does work.

As I lived out this year, I certainly didn't think about how much new responsibility I had or how my professional identity was changing. (How could I? I was way too busy.) Rather, these are things I have thought about in retrospect. Overall, I would say that, most of all, it was a year of personal growth and professional accomplishment. I never found a challenge that I couldn't rise to meet or a problem on which a colleague couldn't help. I believe that having successfully negotiated my way through the demands, politics, and ambiguities of graduate school, I had few surprises as an assistant professor. Some of the stories you may have heard about the life of a first-year professor will be true; you will have to learn how to publish in your field; there will undoubtedly be departmental politics that you'll try to avoid, and you'll have to start a new social life in a new town at a time when you are forced to work long hours. But, by now, you have probably developed good coping skills. Moreover, being in the first year of an assistant professorship does have its advantages. It may be the only year that you don't really have to worry about tenure; there are just too many other things to do.

Getting Along with Colleagues: A Cultural Perspective

Gargi Roysircar Sodowsky

As a third-year assistant professor of counseling psychology, I can refer to some of my early impressions of university academic style, a professorial way of doing things, which I will broadly describe as academic culture. The turnover in the first three years for entry-level assistant professors in research universities is high probably because these newly capped and gowned former graduate students—best described as psychic immigrants to the multidimensional, "superprofessor" system of research, teaching, committee work, grant raising, national networking, political alliances, and administrative duties—are unable to develop a psychological match between their needs, goals, values, achievement potentials, and past training and their newly chosen culture of academia.

Taking stock of my development as an academician, I remember an earlier version of me: the fresh doctorate with reservations about her competence as a professor and with many of the self-doubts of a woman of color who, owing to her differences made obvious in a monocultural white American environment, perceived herself as the "overobserved visible minority." I was hired for the departmental multicultural position which was accompanied by the explicit expectations of multicultural research and teaching that matched my current and long-term goals and the implicit expectation of multicultural service activities, a phenomenon I was unprepared for—especially its unique features of political vulnerability and a high service demand that could have put a junior professor without a power base at great emotional risk.

My personal values about collegiality, professional behavior and language, mutual respect, and fairness were tested the most in multicultural committee work as I experienced the various agendas of diverse racial and ethnic groups regarding what the newly hired minority professor should or should not be and what kind of service activities she should and should not render. In my multicultural service, I might have felt as though I was put on the spot and exposed as I was unflatteringly compared to some higher education minority leaders of "mythical" proportions, talked down to, advised, and even shouted at; interestingly, most of the critical responses came from male members of the minority committee that I chaired and continue to chair. Now in my third year, after many tears and hurts, I have reached a personal ethical decision regarding my cultural identity. I am an autonomous minority woman who aspires to integrate a global and pluralistic perspective on issues related to race, ethnicity, and minority status. By taking the responsibility of redefining my identity at the personal level and not accepting others' definitions of me as the representative of this or that racial or ethnic group and their specific causes, I have prevented myself from quitting my job, having a burnout, or abandoning my commitment to multiculturalism and equity issues.

Thankfully, the trauma of multicultural service did not distract me, which it very well could have, from establishing my research program and settling down to university teaching. However, as in many difficult situations, there is also a good side to being designated as the multicultural person. Unlike many new faculty, I have had the special opportunity to concentrate on and integrate the three important functions of research, teaching, and service in a unified and focused manner, with the functions interacting to the benefit of all three areas and enriching my knowledge and experiential bases, both equally important in the scientist-practitioner model of professional psychology. My mentor has explained to me that one of the requirements for tenure is that a professor should demonstrate a connectedness in his or her activities, development, and future plans; I believe that the breadth of my multicultural involvement will enable me to prepare my tenure papers according to this criterion.

Despite the possibility of some payoffs for the multicultural position, my warning to entering minority academicians is that a vaguely defined multicultural teaching position can set them up for failure if they do not delineate clear boundaries, differentiating their own pretenure academic needs and goals from the needs of the system. A university, being unaware of what a multicultural expert can or cannot do, may have an amorphous and all-encompassing job description for the multicultural position and may, at the same time, leave unmentioned that the "publish or perish" norm applies equally to the untenured multicultural expert.

Multicultural professors also need to consistently remember their original purpose for choosing a university teaching and research career because a central administration official who has a different purpose in the same system may see the multicultural professor's role differently and may thus express contrary expectations, which the beginning multicultural professor might be wise to disregard without feeling guilty.

I would like to return to my earlier use of the term "academic culture" and my statement that entering assistant professors, despite their intelligence and scholarly potentials, experience a complex and difficult process of acculturating to the academic society, often withdrawing, as a result of culture shock and moving to other higher education environs to start anew. The faculty handbook with its formal policies, rules, and instructions, a department's procedures for the annual review or its organizational structure, and the college guidelines for promotion and tenure or its mission statement do not represent the culture of a particular department. A department's culture is an unwritten, unspoken, but strongly felt worldview, a system of values and cognitions that determines how things get interpreted, what decisions are made, and what the quality of actions taken will be. This culture is distinct, separate, and bigger than individuals in the department because those who have been around for some time have been conditioned by the culture. These individuals may even be unconscious of the culture because of its ubiquity and because the individuals are its energy.

However, new professors are keenly aware of the culture, questioning it and perhaps secretly rebelling against it, as they interface its unique personality and energy. Also the dominant culture's influence on new professors will be greater than their influence on the dominant culture because the new professors are the minority. The new professors may often react with stress to the conflict between the dominant culture and their belief system. The cultural conflict could lead to a crisis, arousing normal human fears, insecurities, oversensitivity, dependency, and paranoia-like perceptions, which the new faculty could resolve by either resigning from the job or by choosing to integrate. I propose that experienced faculty who are chosen as mentors for new faculty facilitate the new faculty's cognitive process of exploring and understanding the unnamed academic culture, so that they learn how to read and find reason behind different levels of meaning. If what has meaning in academic culture is not significantly opposed to what makes personal sense, then maybe the new faculty could learn to live with dissimilarities for the sake of creating their own emotional peace. Mentors also need to facilitate the new faculty's process of behaviorally reducing the culture gap between them and the department.

A significant manifestation of a department's culture is its unwritten rules or norms. Owing to such norms, the global terms *research*, *teaching*, or *academic freedom* develop connotations specific to a department. Thus prolific productivity may be given less importance than the kind of journals one gets published in. Despite being strongly focused on publishing, one may avoid mentioning to colleagues one's publication successes, especially when one's current research gets published in the most prestigious refereed journal of one's discipline. There are norms concerning the human aspects of departmental group behavior—for instance, whether one should have social relationships with colleagues or just working relationships; whether one should go for lunch with the faculty on a regular basis to the department's favorite deli; or whether one should socialize at the job. There are norms for faculty-student interactions—for instance, whether one should join graduate students on Friday evening at the local bar; whether one should be on collegial terms with graduate students; whether one should observe a strict professor-student hierarchical structure; or whether one should assume a supervisory role.

Academic freedom could mean one's individualistic freedom, with a departmental faculty supporting norms that favor person-centered needs. Instead of concentrating on private advantages, another department could go strictly by the constitutional First Amendment, for example, with regard to the current sociopolitical controversy regarding culturally appropriate behavior and speech on college campuses. Yet another department could endorse a broadly philosophical perspective about freedom, believing that restraint or compulsion is not needed when one has the power to choose and learn from one's choices. Although most departments require a task orientation, some departments may prefer norms that encourage creativity or innovation; others may prefer to get done only what is required; still others may encourage much sharing and support for everyone's tasks. The frequency and duration of one's presence in one's office (with or without the door open—which is itself another norm) is also influenced by the departmental work ethic norm. Some of the above examples of norms are not mutually exclusive, and combinations could create yet another norm that is characteristic of a department's *esprit de corps*. The new faculty need to secondguess what a department really wants and what norms count to stay out of trouble and finally settle down.

Instead of competing with the actions of the senior faculty, the new faculty could choose to consider the former's objectives, principles, traditions, and behavior for clues to what matters to a department. A department may have a history of critical incidents such as a professor being encouraged to give up a position of power, one not being recommended for tenure, a period of political infighting leading to a departmental turnover, a professor being suspected of sexual harassment, a professor's insensitivity to gender and racial and ethnic minority issues, or the tension caused by stubborn dissenters or provocateurs. These incidents become a part of the department's folklore to which the new faculty may need to be attentive in order to learn the rules of the game. Unless new assistant professors wish to pay a considerable emotional price, they may decide quickly that it is not their role to manage the norms of the department and create a counterculture.

New assistant professors from racial and ethnic minority groups experience a double dose of acculturation problems. They face the challenges of adjustment awaiting new professors as well as the conflict between the values and mores of their cultures of origin and those of white middle-class America, which appears to be well reflected by the academic culture. Although they may be proficient in formal and scientific writing, the new culturally different professors may be unfamiliar, especially if they did not have leadership roles in American university student organizations, with the idiomatic bantering conversational style that comes so fluently to the professors of the majority group and which is not commonly heard in the local community. It appears to be the language of an "Old Boy"/"Old Girl" network and the language of in-group jokes; it is academic dialect. So the issue is how can the new minority assistant professor be collegial or share the collegiality of other faculty when he or she does not even have the language? In interactional situations such as faculty meetings, lunch at the student union, or departmental parties, the new minority assistant professor remains tongue-tied, feeling out of place and lacking social poise. It is hoped that with time, some of the academic wit and jargon will brush off on culturally different professors, so that they may move from the out-group to the in-group and make their upward movement easier in the hierarchical structure.

In the academic culture, the individual freedom of professors is strongly respected and defended. On the other hand, a professor who comes from a culture that places the corporate identity and welfare of the family, community, or organization above the personal identity and welfare of the individual may believe that less personal freedom is needed. This person, if given organizational responsibility, may try to impose some control on individual views and preferences by creating new norms that emphasize discipline, compliance with rules and regulations, group objectives over personal concerns, and loyalty to the organization. The culturally different person, being at an early phase of acculturation, will be at a loss to understand his or her failure at gaining leadership status and collegial cooperation and will be distressed with being labeled as "controlling" and "insensitive" when the department's productivity and prestige was his or her highest priority. Eventually the professor will learn dual flexibility, learning how to be open to the norms of his or her academic culture, while also observing his or her cultural traditions at home and in his or her community. During his or her long, difficult struggle with cultural conflict and adaptive changes, the culturally different professor could be encouraged and supported by empathic senior professors who develop an awareness of and sensitivity to the new professor's cultural background.

I would like to conclude by referring to the dilemmas of a newly hired African American woman professor. Although I have met her only on a couple of occasions at the university, she senses a sisterhood with me and calls me late at night at home, sometimes for more than an hour at a time. All that she wants from me are sympathetic words and a few helpful tips. As she opens up to my empathy, I listen to her telling me that she is deprived of important but commonly known procedural information, including that of due process; that she cannot find a research mentor because senior faculty are deep into their departmental/regional/national commitments and their book-writing projects; that she does not want certain women faculty as mentors because they appear patronizing, as though they want to save the African American race; that she is involved in a power struggle with a faculty coordinator because she believes that she does not have to account for her work to a professor with fewer educational qualifications than she has; that she is uncomfortable addressing her difficulties at program meetings because the program head either responds critically, making her feel put down, or gives her the third degree, interrogating her for additional information; that she has to share a phone with graduate students; that a minority male student has expected a kind of attention from her that she is uncomfortable in giving, and so she has picked up the hint that she is insensitive to her own race; that some students are putting pressure on her to change her grades; and finally, that she is friendless, lonely, and isolated and does not know whom to talk to.

My telephone caller tells me that she has heard rumors that another African American professor experienced ill will in the university until that professor could take it no more and quit. I hear the suggestion that the caller's difficulties are related to racial prejudice and power politics. This

African American woman, if she is to be retained by her department, needs a unique kind of preventative help at the departmental or university level, a help that is perhaps not needed by a new assistant professor from the white middle-class majority, familiar with socially and psychologically sophisticated communications. Additionally, she needs to learn skills to survive the academic culture by finding within her department a mentor whom she believes she could trust and from whom she could learn how to minimize her risks by getting into the soul of her department, its culture and worldview. Finally the intimacy that she is seeking, which cannot be defined as collegiality, is perhaps best found outside the university.

Creating the New Course:
Putting the Show on the Road

The Politics of the Classroom

In creating a new course you will be confronted by tough questions
often without being aware of it. Many of these questions have to do
with freedom—how much freedom do you have in creating and conducting a course? Contrary to what you might think, it's not only academic concerns that can limit your freedom. There are other pressures
as well.

For example, the course may be intended to satisfy scholarly needs
or community needs, which are not always the same. Courses such as
those involving race relations, women's studies, and controversial political issues are subject to many outside, as well as internal, pressures.
These pressures, rather than your initiative, may be the impetus for the
creation of certain courses, and you should be acutely aware that these
pressures do not go away once you institute the course and begin to
teach it. Special interest groups are likely to continually examine the
course contents, your teaching style, and your student evaluations. Be
alert and savvy. You must understand exactly what these special interests are, and you must be able to cooperate with them or counter their
demands effectively and without rancor. Your academic freedom in these
areas is more limited than in others. But special knowledge and competence in the subject matter can give you some protection and strengthen
your defenses.

On the other hand, the community and special interests are not so
likely to pressure you with respect to content and methodology in other
academic areas. For example, the sociologist is more vulnerable to outside

attack than the mathematician because the community simply does not know enough about mathematics to comment on it. There are, however, exceptions in technical areas that have received great publicity. For example, the community may be highly concerned about and attempt to dictate in such matters as genetic engineering, cloning, sociobiology, or research using laboratory animals or fetal tissue. These sensitive scientific areas are subject to strong, and often emotional, political pressure. You have to face reality; the university, in general, is no longer a cloistered world.

In many cases, the pressures and special interests are largely internal—within the faculty. For example, the course content may have to abut with that of other courses or may have to take its place in a sequential ordering of courses. Therefore, faculty members whose courses precede and follow yours may have a voice in its content. Be diplomatic; consult with these people in a spirit of cooperation.

Oftentimes, your task will be to take over a course rather than create a new one. It is a good idea to know the history and context for such courses. For example, a situation you will frequently encounter is one that's been called the "dead horse in the yard" problem. A course has been taught for several semesters or, more likely, for several years and has drawn fewer and fewer students. Students might call it "I love a mystery" or "Trash 101." The course has become an embarrassment to the department and college. Often the faculty or the administration sees the need for the subject and "suggests" to you that you should bring the subject back to life. In many instances, they simply want the "dead horse" removed with as little trauma as possible. It's best handled if the perpetrators, the faculty members who created the original mess, have retired, taken another job, or simply disappeared. In this case, your best bet is to entirely redo the course: new title, new number, new beginning. Your philosophy is "this is now, that was then."

You not only have to redesign the course—because its predecessor was poison—you also have to sell it with a vigorous campaign. First, enlist the aid of the senior faculty members, who often have the power to shift students into it. You have to have students! No matter what deans and chairpersons sometimes say, you need the body count. Second, advertise, advertise, advertise. A professor once came to a state university with instructions to create and popularize a course in a modern foreign language, no small task at an institution that did not consider the language vital. The professor went so far as to advertise the course in the campus newspaper. He sold it. He was also an extremely able instructor. Over a period of semesters, because he was an excellent, charismatic teacher, he popularized the course to the degree that students waited semesters to be able to enroll. Even so, years later he warned new professors to be wary of taking such risks as public advertising. Many had bitterly opposed his marketing of the course, and without the support of a powerful dean, his job might have been in jeopardy. His security lay also in the fact that he was married to a highly paid professional, and he could afford the risk— perhaps better than you can.

Alternatively, you might be asked to take over a course that you are *not* to radically revise. You must basically accept it as is, at least for the time being. There are many courses in the catalogs of all major universities that have not been taught for years. They remain there primarily because the faculty feels that sooner or later they may want to reinvest in one of them, and it is too difficult to get approval for a new course. Or the faculty may wish to hold these courses in reserve as bartering chips. They can appear to be giving up a course to gain a new one. They must, as Mark Twain said, have some baggage to throw overboard. These moribund courses provide the excess baggage that may be sacrificed or bargained away without great loss. The origin of the course may be long forgotten, but you would be wise to study its history and the reason for its existence before you try to institute changes.

Students—The Alpha and the Omega

Of course, in thinking about your courses, you need to think about the students you will be teaching. Those halcyon days when professors, no matter what their ability, were captains of their classrooms are largely gone. The balance of power that gave almost complete autonomy to the faculty in their relationship with students no longer exists.

Several social forces had a hand in the changed relationship. Probably foremost among them was the Vietnam War. The war as a national trauma provided students with a focus for discussions of basic values, and they began to generate knowledge that was largely ignored in the texts that the faculty treasured. This new information and ways of looking at it were yardsticks against which they could measure traditional academic knowledge, and they began their search for individual and national identity through examination of new values superior, they thought, to traditional academic material and rituals, which seemed to them irrelevant. The times were changing. These new forces coupled with the students' conviction that they could and should project their own ideas produced a confrontational atmosphere between students and professors. Students began to realize that they were powerful, insisted that much of the subject matter in the humanities and sciences was not relevant, and demanded the immediate and the proximate instantly. Universities were simply not equipped to deal with problems in this way.

Along with discontent with classroom ritual came a changed student attitude toward authority. In the United States, there has always been a philosophic orientation toward egalitarian, populist beliefs that suggest that all people are on the same level. In the midst of the Vietnam War, young people adopted this philosophy as their own, which inevitably produced confrontation. The authority of the professor and the student-professor relationship that had existed for two or three hundred years were challenged. Increasingly, students expressed the view that "my idea is just as good as yours" in their dealing with faculty members, which began the erosion of professorial authority and the questioning of the concept of academic discipline. And although academic disciplines have always been attacked, the confrontation between old and young brought it to a boil. "Don't trust anyone over thirty" symbolized the rebellion against set ideas with which the academic disciplines were replete. The new sense of egalitarianism disrupted the old academic establishment's ways, mirrored in all subject areas, and it appeared to many professors that the egalitarianism was really anti-intellectualism in that many students felt it essential to denounce and denigrate much of the intellectual achievements of the past. Too, many professors were ambivalent, and because of their own liberal guilt feelings, they encouraged attacks on their own ideas and materials, and they reasoned that since their own thoughts were questionable, it was quite possibly unfair to demand that students know and mouth them. Such ambivalence resulted in pressure to dilute traditional academic requirements and to lower academic standards in both content and evaluation. Increasingly, institutions permitted students to take even more requirements as pass/fail (later changed to pass/no pass because the "fail" was seen as a negative, discriminatory label). According to the prevailing philosophy of the time, because students were just as competent to make academic judgments as were professors, students could plan their own academic programs. And because the knowledge in the academic disciplines was questionable, it was best not to give such material too much consideration. Parallel with content dilution was grade inflation. Today's B+ student is the C+ student of forty years ago, at best. Grade inflation became and is still rampant at most institutions of higher learning.

Open enrollment, which was philosophically compatible with egalitarianism, exacerbated the situation. Anti-establishment professors contributed to their own diminished authority by arguing that all students, irrespective of abilities or academic backgrounds, should be permitted entry into the university. In actuality, such students proved unable to compete with those who were well prepared, and many guilt-ridden faculty members began to tailor their lectures and discussions to these students—changing their roles to social worker or even revolutionary. And although they may have spoken or written of social reform issues in the past, it had been a theoretical involvement. Now many are engaged directly in the social reform process.

The Vietnam War affected academia and the professoriate in two other ways. During the war years, colleges and universities were filled with students attempting to avoid the draft. Once the draft ended, many of these same students dropped out of school. Because of diminished respect for established knowledge, many subject areas began to suffer from a drop in enrollment—a worrisome development for faculty, who feared that low enrollment would be equated with poor teaching ability. The body count was on, which accelerated the already prevailing tendency toward open enrollment, which, in turn, led to a further dilution of the curriculum. Faculty members were under pressure to win the approval of a majority of their students in student evaluations—evaluations that directly affected promotion and tenure decisions.

The media—television, VCRs, rock music—also had a direct impact upon the student-professor relationship in that it fostered students' perception that they should be entertained—whether at a concert hall or in the university hall—and that, consequently, their professors should teach entertainingly and convey ideas pleasantly and enjoyably. In high school, teachers had used field trips, films, and other entertainment activities in their teaching, and now college professors were expected to follow suit or suffer the poor-evaluation consequences.

The civil-rights movement also contributed to the growing complexity of professorial teaching, creating a tension between equal rights of students and intellectual rigor. The question raised is whether discrimination among people of differing intellectual ability is legitimate. The Jeffersonian thesis suggests that there is an intellectual elite and that institutions of higher education should devote themselves to the development of these individuals for the benefit of society and the individual. The civil-rights movement implied that higher education should make accommodations to the same range of intellectual abilities as did the high schools. According to this thesis, an institution was discriminatory if it didn't accommodate this ability range. It was reasoned that if it was discriminatory to penalize on the basis of race, sex, and religion, it was also discriminatory to penalize on the basis of poor academic performance. For example, academic performance might not be a good indicator of ability because of lack of educational opportunity due to economic and social injustices. For some people, this interpretation of discrimination clashed with academic tradition and raised questions about academic content, evaluative processes, and the authority of the professor.

Not all academic subject areas have been equally affected by these factors. The liberal arts, especially the humanities and social sciences, because they are necessarily historically oriented and consequently deal with earlier social class systems and historic gender-based role definitions, are often viewed by students as sexist, racist, or biased in other ways. There were two courses of action open to professors: change course content to emphasize democratic sensibilities or leave course content relatively unchanged, prompting students to boycott those courses to emphasize their disagreement.

Such was not the case for faculty members in subject areas outside the humanities and social sciences. For example, colleges and departments of business within universities expanded their enrollments. It seemed that, mistrusting the foundations on which many of the liberal arts subject areas rested and sensing the doubts of some faculty members, students opted for the pragmatic and vocational, abandoning the freedom and controversy that is synonymous with the liberal arts for more desirable material comfort. This tendency is strong today on many campuses.

What do these historical changes imply for you today? What effect do they have on your teaching methods, evaluations, and subject content?

1. Students are highly sensitized to discrimination in all forms. And although they aren't for the most part crusaders or actively involved in civil rights movements or liberal causes, they *are* keenly aware of any real or imagined implication in your lectures of discrimination or prejudice. Don't tell discriminatory jokes. Handle discussions on controversial issues such as abortion very carefully.
2. Students are highly oriented to personal goals. Their grades, which affect their professional future and thus their financial future, are extremely important to them. Grade appeals are rampant. Cheating and plagiarism are common. Students mean to succeed and, to some, any means is fair.
3. Students are sensitized to consumer issues. The attitude is "I'm paying a lot of money for this class and I mean to get my money's worth." If students feel cheated, they immediately complain to the administrative authorities. Students tend to feel that payment for

classes should guarantee learning. After all, universities sell degrees—don't they?

4. There is an ethos of entitlement prevalent among students. "I'm here to learn, but you, as professor, must construct and convey the material so I can do so." "It's my right." "I'm entitled to it."

5. Students expect you to be able to compete with entertainers and newscasters in conveying knowledge in the classroom. If you can't, they will label you dull, boring, and worse.

6. The student body is a very diverse one. Students are divided on political issues, economic issues, and social issues. They speak with a multiplicity of voices, and those who are not interested speak not at all. They come from many ethnic groups, religious denominations, and social classes. Many are foreign born. They have widely varying intellectual abilities, and the experience base from which they operate is equally wide. Their age range, as well, is increasing and has been doing so for some years. This can present great opportunities, great resources for your teaching. This can also present great challenges.

7. Students are rarely intimidated either by subject content (especially in the humanities and social sciences) or by you. They are likely to bypass your office and head for that of the chairperson, dean, or president in an effort to seek justice or an explanation for having received a low evaluation from you. They are somewhat less likely to seek this remedy if you teach courses such as math, chemistry, or computer science, where more "hard evidence" exists in the discipline. But in courses in which value judgments are involved, students are apt to feel perfectly correct in creating a confrontational atmosphere and calling you to account. Because of their great concern with career preparation and vocational advancement, they are likely to leave nothing to chance that may hinder that rise. They are very unlikely to permit you to close the door on their career aspirations, no matter how quietly.

All of these changes put both new and seasoned professors in a dilemma. Administrators and counselors urge you to be personal, warm, and caring in your relationships with students. You, on the other hand, like the physician, can and will be charged with malpractice if anything goes wrong. There is a paradox here in that although you might be tempted to revise your courses to be more student centered, to do so is to run risks. Because of the changed equation in the student-professor relationship, many professors have chosen strict professionalism, cold objectivity, and distance in relationships. Because they see themselves as increasingly vulnerable, they use professionalism and objectivity as a shield, a strategy that has unfortunate results in the teaching and learning process.

Although you should realize that the rules have changed and the professor's status and prestige have changed, you should also realize that the changes don't mean that teaching cannot be enjoyable. But the profession is more in a state of flux and transition than it once was, and there is no doubt that within the next decade the professional position and its role expectations will differ as sharply from those of today as today's differ from those of 40 years ago. Adapting to this changing structure is the key to your successful teaching on the college and university level.

Course Content

Once you have considered your students, the background of the course you will create or resuscitate, and sized up the degree of political or emotional sensitivity you will run into, you should begin to think seriously about planning the content of the course. It takes time and a great deal of hard work. If you try to fake it or dream it up during the actual presentation, the faculty will brand you a charlatan, and the students will brand you a loser. Both faculty and students will be evaluating you. You cannot hide.

Make sure that you arrive at your new institution with enough lead time to build your new courses or understand existing ones you've been assigned to teach. Think about how to utilize things on hand so that you do not have to do everything from scratch.

Graduate Lecture Notes
A common and effective content source is a good professor's lecture material kept from your own graduate courses. You cannot just use it wholesale, however. You'll need to adjust it to match the level of your students' abilities. You may need to squeeze it or chop it up. But it is prepackaged content that has, to a degree, already been pretested and is of acceptable quality. You must be prepared, though, to accept the fact that the graduate material may not fit your students or does not suit your teaching style. It is rather like putting on someone else's clothes. Don't force it.

Text

Using a text as the chief content of the course provides you an instant structure, and all you have to do is follow it and effectively manage your time in order to finish the course. However, you cannot simply follow the text. Otherwise, students may think, rightly or wrongly, that you are only one chapter ahead of them. So, be sure to supplement with other material.

Cooperative Design

You might teach one or more sections of a course that has multiple sections. Other professors may teach other sections. In this case, there is a certain amount of experiment involved. The group of professors gets together and creates the content. Usually, there must be much compromise. The result probably pleases no one entirely, but at least it provides a similarity in what is being presented in each of the multiple sections of the course. It is not likely that you will find a text to suit the newly designed material, so you have to create one. The material used is often eclectic, and such courses often degenerate quickly once their initiators, who have designed them in a burst of enthusiasm, have left the teaching staff. Such courses tend to have a high faculty turnover. The initiators often become quickly bored with them, and the second generation of instructors often is not able to make satisfactory courses out of the materials originally created or collected.

Another criticism is that a committee-designed course is often bland, containing only noncontroversial material. It has reduced focus and often becomes superficial in its coverage of material. Also, the course may stagnate. The faculty members originally in charge of the course established the parameters. Later instructors do not have the commitment needed to alter the formula.

Personal Creation

A method of building course content that reflects much more scholarship is to develop it yourself. However, for you, a new professor with little or no time to spare, this may prove hazardous. It takes approximately three years to fully develop a course. You have to take the show on the road, try out the lines and the material, and be willing to change. Sometime after the second year, the course begins to take effective form. But all this takes time—lots of it. Course construction is rarely either sequential or orderly. There are gaps. If you try to build a course from scratch early in your career, you might be snidely spoken of as a crusader who has only a point or two to sell and builds the course around them. Too, as a new professor, it is difficult to resist showing impatience and irritation with your students when they are not immediately enthusiastic about your creation. It is hard not to blame someone else when things do not come together, but what you have most likely created at this point is a jigsaw puzzle with lots of missing pieces. So difficulties rarely are the student's fault in a situation like this, and if you persist in blaming them, they may, perhaps correctly, see you as arrogant. In your attempt to create a scholarly work in the form of course content, your ego involvement can get in the way of effective teaching.

And there are other problems. As a new professor, you may concentrate so much on delivering the material that you are likely to lose the interpersonal contact so essential with students. You become too wrapped up in the material and forget about the people. Furthermore, once you have the material perfected, it is hard to bring yourself to change it, even if circumstances in your classes demand it. It was too tough a job putting it together in the first place, you think. So you hang on to those old yellow lecture notes—appropriate or not.

Student Creation

Courses might be more or less student created. Many courses employing field research use this method. In some instances, there is an element of grounded research involved in creating the content. If the students are well qualified and intellectually able, it is neither an impossible task nor does it create the worst of courses. However, student creation of course content usually works only with upper-division undergraduates and graduate students.

Independent study, in which you and the student develop the study program, can also be part of this method. Some tutorial sessions are very effective and learning is significant, but this is not always the case. It depends largely upon your professionalism and concern and the intellectual level of the class. If that's too low, the course will suffer. The dialogue carried on in the class may degenerate into interminable and meaningless gossip and storytelling. At its best, independent study uses the Socratic method in which you build on students' questions and answers, providing an environment in which students are truly challenged. These teaching methods are also highly personalized, and students may recall for many years thereafter the magic of such learning. Be aware that independent studies must be carefully supervised. Don't get the idea that you simply can turn students loose.

Teaching Is More Than Presenting Content

Obviously, course content is important. But you have to realize that good teaching involves more than just presenting the content. In the past it was easier to find the correct level at which to pitch a college or university class than it is today. Students used to come generally from the same social class and were all about the same age. There was a certain homogeneity in the classroom population. That is no longer true. Today's colleges and universities serve people from all social classes and age ranges—from students in their early teens to those in their forties, fifties, and even sixties. Their cultural backgrounds, academic goals, and career plans are diverse.

Therefore, you may be in a quandary when you try to decide at what level to teach the material. Only rarely can you individualize the material to meet everyone's needs. For that matter, individualization may not be appropriate for everyone even if it were possible. For example, groups such as Native Americans may be collateral or group oriented in their learning styles.

To add to the problem, in any given classroom, some students will be subject-matter neophytes, while others have quite a sophisticated grasp of it. If you teach to the beginners, the accomplished learners will find the material boring, and they will say so on your evaluations. If you try to meet the advanced students' needs, you are bound to lose the beginners.

To determine what level will be best, you need to ask and answer some pertinent questions about the institutional function of the course. Is this an advanced course for departmental or college majors? Or is the course one that contains large sections and is required for all students in the institution? Is it one of those courses, found on every campus, that is meant to ensure that not all students will meet the prerequisites for study in the professions such as medicine, law, and dentistry? For example, such a course for potential M.D.s is usually one in life science or chemistry that is intentionally designed to weed out the multitudes. Everyone on the faculty knows its function and, therefore, appreciates the academic level which at which the course is taught. Teaching courses like these is not for everyone.

Or is the function of your course to attract students rather than weed them out? Perhaps your department is neglected, forgotten, or nearing extinction. Its resuscitation may depend upon a course that is popular enough to draw large number of students. In this instance your course is probably an elective, and it must draw students on its own merits.

All this may give the impression that your courses will be dictated by outside forces. And to an extent, that is true. But remember, your personality, your personal strengths and weaknesses, also play a major role in the structure and tone of your classes. Focus on doing what you can do better than other teachers can. You may be a top-notch lecturer; the Socratic method might suit you best; or you might be a whiz at demonstrating. Great professors create an art form in their teaching, and this is largely a personal endeavor.

Even if you are told to teach a cut-and-dried offering already listed in the catalog, in one sense you have little choice but to create a new course. It has to suit you if you're going to teach it successfully, and you may well have to alter the syllabus considerably. Most pre-formulated courses are too rigid for you to use your special talents. You are being asked to play a part that is not right for you. You must come armed with as much information as possible, and you must attend to pressures, special interests, and university, faculty, and student needs, yet you must also do what is necessary to make a course your own.

It is incumbent upon you to develop teaching concepts through which you can generate maximum learning in your students. Your personality, the qualities and quantities of students, the environment, and the nature of the subject matter will together suggest the most desirable teaching methods.

Remember that no course, or almost no course, is really stable. The content changes. And it should. Veterans of academia suggest that about 10 percent of the course content changes each year. Thus, over a period of ten years, the entire course has evolved into something else. Of course, change can be negative or positive. Examine the evolutionary process in your courses periodically. Discourage negative drift, but encourage constructive and positive change, and use well-planned research to provide new content that meshes well with the best you already have.

Navigating the Wood:
An Essay on Course Planning

Anthony S. Abbott

The second time is easier than the first, the third time is easier than the second, the fourth time is easier than the third. As you read this essay and reflect on it, please remember these words. Nothing that I say will be more heartening. We grow as we teach, and the process of planning a course, which seems as awkward as a novice's golf swing, starts to become natural with time, growing to fit the teacher's understanding of her own particular contribution to a field which she is coming to know better and better through experience. At the beginning it's like the opening of Dante's *Divine Comedy*. You're wandering in a dark wood. This essay won't get you out of the wood, but it will help you to navigate through some of the denser parts of it.

I must start with a few assumptions if my essay is to be of any real help. The first is that you are a graduate student or a teacher in your first college or university appointment and that you care about being a good teacher. The second is that the bulk of your teaching assignment is in beginning and lower-level courses—things like freshman composition, calculus, introduction to economics or psychology, survey courses, freshman biology and chemistry. You might have some advanced courses, but if you do they are still directed largely toward undergraduates.

And so I begin with Rule 1: Forget everything you learned in graduate school. Of course, I say this half tongue in cheek but only half. The world of graduate school is about as far away from the world of freshmen and sophomores as it can be. The most common complaint I hear from students about young teachers is that they are too academic and think they are teaching graduate students. They assign too much work, work which the students can't master because they don't have the rudimentary skills necessary to understand it. One student told me just this spring that her Introduction to Literature professor assumed she knew all the terms which she had taken the course to learn. To put together an effective undergraduate course, you must take yourself back to a time when fraternities and Monday night football jostled with extracurricular activities, dates, and—oh, yes—academics (as they like to call their studies) for priority in your mind. Perhaps studies always held the highest priority for you, and that is why you are a Ph.D. going into teaching. But remember, very few of your students are like you, and if you're going to reach them in your course, you've got to find them where they are. That doesn't mean you should be easy or patronizing or that you shouldn't have very high standards; it does mean that you've got to address the fundamental and basic issues of your field in language that they, as beginners, can understand.

They are smart, most of them, but they just don't know very much. As Messrs. Bloom, Bennett and company have reminded us, there is no longer a common cultural language with which they came to college. So you have to teach it to them. I tried to teach Tom Stoppard's zany, wonderful *Rosencrantz and Guildenstern Are Dead* in my modern drama course, and found that over half the class had never read *Hamlet*, upon which Stoppard's play is based. I will not teach the Stoppard play again without requiring *Hamlet* as well. The point is: know your audience. There's no purpose in gearing a course over their heads and flunking everyone because they fail. Whose failure is it, anyway?

Before you actually sit down to design a syllabus, you will want to do some preliminary research about reading. Much of what you are able to do depends upon the availability of texts and your preference for one set of texts over another. In many of the courses that you will be asked to teach, there are standard texts. In some cases, especially in courses with multiple sections, texts are chosen by your department. In these cases, your problem will not be choice of text but how much to assign and in what order to assign it. Where you are given a choice of text, it is extremely important that you do some solid research on the merits and drawbacks of different texts before selecting one. Your first and most important resource will be the department which has hired you. Communicating with your new colleagues about texts is a wonderful way to get to know them and their values. If they are not helpful, that in itself will tell you something. Find out which other faculty members at your institution have taught or are teaching the same courses. Ask them to send you their syllabi.

Cooperating with professors at your institution can be a useful lesson in the need for compromise. For example, if you and another teacher are given different sections of the same course, an agreement to use the same text will facilitate resale of used books to students and permit them to change sections without penalty. It will also encourage communication about the course between you and other people teaching it. Much of what I learned about the teaching of freshman composition came from listening to my colleagues and trying out either readings or classroom techniques they suggested. If you are still in graduate school, communication with your future colleagues may be difficult or impossible, but I believe it is worth your while to write to them or telephone them for ideas. Faxs and e-mail make such communication much easier and quicker than it ever was.

Sometimes your new cohorts will not be using the most up-to-date texts. Old texts sometimes fit old professors like the proverbial tweed coats with elbow patches. We become comfortable with what we have been doing and don't want to go through the pain of changing. Perhaps the texts being used at your new institution do not reflect current attitudes toward curriculum. How are women and minorities represented in such texts? If poorly, then how do you find better ones? In short, how do you find out what the best beginning psychology, economics, or biology text is? Every major publisher has one and wants to sell it to you. One avenue is the chair of your graduate department; another is the professor who teaches the course at either your undergraduate college or the university where you did your graduate work. Rule 2 seems to be: Don't be afraid to ask questions.

Rule 3 is: Do your reading. Do not attempt to design a syllabus until you have spent substantial time reading the text or texts that you have selected. Texts today, especially anthologies, have become larger and larger. Second and third editions proudly announce the addition of 400 more pages (more women writers, more minorities, more special topics of particular interest to current readers). The problem is you can't teach it all. You can't even teach half of it. Because you have to select and select with some degree of severity, there's no way around the problem of doing the reading. You can't trust the chapter titles or unit introductions; things are not always what they seem. Promising ideas fizzle, and the best essay or story in an anthology might be one you have never heard of and would therefore not have chosen had you not read it. Select things that move you; select works that you genuinely care about. If you care deeply enough about something, the probability is that you will be able to make the students care.

At the same time don't carry the process of personal selection to the point of eccentricity. A course in twentieth-century American fiction that omitted Faulkner because the instructor didn't like him would be like trying to make bread rise without yeast. Faulkner is the most important American fiction writer of the twentieth century whether you like it or not. The same situation holds true in other fields. You must do your very best to give the centrally important figures in your field a fair hearing. If you don't, the students will never have the chance to decide for themselves, because you will already have decided for them.

It's now time to design a syllabus, but before you actually start the word processor, you need to make some important decisions about how you're going to evaluate the students. Rule 4: Evaluate student work fairly and under conditions that give them the opportunity to perform at their best. The most common tasks assigned students are (a) essays, (b) tests and examinations, and (c) class attendance and discussion. I am an English teacher, therefore, I favor as much essay writing as the professor can reasonably expect to read and evaluate. In some fields, like math and science, essay writing may be less appropriate, but for the most part, the more students write, the more they learn. Law schools today have organized classes in composition for first-year law students who cannot write. Businesses are hungry for students who know how to write. The writing and revision of essays will benefit your students more than any other single activity. Writing essays will teach them to think clearly, to analyze complex questions, and to frame their analysis in the clearest prose possible. Tests and examinations can also be extremely useful, especially when the professor shows some imagination in their creation. Examinations should not frustrate students by forcing them to try to remember obscure details from the course but rather should encourage them to synthesize material studied and come to conclusions not obvious to them until they have taken the examination. The final examination, in particular, should be a significant part of the learning process, an opportunity for students to leave the course with a sense of exhilaration rather than despair. An examination should not be a demonstration by the professor of how smart he is or of how many questions she can cram onto one side of an 8 1/2" X 11" sheet of paper.

The issue of class discussion is a thorny one. You will have to decide how much weight you will give discussion in the overall grade, and you will have to explain your policy clearly in the syllabus. You will also have to make clear what your attendance policy is and how it relates to your discussion policy. It may well be that you are teaching a large lecture course in which attendance is taken and no discussion expected. The likelihood is, however, that you will have at least one or two classes small enough to involve discussion on a regular basis. The more active students are in class, the more likely they are to do well. Students who participate vigorously in discussion have more of a commitment to the class. The exception is the extremely bright but very shy student who writes brilliant examinations but never talks. My policy is to encourage discussion and to reward those who participate; at the same time I try not to penalize the genuinely shy student who is doing otherwise superior work.

The most important point I can make in this section might be summarized as Rule 5: Be consistent with the policies and practices you have stated in the syllabus. If you say you are going to give two tests and two papers, then don't change your mind in midstream and give four tests and one paper. If you say that you expect regular attendance and participation, then hold the students to it. Many young professors get into serious trouble with their classes by either not having a written syllabus (which is fundamentally unfair to the student) or by cavalierly violating the syllabus when it suits their fancies. And please, when you are planning the due dates for essays and the dates for major tests like the midterm examination, take the time to consult the college's master schedule. You will not win any friends by scheduling the midterm examination on the Monday after Homecoming Weekend in the fall or the major spring party weekend in the second semester. Nor will you endear yourselves to your classes by requiring attendance on Good Friday or Easter Monday. We are not engaged in trying to win popularity contests, but common consideration and a desire by the teacher to give the student a chance to do her best work ought to rule our choices about due dates.

Having made some decisions about the reading, the form and frequency of evaluation, and the dates for tests and essays, you are ready to sketch out a syllabus. What should the syllabus contain?

1. A list of required texts and reserve reading. You should make it clear which books should be purchased and brought to class and which may be read in the library. In requiring titles for purchase, be aware that books are expensive and that you ought not to require the student to buy a $20.95 volume for a one-day reading assignment of 30 pages. Before you commit yourself to texts, confirm with the college bookstore that titles are in print.

2. A class-by-class listing of reading assignments, tests, essays, and other class exercises. You may not know what you are actually

going to do on each of these days when you list the reading on the syllabus. You can plan each class later. But if you commit yourself to a specific reading for discussion or analysis, you will then free yourself to work specifically on that assignment and not waste time trying to figure out what you want to assign. If you give yourself too much flexibility, you may simply end up creating more work for yourself.

Make sure that the syllabus has a structure that is clearly discernible both to you and the student. The three most frequent student criticisms of young teachers are that they assign too much work, that their tests are too hard, and that the structures of their courses are unclear. I would urge you on the first day of class to go over the syllabus with the students pointing out the major units, the focus and purpose of each, and why each is important to the course as a whole. Students want to know where they are going and why each point along the way is a necessary part of the journey. Show your syllabus to other professors in your department and see if they can discern your structure and purpose. What is clear to you may not be clear to others. I had an English teacher in high school who always wrote in the margins of student essays: PYIRP. It meant "Put Yourself in the Reader's Place." In designing a syllabus, put yourself in the student's place. Remember that the student hasn't had the course before. Clarity of design is of utmost importance to him.

3. A list of course requirements including attendance, discussion, essay topics, examination procedures, conferences, etc. This is extremely important. Often students will not read this section, but that is all the more reason to have it. If a student comes to you later and says, "You never told us that . . ." you can say, legitimately, "It's right there in the syllabus." I would encourage you to read this section of the syllabus on the first day of class so that there can be no misunderstanding about what is required. If students don't like it, then they are free to change to another class. In this section you ought to describe the length and nature of essays, the type of examinations you will give, and the place and duration of your office hours.

Rule 6, then, is: Be accessible. List office hours in the syllabus and on the blackboard and post them on your door. Then keep them. If you have an emergency, then let the students know you will be away on a particular day. It is particularly important that you have adequate office hours immediately after you have returned tests or essays. These are the times you will do your most valuable work as a teacher.

And finally, as you are planning your syllabus, observe Rule 7: Return all written work promptly with useful comments as well as grades. Students should get their first essay back from you before a second one is due. If you are not able to get the work back in a reasonable amount of time with written comments, then you are probably assigning too much work. The first time you plan a syllabus, you may not know how much is too much. Don't be afraid to make adjustments as you go. No one will complain if you cancel Essay 3 because you are still reading Essay 2. Be willing to admit mistakes. Students admire honesty and your willingness to communicate with them in a forthright manner.

You are now ready to start working on daily plans. With the syllabus in hand and the purpose of the course in mind, you will do much better than you would have earlier. My advice here might be summarized under three rules—Rule 8: Do what you do best; Rule 9: Be open; and Rule 10: Less is usually better.

"Do what you do best." I have one colleague who always lectures. His courses are always full, even at eight in the morning, and he continues, after twenty years, to be both popular and respected, for his wit, his knowledge, and his style. I have another colleague who NEVER lectures. He asks questions and bounces one question off another, tumbling his students through a give and take that is both exciting and a little frightening to novices. I like to lecture on general issues at the beginning of units and discuss specific texts. What you do will depend on your personality, your style, your subject, and your circumstances. So all you can do is to "be open." It is especially important to be open to what the students have to teach you. Of all the teacher's skills, the most important may be listening. You must listen to what they are saying and learn to use what they are saying as a way of engaging them with the material. Be open to change. If something doesn't work, then try it a different way the second time. Reading student evaluations can be a humbling experience, but it can tell us what needs changing and why. Be open to what's going on around you. One of the best teaching resources is the university itself and the speakers, concerts, and other events planned there. If the political science department is having a symposium on the upcoming presidential election, as a history teacher or English composition teacher you might ask your students to attend the symposium and then discuss it or write about it in your class. Use what's happening in the world to stimulate student interest, and make changes in the syllabus if necessary to incorporate student participation in the events going on around them. Even better, find out what's going on ahead of time and build it into the syllabus.

"Less is better." We never know how much is enough until we've done it once or twice, but you will find that each year it takes you longer to cover the same material. That's because you begin to incorporate what you've learned from previous experience. Where you once taught five poems in an hour, now you can cover only two. The concept of "coverage" is one of the most widely debated in college and university curriculum discussions, and more and more people are agreeing that all curricular choices involve the prejudices of time and place and that omissions once thought serious are no longer considered a problem. Students can only retain so much, and a thorough discussion of fewer texts may teach them much more than superficial coverage of a large, traditionally canonized, body of material.

One of the great joys of teaching is the spontaneity of the classroom when the give and take between student and professor becomes so natural that the hour passes without anyone stopping to see if Point I.B.2 on the outline was covered. I believe that you will be able to achieve that spontaneity more quickly and more easily if you are well organized. Your organization gives you a coherent framework within which you have the freedom to improvise. The critical function of planning is the construction of that framework. The time and energy you put into that planning will bear fruit in the pleasure of the day-to-day experience of the classroom, which is, after all, one primary reason that we teach.

Some Considerations for the University Teaching Faculty

Dean K. Whitla

As a founder and former director of The Harvard-Danforth Center for Teaching and Learning, I watched a number of faculty members dramatically improve the quality of their teaching. Good teachers and bad teachers really behave quite differently. Once you understand these differences, you can master the useful behaviors and extinguish the rest. Once mastered, they will serve you effectively for the rest of your life. Good teaching takes no more time than poor teaching, and it is enormously satisfying.

Let me list a few pointers to encourage you in this pursuit. Leading discussions is probably the biggest problem of beginning teachers. Discussion, a civilized conversation in which each member of the class builds on the previous contributions, can raise the general level of understanding beyond that of any single individual. Participating in such intellectual discourse and helping students master this art are some of the pleasures of the life of the mind. New teachers try but often fail to achieve such a goal; sometimes they even fail to get students to participate and out of frustration end up lecturing. Teachers who have such problems can master a number of techniques which will help. For example, they can learn how to set up a situation which invites discussion by developing a series of questions, beginning with those that are simple and factual and following with those that are more thought provoking. Illustrations can make abstract ideas more concrete. Learn when to summarize, know which ideas should be put on the board, learn how to use space, and how to minimize the distractions of irrelevant comments.

How one uses space, for example, can be very important. Standing behind a desk adds formality to the class, and sitting on the edge reduces it; use each appropriately. Actually moving toward a student when asking a question can be intimidating; you can invite a student to share your space by asking him or her to write on the board. There is always a student who wants to demonstrate that his or her mastery of the material is well beyond that of the rest of the class. One must not, at the risk of losing everyone else, answer that student's question, but do promise to answer it after class. Such techniques are ones that good teachers call upon to facilitate student learning.

One specific method of improving teaching is to have a videotape made of your teaching. Reviewing the tape with a colleague or consultant can be of enormous benefit. This process not only facilitates improving your teaching but at the same time provides you a quasi-experimental record of your changes. It can be thought of essentially as a pre—post—post—postexperimental design, for each taping is followed by another with an intervening viewing session. This cycle can be repeated as many times as is helpful. In the Center, we found that the learning curve is still very steep after the first two or three sessions. Even after four sessions most professors will have had more opportunity to explore ideas in their classrooms and begin to consolidate their learning. From experience, we know that this process can lead to dramatic improvement. One instructor became a regular user of the Center and made his lectures so effective that he received a round of applause at the end of each class.

Student ratings also improved markedly for teachers who worked with the Center. When teaching begins to improve, it is encouraged and supported every day by students. They appreciate better-organized classes, clearer explanations, and discussions that are well led. They will spend more time on class preparation and participate more eagerly. What teacher needs more encouragement?

To help faculty members become better teachers, we compiled a list of behaviors that good teachers do and that poor teachers fail to do. The list came from watching videotapes of good and mediocre teachers until we had a sense of why they differed.

1. Organized teachers are better teachers; creative teaching can occur in the classroom, but one cannot count on the muse to awaken spontaneously.
2. The best teachers are aggressively full of enthusiasm for their subject. Diffidence and distance do not convince students that they should become actively engaged in the subject.
3. The best teachers know how to ask and answer important questions; they know which questions are important—answering

questions which do not contribute to the central argument interrupts the flow of the discussion.

4. The best teachers inspire. They present ideas in such an intriguing fashion that the students continue to discuss them after class. David Riesman taught only from 12:00 to 1:00 so that students would not schedule another class immediately after his lecture but, rather, would talk about it over lunch. He and his teaching fellows (I once was one) encouraged this by lunching with students at Quincy House once a week after the lecture.

5. The best teachers help students achieve, even beyond their expectations. It is easier to play to the best students in the class, but it is ultimately more inspiring to teach the whole class. One professor of chemistry uses key students to help him pace his lectures—if an average student whom he has located (and students always sit in the same location) is nodding in agreement, he can then go a bit faster. If he or she appears lost, he slows down.

We also decided to explore the qualities of gifted and mediocre teachers through the voice of students. They wrote about gifted teachers as follows:

- He presented entertaining lectures that reflect his interest in and enthusiasm for the material.
- He is an expert in the field.
- He has an impressive depth of knowledge.
- She has a great attitude toward her students.
- He has an impressive depth of knowledge.
- He is friendly toward students.
- Her lectures are well organized and information packed.
- Her clear, well-prepared lectures are a delight.
- Her enthusiasm, friendly attitude, accessibility, and consistent helpfulness are just great.
- Her lectures are well organized and clear, and she occasionally peppers her lectures with personal anecdotes which enliven the potentially dry material.
- His lectures are compelling, systematic, extraordinarily lucid and almost impeccably delivered.
- He keeps his lectures unbiased and maintains a positive attitude toward students.
- She has a particularly impressive command of the material.

- He gives clear, informative lectures and is well organized.
- His organization, enthusiasm, self-assuredness, and wit all contribute to make his presentations captivating and informative.
- He is exceptionally clear, concise, and accessible.
- She is accessible and willing to spend time after lecture answering questions.
- He has a great wit and is clear in his presentation.
- He is an organized, affable, and enthusiastic lecturer.
- She is concerned and gives clear explanations.
- She is clear and organized, friendly, and accessible.
- He delivers interesting, lucid, and amusing presentations.
- He is approachable and helpful

About mediocre teachers, students said:

- His presentations are especially confusing and often dull and uninspiring.
- His presentations were disjointed and difficult to follow.
- His presentations are too fast paced, and his lectures are dry.
- Her presentations are dry and her attitude toward students detached.
- His lectures are dry, slow, and poorly structured.
- His presentations are confusing and dull.
- Her lectures are disjointed and difficult to follow.
- He gives disorganized and rambling presentations.
- She makes too many generalizations.
- His lectures are repetitive and unfocused.
- Lectures are repetitive and structurally weak.
- Her delivery style is stiff and distant.
- The habit of reading from her notes makes presentations dry and overly formal.
- The course is weakly structured and lacks coherence.
- She allows discussion to get bogged down by trivial questions.
- He is aloof and unapproachable.

Simply reading a number of student comments illustrates that there are a few fundamental dimensions which distinguish outstanding teaching from the mediocre. Students make it abundantly clear that good teachers provide cogent explanations of complicated materials, they are well organized, personable, articulate, and interested in student progress. Mediocre teachers in contrast are disorganized, unclear, unnecessarily complicated, aloof, and dry. The message could not be more clear.[1]

What are the limitations of such a definition of good teaching? Some would suggest that alumni, not students, should supply the criteria for judging teachers, for they really know who taught material that withstood the test of time. Some reject both, stating that allowing either students or alumni to set criteria for teaching implies a consumer-oriented college when it is the faculty who have the responsibility for setting the standards in the academy. Both of these arguments are simply rationales for poor teaching. For example, establishing standards which are beyond your students (a common complaint about poor teachers) is quite inappropriate. One must start where students are, but one has every right to expect serious improvement during the term and hold students accountable for a high level of mastery at the end of the course. That is an appropriate use of standards. From my experience, I believe that students do have a good sense of criteria for teaching and what facilitates their learning. They, according to our evidence, are attracted to demanding courses, if they are well taught.

One of the more complex topics with which to deal is the delayed effect phenomenon. Christensen draws upon the words of the poet Amy Lowell to illustrate this point, "You know when a letter is posted but you never know when it will be delivered."[2] In my course Individual Psychological Assessment, I have had students for whom assessment, evaluation, and testing are an anathema; they plod through the course with disdain but oftentimes two to three years later come back to express how much the course meant to them now that they are actually in the field and working with children and adolescents.

Clearly there are courses where the impact is slow in coming, but in general I tend to question the value of a course when a year later there is very little memory of it. Some years ago an experiment was conducted in which students were re-examined a year after they had completed Economics 10, Harvard's beginning course in economics. Results indicated that students had forgotten much of the nomenclature on which they had been carefully drilled, and they had not read any economics since the course ended. The one thing they did remember was the analytical methodology taught in the course. These findings provided information useful in restructuring the course. Professional terminology was minimized; illustrations were drawn from contemporary issues rather than the classical economic problems to encourage students to continue reading in the field, and the analytical approach was emphasized even more.

Outcome research which restructures teaching is in particularly short supply. We examined the seven leading journals on college teaching and found virtually no articles of experimental research on teaching. Why is so little research done on teaching? If this holds any interest for you, it can become an area where you could make a major contribution.

Teaching is an art and a craft. Every teacher cannot necessarily be a gifted artist, but it behooves all of us to master the craft of teaching. If we have at our command the skills that help us control the classroom, then we can facilitate the learning process. Although these are secondary to having a mastery of the material itself, such skills are central in creating an environment which enhances student learning.

Notes

1. Quotes have been drawn from the Course Evaluation Guide published by the Committee on Undergraduate Education, Harvard University (1990).

2. C. Roland Christensen, University Professor at Harvard, was the source of inspiration for many of these ideas. His contributions to helping teachers improve their talents are legion; his book *Teaching and the Case Method* was published by the Harvard Business School, Publishing Division.

Research Agenda for the Beginner: When Your Feet Hit the Ground, Start Running

You must hit the ground running with respect to research. There was a time when the leisurely life was permitted. As a new professor, you could afford to spend most of your time getting acquainted with colleagues over coffee breaks; learning to deal with complaints, romances, and successes of students; building your image (one assumes a popular one) on campus; or dealing with community residents. These activities are still valued, but they are subordinate to the necessity of publishing. This is particularly true at the large state and private universities. Unquestionably, there are institutions at which teaching and service (broadly defined) are the primary focus of the college. And it may be that the role of research is being reconsidered at some of the larger state and private universities. However, research continues to be a central activity for many professors and is still the key for professional advancement.

All universities today do have a group of professors who have published little or nothing. Usually they were brought into the institution when there were very different standards for promotion and tenure. These professors are frozen in place by their lack of publications and are usually at the bottom of the salary range for their academic rank. They carry water and keep the store. Frequently, they defend their importance by teaching large classes and advising huge numbers of students. This work is appreciated locally but not valued professionally. What will make you, as a beginning professor, exciting to the institution and marketable to other universities is nothing more or less than your research productivity. Emphasis on faculty research productivity results from the fact that universities themselves are usually ranked on it.

Senior faculty members at any institution can cite cases in which beginning professors disregarded the research requirement and suffered the consequences of that disregard. If it's at all possible, arrive on campus with two or three publications in your portfolio. You'll have done these during your graduate school days, and often they're joint publications shared with your doctoral advisor. To have aligned yourself with a publishing professor during your graduate school days buys you time. You can delay research production in this case until you can establish yourself at your new institution.

Increasingly, research is coauthored. There was a time when coauthorship didn't count much toward a professor's research production; however, with the increasing difficulty of placing articles in quality journals, evaluation committees in departments and colleges have looked favorably upon coauthoring. It is a good means of encouraging junior faculty members to begin their research careers, because in such efforts, the beginner may often rely heavily upon the senior author and learn the ropes.

Outlets for Scholarship

There are several ways to disseminate your scholarship. You need to be smart about the outlets for your work, though. All have some value, but you need to look for the venues that have the most value for you.

Refereed Journals

The most important outlets are nationally or internationally respected journals that maintain boards of editors and boards of referees. Usually, the referees do not know the names of the authors of the papers they review. Similarly, authors do not know who reviewed their paper. So, the referees' judgment is based on the quality of authors' work rather than their "name" or the threat of retaliation from disgruntled authors. Obviously, you would do well to publish in such journals. They do much to enhance your professional status.

Nonrefereed Journals

There are some journals of national reputation that do not use referees. Acceptance decisions are made by the editor. Such research articles do not weigh as heavily with promotion and tenure committees as do the refereed articles. Most promotion and tenure committees insist that research be identified as published by refereed or nonrefereed journals.

Authored or Edited Book

Depending on the institution and the book, an authored or edited book will receive credit ranging in value from three to possibly seven articles. It may or may not contain original research. If you're the sole author, the book generally will count more than an edited book. Also, a scholarly book generally will count more than a textbook. In some instances, a book is easier to put together than a series of articles. However, as a new professor, you'll need considerable confidence to commit yourself to the amount of time and effort that is required to produce a book. Nonetheless, if you successfully complete such a project, you'll be assured of a far greater amount of attention by the administration and your colleagues than you would normally gain through the publication of a series of refereed articles.

Local and Regional Publications

Many very fine research articles are published in state or local magazines and professional journals. Oftentimes, these are service publications that contain research aimed at helping local practitioners. These sorts of papers can count toward service. However, these publications usually do not count for a whole lot in terms of scholarship. Typically, such papers emphasize "how to do it" information and are not considered to be on the cutting edge of knowledge. Local publications can get you noticed and be of service to others, but you would be wise not to make them the principal outlet for your scholarship.

Presentations

Most universities consider a paper read at a professional association meeting a legitimate form of scholarship. Much depends on the review process for the conference, however. Presentations that are not peer reviewed do not count as much as peer-reviewed presentations. Sometimes, presenters only submit abstracts for review and not completed papers. Those sorts of presentations count for less. Also, the presentation counts more if it is published eventually. Many times, associations will publish the proceedings of their meeting. That isn't always the case. If your presentation is not published in a conference proceedings, be sure to think about journals where you might publish it. This might require some rewriting of the paper. If you do publish peer-reviewed papers from conferences, be sure you have ways to document the review process for your tenure and promotion file.

The upshot of all this is that you must keep these different research forms in mind when you decide on your own research projects.

Getting Started

Clearly, one possible starting place for your research program is your dissertation. Considerable difference of opinion exists as to the desirability of crafting your dissertation into a book or series of articles. Earlier we suggested that, rather than starting from scratch, you may wish to explore areas of the thesis that may lead to further research. Several contributors in the present work strongly urge the beginning professor to publish an article or two from the doctoral thesis. Dean Whitla says that at some institutions new professors must make the dissertation into a book. Much, of course, depends upon the quality of the thesis itself. The reputation of the publishing house is important, too. Avoid publishing in vanity presses (which require authors to guarantee sale of a certain number of books).

A counterargument suggests that it's usually wise to abandon your dissertation temporarily even though you may examine the material a few years later and publish in the area. If you publish your dissertation materials early, it often leaves the promotion and tenure committee with a poor image of you. Extensive multiple publication from a dissertation is oftentimes considered to be a "cheap shot." It is expected that you will publish an article or two on dissertation material; that's considered to be in line with cutting your teeth academically, but heavy dependence on such materials leaves the wrong impression.

A second reason for not relying too much on your dissertation in the initial phase of your research productivity is that you'll usually need to begin anew. The writing of a dissertation is often more important as a method of learning the process than in developing important theory. Break loose now and use the process on new material and new ideas. Cut the umbilical cord. Evaluation committees and administrators want to see growth beyond your dissertation. An old and respected dean once commented to his young colleagues that the doctoral degree was good for only about ten years, at which time the learning attained to achieve the degree was out of date.

As you determine a research agenda, ask yourself first why you're doing the research. As a young professor noted, you have the opportunity to seek (a) fame or (b) authority. If you're looking for fame, select a hot topic for research and pursue it. If you're after authority, become the initiator in a specialized area, and others will follow your lead. Authority might not lead to fame, or at least not broad recognition, as your area of expertise might be quite narrow. However, authority surely can lead to fame. When the innovative research is not too controversial, then, you often can count on a number of followup articles by others who join the discussion of what has now become a hot topic. This spreads your reputation. (There are, however, instances when the initiator of original research selects a topic that in itself is too hot to handle. This is exemplified by the research of Christopher Jencks.)

For example, one way of gaining publications can be referred to as the "ping-pong game." This "picking-a-fight" approach often proves to be a gutsy game. In this instance, you publish a controversial article. Other writers pick up your theme and refute it or criticize it. Of course, you must now defend your original stance and must publish a refutation of the refutation. The second wave insists how wrong you were, and sometimes waves and cycles continue until the subject is resolved or more likely done to death. A number of publications can be generated in the process although journals tend to limit the space they devote to these exchanges. Still, this is a method of generating publications.

A variation of the "pick-a-fight" strategy is disagreeing with a deceased authority, which can be safer than disagreeing with the living. The dead may turn over in their graves, but they rarely talk back. A new young professor once took on the late Frederick Jackson Turner, whose "safety-valve" thesis had dominated interpretations of western U.S. history for generations. He suggested a very different analysis of the westward movement. Thus, he engaged in "unfaming" a person and, by attacking a prevailing theory, gained fame for himself.

However, such a strategy can promote a disjointed eclecticism in your writing. It's best to begin early to achieve focus in your research effort. "Focus" is more likely to appear in evaluations than any other word. If you publish widely under every topic known to man or woman, you'll be criticized for your lack of focus. Research institutions today wish to have their faculties on the cutting edge of knowledge, which you can achieve only by intense effort in a specific area. They want you to become an authority on something. In fact, they really want you to become "the" authority on that something.

Of course, even after you've determined a research agenda and produced articles, it doesn't mean the end of your worries. The work still must be accepted for publication.

Submitting Your Research for Publication

In submitting research articles to journals, be aware of certain ethics within the academic profession. One of the most important of these is that you can't submit the same article for publication to more than one journal at a time (although it would certainly save you time to do so). Dual publications of the same material can lead to your professional disgrace. Be patient. You may not hear from the editorial staff as to the receipt of your article for some time. Some don't send the expected postcard at all. Some may take up to a year to evaluate the article; the minimum amount of time is about three months.

You'll probably be puzzled over why a particular article you submitted for publication is not accepted by a journal. And, indeed, many good articles are not published. There are several explanations. It's an increasingly tight marketplace. As universities and colleges increasingly emphasize faculty research productivity, the number of journals available for publications is insufficient. Increasing costs of publication have driven many out of business. In some academic areas, there may be only two or three recognized journals to serve an increasingly large group of researchers. Critics often charge that the journals and their editorial staffs regard themselves as gatekeepers whose mission is to maintain orthodoxy. If you submit articles that differ from the views of the editorial staff, they may be rejected. There is a suspicion that some journal staffs concern themselves primarily with their own career advancement or that of their friends. The deck may be stacked. You should prepare yourself for rejections. All research veterans are familiar with that dreadful moment when the article they've worked on for months, possibly years, is returned in a large brown envelope with the rest of the day's mail. The thump of the heavy envelope is sufficient to frighten even the bravest soul.

When they reject a paper, some editorial boards will recommend another journal to which you should submit your research article or offer to accept it with substantial revisions. Sometimes included with the rejected paper are critical comments from reviewers. A majority of these comments are apt to be negative, and a few may even be devastating. The research experience is often painful and not for the timid or thinskinned. But you can take advantage of these criticisms, revise the paper, and resubmit it to the same or a different journal.

Obviously, the costs of rejection may be steep, but so may the costs of acceptance. With increasing publication costs, some journals require that you, the author, share the cost of publication. Sometimes you must pay page costs prior to publication. Many academic departments or colleges will pay such costs. The support system provided by the department may be crucial in advancing the research production of its faculty.

Before the advent of the word processor and other computerized technology, the research professor was frequently forced to pay large amounts for research publications. Two hundred and fifty dollars out of the individual's own pocket was not an uncommon expenditure for a typical publication. Costs consisted of pay to a secretary for typing, basic research, possibly in the form of questionnaires, statistical help, etc. However, with today's technology and with the support systems provided by research-minded departments, you need no longer absorb these costs. In the past, research productivity was often hindered by a professor's low salary. Often there simply was not the money available to invest in the career.

There are ways to maximize the return on your investment of time, energy, and money. It's possible on occasion, if you're lucky, to get substantial credit through a single well-written article. First, the original is published by a respected journal. Then, the article is reprinted in a digest journal or is selected for an anthology someone is putting together. If it's really good, the paper may be reprinted in several places. This gets you recognition, but tenure committees will recognize that these are reprints. You will get credit for publishing a widely read article. That is important, because it's a measure of the quality of your work. But do not try to pass these other printings off as several different articles. Be proud of the reprints, but be sure to make it clear that they are reprints.

You don't always have to rely on luck. One professor, indicating how he solved the cost problem, suggested that his research article served three purposes: It would be a lecture in his regular class, a paper he read at a national professional meeting, and a published research article. Maximum return on a single investment.

It also is possible to revise a published paper and submit it as a new paper to a different journal. The core ideas and arguments might be the same, but they are packaged differently, perhaps applied to different problems or contexts. This is ethically acceptable so long as the publications really are appreciably different.

Also, to make efficient use of your time, study the journals to which you are submitting your work. Spend time at the library analyzing the market for your writings and research. You may find to your dismay that some academic fields have few refereed journals. On the other hand, the number of journals in traditional fields such as history, sociology, or philosophy may be very great. If you're in these academic areas, you'll have an easier time than those in areas in which few journals of distinction exist.

The remarkable research publication record of an old and endearing professor can be cited. It far exceeded the record of most of those who might be considered more able and more eager. The professor's detective work had uncovered little-known and obscure but legitimate journals that had a high acceptance rate. He created a successful career for himself by taking advantage of that fact.

Acceptance rate varies radically from journal to journal. The more prestigious journals may accept only one out of twenty articles submitted. Others, of lesser reputation, may accept one of five. Study what the journal looks for in terms of style, content, length, and topic. Journalistic policies differ. Know that difference.

Another way to recoup research costs is to take advantage of research grants, both from your institution and elsewhere. A university makes a substantial investment when it hires you. If you're hired at the assistant level at age thirty and continue at the university (assuming you earn the rank of full professor) until you're sixty-five, the university will have invested a couple million dollars in you (including salary, support system, office space, etc.). That's no trifling amount. The university wants value received for money spent. At research-oriented institutions, you can petition the university for seed money in form of grants for the purpose of starting your research career. These grants may be relatively small, and your research proposal will be inspected critically before the grant is awarded. A midwestern institution once held in escrow a quarter of a million dollars to be used purely as seed money for new professors with acceptable research proposals. However, as is often the case, research priorities were heavily skewed in the direction of the pure sciences. Seventy percent of the quarter of a million dollars went to one department, chemistry.

There are many varieties of grants that you can seek—federal grants, philanthropic institution grants, state-subsidized grants, professional association grants, corporation and business grants, and grants supported by wealthy alumni or friends of the college or university. In this last instance the grants usually carry titles honoring former professors or alumni. One department chairperson always made it a habit to take every doctoral candidate (at the candidate's expense) to Washington, D.C., for a week's visit. During the week, the candidate was taken to all those bureaus and departments of the federal government that had appropriate grants to award. The candidate was educated on the spot on how and where to go in seeking grants and was introduced to a number of senators and representatives whose influence would be helpful in securing them.

You have a short but important lesson to learn: Those who have get more, and those who have never had rarely get. The first olive out of the bottle is the most difficult to spear. Grants work in exactly the same way. Try to get a modest grant first—perhaps one of less than a thousand dollars. Probably the first two or three grants should be modest. You'll build up your reputation and skill before you try for the large and prestigious ones.

The *Federal Register* contains a listing of available grants. However, such information usually is distributed to the public with little time for proposal preparation. Insiders are far wiser and much more successful in obtaining research grants. If you associate with the right bureau and departmental officials, they'll give you clues about what research is likely to be called for long before official requests are mailed to the general public.

"Grant eaters," researchers whose batting average in securing grants is well over five hundred, generally use a boiler plate. When you apply for a grant you must list your faculty resources, office space, computer equipment, and so on. So it's good practice to have the boiler plate, a generic list that you can use for any proposal, readily available.

Some researchers are highly selective in seeking grants; thus, they preserve their focus. Others tend to drift with the various cycles or development of hot topics and shift their research accordingly. At the beginning of your career, it's best to seek the more modest research grants and establish your track record. After you establish the fact that you do good research with your grant money, you can go where you will.

Grants from outside sources are much sought after by universities. If the research grant is significant in the prestige of its topic or project, many university administrators will go all out to help you secure it. Normally, the university will skim off a percentage of the grant to compensate for your use of the university support system—secretarial help, and so on. But if the university ardently desires the prestige of a nationally or internationally recognized project or piece of research, the trustees may vote to finance the grant at 110 percent or 125 percent of the grant amount— that is, they'll pay an additional 10 percent or 25 percent of the cost over and above the actual grant itself.

If you're a beginning professor in the classics, philosophy, or foreign language, you may become frustrated with the inequality of the grant system. There are few grants available in these academic areas. There is also, undoubtedly, a relationship between the amount of money brought to the university by professors in the sciences and in mathematics and the salaries awarded to them. The federal government and others are highly interested in research in chemistry, physics, and engineering. Professors in these select academic divisions may well have at their disposal grants amounting to millions of dollars. They may, with good reason, have considerable clout within their departments and within the university generally. The university does not pay them; they, in reality, pay the university by supporting possibly a dozen or more excellent graduate students who contribute to the research project. A Latin professor rarely exercises such power or productivity. The availability and size of grants reflect the marketplace.

Scholarly Publications: It's Still Publish or Perish

John A. Glover

At the beginning of my career, I believed the most important part of my professional life was teaching. After all, colleges and universities exist to educate students, and, as a faculty member, it seemed nothing could be more important than holding up my end of the educational bargain through good teaching. My views on the importance of teaching have changed dramatically over the years. I'm still committed to excellence in instruction, but I've learned other things are more important for personal and professional survival.

The Importance of Scholarly Publications

I once believed instruction was the most important part of a professor's career; I now believe the publication of scholarly works is more important than teaching. There are four reasons why I hold this belief. First, the likelihood of obtaining a position at a college or university upon graduation is directly related to a person's potential for scholarly productivity. Second, salary, promotion, and tenure decisions weigh scholarly productivity more heavily than any other factor. Third, the ability to leave one institution for a faculty position at another is almost totally dependent on the job seeker's publication record. Fourth, the recognition and prestige attained within any domain (e.g., chemistry, foreign affairs, psychology, art history) is a direct function of the quantity and quality of a professor's scholarly publications.

These four assertions may seem radical, even irrational. Indeed many highly able faculty members would scoff at my position, arguing I was closer to the truth when I was a beginning assistant professor—the nurturance of students is the reason for our existence. The problem really isn't one of who is right and who is wrong, though. Philosophically and theoretically, people who espouse teaching as the reason for our existence are correct. Pragmatically and perhaps cynically, though, scholarly productivity has become preeminent and a brief discussion of my four assertions should help me make that case.

Obtaining The First Position

I've met a large number of naive doctoral students who believed merely completing their coursework with good grades and writing a nice dissertation would lead them to a satisfactory academic position. This belief simply isn't true in any area where there is competition for jobs. Some people get jobs; others don't. What separates successful applicants for first-time academic positions from unsuccessful applicants?

The answer, not surprisingly, is scholarly productivity. Consider two equivalent candidates, one of whom has published three or four papers prior to the dissertation, the other of whom has not. Every search committee I've ever known or heard of has opted for the candidate with publications—even in institutions in which research presumably is a minor consideration.

As I'm sure is mentioned elsewhere in this volume, a great number of variables are involved in finding a first position in academe. Among these variables are the institution of the student's dissertation adviser, and, at least in a few areas, the person's previous teaching experience. Deficits in these areas and more can be overcome by a good publication track record. Search committees want to find the best possible additions to their faculty. As I'll argue later, there are no good ways of objectifying teaching ability, and the reputations of schools and major advisers often have not been predictive of students' subsequent scholarly abilities. Early publication, however, is seen as a clear and direct demonstration of scholarly ability and commitment to a scholarly career. Not surprisingly, the single most important factor in hiring new Ph.D.s is the quality of their scholarly productivity.

Salary, Promotion, and Tenure Decisions

The role of publications does not end once a person has obtained a faculty position. Others (department chairs, deans, assorted vice presidents for one thing or another) will be making critical decisions about the new faculty member related to yearly evaluations (salary), promotions in rank, and permanent appointments (tenure). A fair question is what factors are associated with getting good raises, being promoted, and attaining the state of grace known as tenure. Let's consider the kind of evidence decision makers work from in making these choices.

Any institution, from the most research driven to the most teaching oriented, will publicly acknowledge three general factors in evaluating faculty: teaching, service, and scholarly productivity (commonly referred to merely as research). A careful examination of these factors will reveal only research yields relatively objective data.

Data on teaching must come from the following: student evaluations of the faculty member, peer and supervisor observations of the person's teaching, students' scores on some standardized measures of achievement, and instructional materials generated by the professor. Although I won't argue against the utility of student evaluations, their value in assessing an instructor's competence leaves much to be desired. One shortcoming is that the nature of content strongly influences evaluations. For example, it is quite possible for a person to teach a marvelous course, in say, introductory chemistry and obtain much poorer evaluations than another person who gives little effort to a course in abnormal psychology. Further, student ratings load very heavily on the perceived personality of the instructor. This hardly seems fair as shy, introverted professors might actually offer more valuable courses than their more dynamic colleagues.

Peer and supervisor evaluations also may give a good indication of how well that person can organize materials, but I know of no research tying this source of data to teaching ability. Standardized test scores might be a good solution, but there are several issues preventing their use (e.g., availability, cost, issues of academic freedom).

The long and short of things is that teaching data are not very helpful in making critical decisions about faculty members. Generally, as long as a person is teaching well enough to stay out of trouble, teaching is viewed as adequate.

The evaluation of service poses many of the same problems as evaluating teaching. What is good service? Who is to be served? How much is enough service? Should the service be free or paid? Using data from a faculty member's service to the community also is a problem because some disciplines better lend themselves to service than others. For example, engineering, architecture, psychology, education, and business faculty typically can find satisfying and appropriate ways to serve a community. Faculty who teach Latin, the classics, philosophy, and so on may have a much more difficult time finding someone who needs their special skills and knowledge.

Because data from teaching and service inevitably are flawed, administrators turn to faculty publications in their decision making. Although publications may have absolutely no relevance to teaching, they offer an objective, quantifiable source of data. Clearly, publications carry different weights at different institutions. Still, even the most teaching-oriented institution rewards publication. If you want raises, if you want to be promoted, and if you want to attain tenure, there is one strategy that will facilitate your quest for these goals: publish and publish frequently. Mediocre teachers who do not provide community service are tenurable if they have publication track records. On the other hand, at most institutions of higher education, even the very best teaching will not save you if you do not publish.

Don't take my word for it. Find people who did not make tenure and lost their jobs—people who did not publish and perished as a result. Compare those who were fired for poor teaching (if you can find any) to those who were fired for lack of publication. Colleges and universities may exist for the purpose of educating students, but the most critical component of faculty evaluation is publication. I won't argue this state of affairs is appropriate or acceptable. However, it is the way of the academic world. Teach well, teach very well, but don't forget it is publications that will get you tenure.

The Ability to Change Jobs

As it sometimes happens, people may want to change jobs. The reasons for wanting to make a change really aren't important. Only one thing matters. Why should an institution hire someone with several years of experience instead of hiring a new Ph.D.? Consider: New Ph.D.s are cheaper. New Ph.D.s should be highly motivated to perform well in order to attain promotions. New Ph.D.s are easier to mold into an institution's idea of what a faculty person should be like. In contrast, the only advantage of hiring experienced faculty is that they've taught more. Maybe this is an important factor, but as I've argued before, the evaluation of teaching ability is a very, very difficult thing. Further, why should an administrator pay $10,000 to $15,000 more a year for a senior faculty member when the potential of hiring such a person is so very difficult to verify?

Well, the answer to my question is they don't. Look at the advertisements in the *Chronicle of Higher Education*. Fully 90 percent of the jobs listed are at the level of beginning assistant professor. Each year only a small minority of positions in academe are at senior levels.

How does an experienced person find a new job, then? There are three ways. First, go into administration. Second, convince an institution there's no hidden reason why you're willing to take a cut in salary and rank to move. Third, build an exit vita.

Going into administration may be a reasonable career move. After all, somebody *has* to do these things. You'll need to build a proven track record in administration and the ability to get along with others to make such a move. I won't say more about the transition to administration here because it is outside the scope of this essay.

Convincing another institution you really don't mind a several thousand dollar cut in salary, a reduction in rank, or giving up your tenure is not a strategy I recommend. Inevitably, potential employers want to know what has gone wrong. Furthermore, the majority of experienced people competing for beginning assistant professor positions are those who failed to make tenure. I've known a few people who were able to move this way. All had failed to make tenure at their original, more prestigious institutions and had applied for positions at "lesser" institutions. Luckily, these people had friends or good acquaintances at the institutions they joined who convinced the search committees to gamble on "failed" careers. Still, these people had to go back and start over as beginning assistant professors. Each also gave up thousands of dollars in current and future earnings, and had to endure the heartache of having to once again prove themselves fit for permanent appointment. Sadly, most of the people I've known who did not make tenure had to leave academe for other positions. Only a lucky few professors who fail to make tenure are able to find other academic jobs.

Building an exit vita really is the best approach. An exit vita is exactly what it sounds like—a vita built to find you a senior position at another institution. You see, I misspoke earlier when I stated the only advantage senior faculty have over their junior colleagues is teaching experience. This is only true if faculty members do not publish. If faculty members publish, senior faculty should have the enormous advantage of a clearly articulated, thematic, and nationally visible program of scholarship. Senior faculty are not hired to teach—brand new Ph.D.s are cheaper and easier to deal with. Senior faculty are hired to give prestige to a program or to provide intellectual leadership to a department or area. The only way to convince a search committee you will be able to provide intellectual leadership is to publish. Nothing else can suffice. Even a Harvard Ph.D. loses its glamour when its holder fails to publish.

Related to the general issue of finding a senior position in academe is the question of how one advances from one institution to another. It is common knowledge some institutions are more prestigious than others and provide certain advantages to their faculty. Moving from a less prestigious school to a more prestigious school requires an extraordinarily good exit vita.

Recognition in One's Field

I am unaware of any person in any discipline who has attained a position of intellectual or scholarly eminence on the basis of teaching or service alone. If you want to be recognized within your academic discipline, there is no way to attain this goal save scholarly publication. Of course, once you are recognized in your field, issues such as promotion and tenure, salary, and changing positions become much, much easier.

How Much Is Enough?

I have a good friend in his 11th year post-Ph.D. During this time he has averaged more than 30 publications a year. His climb within his profession was meteoric, and he has earned every major accolade available from his discipline. At the same time, he has taught well and been an outstanding advisor to graduate students. This friend represents one extreme on the continuum of scholarly productivity. At the other extreme, of course, are individuals who publish nothing. Despite my admiration for my friend, I recommend neither extreme to young faculty. On the one hand, 100-hour weeks are more than most of us can give. On the other hand, failure to publish is self-destructive.

There is no answer to how much a person should publish. There are differences across disciplines and different demands at different institutions. Further, there should be very real differences in a professor's goals for publication at different times in his or her career. Trying to take these things into account, my overall advice is to publish one or two papers a year in good journals and give one paper a year at the convention of a major organization within one's field.

One or two papers a year may not sound like much, but taken over a 30-year career, 60 papers is a substantive contribution to a literature that cannot be overlooked by later scholars reviewing the area. A paper or so a year at a major convention also helps keep scholars in the minds of their peers at other institutions. If a move has to be made or if a letter or two of support for promotion must be obtained externally, the expenses involved in regularly presenting are more than worth it.

Quality or Quantity?

Ultimately, the question of quality versus quantity must come up. Like almost everyone else, I believe quality is more important than quantity. Still, there are other factors to be considered. For a graduate student and early in one's faculty career (the first five years or so), numbers of publications probably are more important than the quality of those publications. No reasonable person expects graduate students or beginning assistant professors to have the knowledge and skill to do first-rank research. Indeed, John Hayes of Carnegie-Mellon has studied the issue and suggests it takes about eight to ten years post-Ph.D. for scholars to learn enough to make significant contributions to their literatures. My experience is in direct accord with Hayes' research findings.

The reason I emphasize quantity for young scholars is the need they have to demonstrate the ability to do research. At this stage in their careers, graduate students and young faculty must show they have potential. Because decisions to hire and tenure faculty are made so early, they inevitably are made on the basis of potential.

Despite the emphasis I put on prolific publication early in one's career, it is important to keep in mind high-quality work always wins out over work of poorer quality. A new Ph.D. with two publications in the major journal in his or her field will attract much more attention than a graduate student with five or six publications in marginal journals. The idea is to be as prolific as possible while, at the same time, maintaining the highest standards possible.

After tenure has been obtained, quality of publications becomes much more important than numbers of publications. Remaining marketable and attaining recognition within one's field depend on the quality of one's work. Quantity probably also is an issue, but there is no substitute for quality. Senior positions go to individuals who have demonstrated high-quality scholarship.

What Kind of Publication?

Fields differ in the emphases they give to empirical reports, syntheses, books, funded grant proposals, and other means of demonstrating scholarship. In general, however, grant proposals and books are relatively low-payoff projects early in one's career. Writing grant proposals is a particularly bad way for an assistant professor to spend his or her time. Unfunded grant proposals take just as much time and effort as funded proposals. These "failures," however, seldom are of much value. Decision makers are unlikely to reward faculty who fail to write successful proposals. They don't care how much effort went into the task—a failure is a failure—even if 97 percent of all proposals to a funding agency go unfunded. The odds of writing successful proposals are long, and, unless the writing of grant proposals is a specific part of an assistant professor's job description, I would avoid the task. Even funded proposals may not carry the same weight as one brief report in a good journal. Finally, if a proposal actually is funded, the assistant professor is stuck carrying out the granted activity—a task that may not be very enjoyable.

A last word about grants also is needed here. Never, never believe you must have a grant to do research. If certain kinds of research activities are impossible without grant funds, find another area of work. If you tell yourself you must have funds to do research and then fail to write a funded proposal, you are dooming yourself to failure. Sure, you can blame the granting agency, but the agency isn't going for tenure—you are. Make do without funding. I have seen too many faculty who tried to hide their lack of scholarship behind the lack of funds. In contrast, one of my friends, a physicist by trade, began her career at a small school with inadequate laboratory facilities. She could not attract external funding, but still did not give up. Over the course of the next five years, she published eight empirical papers on the teaching of physics, two notes in astronomy journals concerning her amateur observations, and three papers (as second author) with a former classmate who taught at a state university. Not only was she promoted and tenured, she also was courted by several major institutions looking for a good senior faculty member. She didn't leave, but she is paid very well.

Writing books is a far better way to spend one's time than writing grant proposals. However, in many fields, the publication of empirical reports is much more important. Writing books takes a great deal of time and effort. At many major research-oriented institutions, 10 to 12 publications in major journals over a five-year period are enough for faculty to gain promotion and tenure. The time, effort, and energy needed for these reports almost inevitably will be far less than what is needed to write one book in most fields; writing books is better put off as a posttenure activity.

The choice of scholarly activity should be made on a single pragmatic basis. What set of activities will most likely help the faculty member succeed at his or her current position, gain promotion, earn tenure, and remain marketable in the field? I cannot prescribe this choice across disciplines, but it is clear the issue deserves considerable study at the beginning of one's career.

Summary

Scholarly publication is critical to finding a first job, succeeding in that position, finding a new job, and attaining recognition within a field. Teaching may be what the professoriate should be about—I cannot argue against this assertion. However, professional survival and advancement do not depend on teaching well. In fact, survival and advancement depend on scholarly publication. With only a modest program of publication, one can be a mediocre teacher and still be very well rewarded. Ultimately, I encourage all new faculty to distrust any person who tells them research is unimportant or that teaching is everything. Such rhetoric may be very beguiling, but it is patently false. Academe has changed in many ways over the years, but one dictum still is true: "Publish or Perish."

Promotion and Tenure:
Keys to the Kingdom

At your job interview, you should examine closely the promotion and tenure process at the institution. Ask to have copies of the documents that describe procedures and expectations. Talk to the department chairperson, the dean, and faculty about tenure and promotion. Promotion and tenure practices vary widely, and they will determine your professional advancement and, indeed, whether you'll be permitted to remain at the institution at all.

For many years, at many institutions, tenure, the process of giving you a legal right to your job and permitting dismissal only for cause, was automatic after a period of time and was considered no great thing. Increasingly, this is no longer the case. Standards for tenure and promotion are becoming more rigorous, and you must work steadily and seriously toward meeting them. Quite literally, your professional life depends on it. Most institutions stipulate that you must attain tenure within a certain number of years or else be dismissed at the end of that time.

No doubt, at this point in your life you are weary. You have written your thesis, found your job, gone through multiple interviews—all adding up to a great deal of worry and stress. You probably want to just sit for a year or two, get used to teaching at the college level, reacquaint yourself with your family, and just plain take it easy after the exhausting experience of graduate school. Mistake. Don't do it.

The Importance of Promotion and Tenure

Why are promotion and tenure so important? Perhaps the most obvious consideration is job security. Having achieved tenure, you are protected from dismissal except for cause. The basic intent of tenure is to protect your academic freedom. (Academic freedom is discussed further in Part III.) You cannot be fired just because people disagree with views you express or issues you study.

Promotion (which may not include tenure) will usually bring you a salary increase, but the amount varies enormously, depending on the institution's budget. When money's available, you can expect a significant salary increase. In lean times, you may be given congratulations, and that is it. At some institutions, faculty promotion is undoubtedly directly tied to the institution's overall financial health. Administrators may try to reduce deficits or maintain balanced budgets by slowing down the promotion rate—for example, by increasing the number of publications required.

There are penalties (other than monetary ones) for you if you are not promoted on time. All too often, faculty members reach the rank of associate professor and die on the vine. Many never make full professor—for many reasons: Now middle aged, they find the requirements for advancement too difficult; their careers have tended toward application rather than theory; their time is taken up with heavy teaching loads; or family demands or divorce interferes with their career progress. Few reach the rank of full professor after age forty-five. The administration, knowing that the likelihood of their doing so is slight, tend to make it even more difficult for them by making them "storekeepers."

If you find yourself in this position, you will hold the fort while others enjoy the more prestigious and rewarding duties. And once you've reached forty-five with no prospects of becoming a full professor, the job market quickly dries up for you. You are stuck; you are a second-class citizen; no one cares what you want; you may be forced into being a generalist who, with or without your consent, is expected to teach and counsel. You might enjoy this enormously—you also might be bitter and resentful.

If you achieve the rank of full professor you will find that now, at last, you do have academic freedom, that you may risk studying or researching just about anything, controversial or not. You are expected to help run the institution. You have clout. In most institutions, only those who hold rank equal to or higher than yours will vote on your tenure or promotion. Obviously, full professors get to vote on everyone. Their power and perks can be disproportionate. On the other hand, some institutions tend to be more concerned with junior faculty. They expect senior faculty to be leaders, but all the breaks—reduced teaching duties, money for research—go to the untenured faculty.

Increasingly, with budget crunches and with institutions' overriding concern with faculty research productivity, there is growing pressure for tenure and promotion reform. It is suggested that promotion, and even tenure, should be for a limited period of time, such as five years, and that at the end of that time, all those occupying a particular rank, especially that of full professor, must apply again for rank or tenure. Such proposals have little or no chance of being instituted, however. Even so, professors will be under even greater scrutiny than in the past. For example, even if they do not have to reapply for rank and tenure, fully promoted professors do go through annual reviews of their performance.

Expectations and Evidence

You will normally have five or six years to produce the research, teaching, and service records that are essential to earn tenure and/or your first promotion—three areas which may be subdivided into a large number of categories by some tenure and promotion committees. One well-known state university uses 49 separate cells for categorizing and evaluating candidates. Various activities are listed, with a five-point scale used to assess the candidate's qualifications, which may be nationally or internationally known or known only inside the institution. The scale may reflect responses from excellent to poor. Such a scale will result in a quantifiable score or set of scores.

Another institution uses a 14-point set of activities largely taken from the teaching, research, and service criteria. To be eligible for tenure or promotion, the candidate must score an "excellent" in one of the three major categories and at least a "good" in the other two. If the individual eventually becomes a candidate for full professor, he or she must score an "excellent" in all three.

The three categories do not always receive the same emphasis. If you find yourself at one of the larger and more prestigious colleges and universities, your tenure and promotion will depend, more than at other institutions, on your research productivity.

The point here is that to be successful in the process you have to know the specifics of the process at your institution. You will need to document that you meet and hopefully exceed the expectations for tenure and promotion. Early on, make some file folders that correspond to major categories of expectations you find in your institution's tenure and promotion documents. That way, you'll have a convenient place to collect evidence.

Should you become a candidate for both tenure and promotion at the same time, you can use the same portfolio of material for both processes.

Many institutions tie tenure and promotion together. At one time, promotion to the rank of associate professor automatically signified the granting of tenure as well. Today, the processes are differentiated and voted on separately at most institutions.

You will need a year of preparatory time to get ready to apply for tenure and promotion. Most departments will provide you the necessary secretarial help and budget. In many instances, the chairperson will lighten your teaching load or other duties to allow you to spend as much time as possible in collecting your evidence. If not, you will have to use your private time and income.

To maneuver through the very complex and lengthy process, find yourself a "campaign manager." He or she should be thoroughly experienced in the process and committed to your promotion and tenure—a close colleague who has already gone through the process. Your manager acts as your trainer, handler, and agent and keeps you working, typing, and assembling the requisite materials and documentation.

What sort of evidence should you collect? Evidence for research might seem fairly straightforward. Obviously, you'll include papers and other things you have written. The trickier task is to show that your work is good quality. One indicator is that you publish in refereed journals. Collect data on the journals' review boards and acceptance rates. Outside evaluations of your research are sometimes required. A representative sample of your papers may be sent to authorities unknown to you who are employed at other, possibly distant, colleges and universities. Sometimes you are asked to nominate a list of possible evaluators at other institutions, and the departmental committee selects the ones to do the outside evaluations.

Evidence of teaching effectiveness may come from a variety of sources—student evaluations, colleague evaluations, or presentation of creative teaching materials or processes. You may have done graphs and charts on teaching effectiveness over a period of semesters or years. You might work out statistical techniques to indicate your degree of effectiveness, some of which may be quite elaborate. The problem for the committee is that it has almost no criteria to evaluate your teaching. Although student evaluations of teaching are very popular today, they are also difficult to interpret and are sometimes suspect as accurate teaching assessments, and committees whose duty it is to interpret them may need the wisdom of Solomon.

You may have even more difficulty documenting your service activities. Your academic field may not naturally include them; you may not be sought after by the community as a speaker or consultant. Disciplines such as sociology, criminal justice, psychology, or political science are relevant to community interests, but many others are not—at least in the public's mind. Faculty of schools and colleges of education always have an advantage in the service category, as do psychologists who serve part time at clinics or workshops. In any case, you must list all of your speeches, debates, workshops, commencement addresses, etc.—keep a list of them from the beginning of your career. Your committee appointments at the departmental, college, and university level also count as service. But rarely will your number of doctoral candidates or your advisory load count. If you're heavily involved in these, you're probably going to be shortchanged.

The Review Process

Usually, there are several layers or levels in the review process. Tenure and promotion committees are formed on the departmental level, the college level, and sometimes the university level. An applicant's file first goes to the department committee. If that committee supports the application, the file goes to the college committee, and so on. Typically, upper administration is involved also. For example, the college committee may be one of two types: an independent committee, which makes its judgments and passes the material to the university committee, or an advisory committee, which reports to the dean of the college, who may confirm the committee's judgment or reject it entirely. Final approval usually rests with the board of regents or board of trustees.

Tenure and promotion committees almost always operate secretly and discreetly. Junior members are usually warned by their senior colleagues of the necessity of debating and discussing applicants' qualifications with complete confidentiality and seriousness. People's academic lives are on the line. In meetings, a member of your department may speak up to clarify a question raised; however, he or she is expected to be as objective as possible in all judgments and in no way act as a campaign manager. Usually, the personal notes of committee members are destroyed when work is completed. On the other hand, in controversial cases, taperecorders may be used to preserve evidence presented.

Should your petition for tenure or promotion be rejected at some step in the process, you always have the right to appeal. You will find the mechanism of the appeal process in the bylaws or a similar document.

This whole process may seem cumbersome. But it is a process that does a lot to protect your interests in your own career and in faculty governance (although, it doesn't always work perfectly, of course). At one time, promotion of faculty members was in the college dean's domain. A dean at a state university once decided to make some midnight appointments before he left for another position. In particular, he intended to promote an assistant professor to associate. The man had been on the faculty for 30 years, and the dean was going to do him a favor before he left.

Another dean, a week away from retirement, planned to promote a half dozen of his close associates who had been forever at the rank of associate professor to full professor. It was obviously a "Good Old Boys" sort of thing. This kind of favoritism is largely a thing of the past because institutional committees and tight budgets have made it prohibitive.

Rank and Tenure Hierarchies

Some institutions use a quota system for both promotion and tenure although most don't. Where one exists, the institution usually indicates that no more than, say, 25 percent of the faculty members may hold the rank of full professor. Such a rule could spell trouble for you as a new faculty member because faculties are notoriously long lived. So competition to fill a vacant position is extremely tough. Many institutions like to keep a balance of rank in the faculty. In many European systems of higher education, it has been traditional for only an allocated number of full professorships to exist. Consequently, some faculty members never become full professors.

In many of the more prestigious universities in the United States, two separate faculties of equal rank exist. One is tenured, and the other is not. This situation permits the institution to expand or contract as needed without having to make difficult dismissals, relieving untenured faculty members, irrespective of rank, of their positions with little notice. In a sense, they are always on soft money. Of course, few are tossed out on the streets or forced onto food stamps. They may use the prestige of their untenured positions to market themselves with an institution that will give them tenure, rank, and full appreciation.

At one relatively new state university, an even more unique method of giving rank and tenure has developed. Three faculties exist side by side. The first (about 10 percent of the total) is a traditional one in which the faculty members come routinely through the ranks and apply for tenure. A second faculty (about 25 percent of the total) could be called the circuit-rider professors, who travel weekly from their base station at another in-state university, teach at the new institution, and hold rank and tenure only at the base institution. The third faculty (about 65 percent of the total) is an adjunct one in that the large city has enough holders of doctorates in its public school system and its community to provide a nighttime faculty. The members of this third faculty hold the rank of assistant, associate, or full professor but do not have tenure and are not eligible for it. This may, indeed, be the pattern of the future.

Some Difficulties

Probably more litigation in colleges and universities originates in the promotion and tenure process than in any other area of activity. The administration is under pressure to encourage the promotion and tenure of faculty members whose ethnic group or gender has in the past been discriminated against. But even though our society has changed radically in the past two decades, promotion and tenure promotion and tenure rules have remained the same or have increased in the stringency of their requirements. Sometimes a difficult situation of tension between the values of affirmative action and academic rigor is created.

You may be forced to hold dual appointments in different departments or even different colleges within the same university. You may come into both departments or colleges as an assistant professor, but you may have to go through two totally different processes to gain promotion or tenure in the two divisions, or you may elect to seek promotion or tenure in only one of them. The questions of what percentage of salary comes from which department and whether there should be differences in your rank in the two departments will undoubtedly crop up. As a new professor especially, you may find this situation difficult to cope with. You will undoubtedly be more isolated and have less support than if your appointment is contained in a single department.

The tenure and promotion process is not only intense but can, if not handled objectively and diplomatically, create faculty divisions, enmity, and jealousy that can last decades or until the participants are dead or gone. Unresolved quarrels over the fairness of the process disrupt the institution's productivity. In one small college, a professor, having been bypassed for promotion and having stewed in the bitter juices of the injustice, shot and killed the chairperson, who, he assumed, had been instrumental in the bypassing. Then he proceeded to the president's office and murdered him as well. Thankfully, such cases are rare, but the point is that the tenure and promotion process must be taken seriously by all the people involved in it.

Promotion and Tenure

Paul E. Kelly

Promotion and tenure are vitally important topics for all those embarking on academic careers. They provide job security and the only guarantee one has of academic freedom and are primary determinants of one's compensation. To think otherwise is naive.

For most people, the successful completion of a doctorate requires the kind of single-mindedness that relegates most other considerations to those shadowed areas at the back of the mind. It is no surprise, therefore, that the degree becomes almost an end in itself. One can easily lose sight of the fact that the doctorate is a means to an end and merely the first step in a career that may span 40 or more years. Early promotion and tenure require looking beyond the doctorate.

Given the foregoing facts, a wise doctoral student chooses a dissertation topic that has potential for future development. Whole careers have sometimes been built on research initiated in graduate school, with the first publications coming from the dissertation research. A good dissertation, especially one that generates a published article or two on a hot topic, gives the newly-minted Ph.D. a leg up on the competition in his or her job quest.

Choosing the right position has for the beginner the same importance that choosing the right graduate school, the right major professor, and the right dissertation topic once had. One must use to good advantage whatever assets one has, and having a few reprints of published articles can be very impressive, provided that they are good and from respectable and relevant journals. If one has attended a prestigious graduate school, it is important to remember that it is possible to be from there only once. Afterward, one is from that institution in which he or she is employed and is judged primarily on the work done after the receipt of the doctorate. It might be added that being from a prestigious graduate school is sometimes a mixed blessing, and this may also be the case, not only in seeking a position but in being considered for promotion or tenure. For example, no one seems really to notice when a faculty member talks about his years of graduate study at a perfectly respectable but not especially distinguished graduate school, but one who dares mention his years at a highly respected institution of national or international standing is seen as a name dropper. Envy and jealousy come into play, especially from those who might have aspired to attend such an institution and were denied admission. If these people are in a position to deny employment, promotion, or tenure, they may subconsciously or even consciously apply unreasonable standards in judging those who had once been judged superior to them. It is a way of getting even for their past rejection. It is probably made easier by the fact that it is much more difficult to get a high grade-point average and really strong letters of recommendation from the more prestigious graduate schools than from others because of the competition. A student who may have been outstanding at one institution may be only average at another more selective one.

Yet another problem involves the unethical practice of advertising positions that are going to be filled by preselected individuals, but for which candidates are nevertheless invited and interviewed. It is helpful to be able to say that some of those who were interviewed and rejected were from top-flight institutions. It may be argued, of course, that these disadvantages are offset by superior preparation, a preference on the part of some to hire people from big-name institutions, and a superior network, generating more employment opportunities.

When the novice considers promotion and tenure, should he or she choose a position with further learning opportunities but no long-term future (say, a three-year, nontenure, nonrenewable appointment) or one with the possibility of long-term career development (a tenure-track position)? This is a hard question to which there is no easy answer. The wisest course would likely be that of taking the position where there would be the better chance of having some published research within the next two or three years. Unfortunately, it is often impossible to predict which position that might be. In the one instance, the beginner may find himself or herself part of a team engaged in a research program spanning a relatively long period of time, with few opportunities for his or her own work and little recognition for contributions made to the group enterprise. In that case, the individual might be less marketable at the end of the appointment than at the beginning. Three years go by very quickly, and the time pressure would be something to consider, especially because of the length of time required to get research done, articles written, accepted, and actually published. In the other instance, in the tenure-track position, one may have more time before facing an "up or out" situation, perhaps five years instead of three, in which to get something done. One may, however, be saddled with a heavy teaching load, student advisement, and time-consuming committee work and other duties that leave little time for research. It is a difficult choice.

So far, little has been said about teaching and service, which, together with research, are normally considered to make up the primary functions of a professor and are ostensibly considered when a person is up for promotion or tenure. The three functions are sometimes said to be of equal importance and given equal consideration. A great deal of lip service is often given to the importance of teaching, and recognition in the form of plaques is not uncommon, but the big money lies in the area of research, especially research supported by grants and resulting in significant publications in top journals. Except in liberal arts colleges, outstanding teaching runs the risk of going unnoticed and unrewarded. Service doesn't usually count for much either, except in those fields where it is directly rewarded by substantial consulting fees. To the extent that teaching and service interfere with research, they are usually counterproductive in most large universities. To be sure, this is unfortunate, but it is true, nevertheless, even in states in which the education of the populace ought obviously to have the very highest priority. Big-name, highly paid professors in some of the larger state universities may have little contact with students from the state and may be engaged in research that has no direct relevance to any of the primary concerns of the state. The few students with whom they work may be from China, India, Kenya, or some other foreign country, and they may be the ones assigned to teach large undergraduate sections, thus freeing the professors to pursue their research.

Teaching can be very discouraging, especially when it is not regarded as being very important and is so poorly rewarded. The fewer classes one has to teach and the fewer students one has to deal with, the better, provided the time saved is put to good use in more rewarding activities, chief among them research and publications. When one is up for promotion or tenure, that is what the committee will look at. Provided there have been no complaints about one's teaching, very little is likely to be said about it one way or the other.

Where teaching evaluations are used, they often take the form of student evaluations, with anonymity guaranteed and the evaluations made available to faculty members only after grades have been turned in. Students are often unfair and lacking in objectivity. They can be especially hard on instructors or professors in courses outside their major fields of interest, which they often dislike and resent having to take. It can become a kind of popularity contest; a course may be judged more on its entertainment value than on its true merits, and professors may be punished for difficult assignments, outside reading, papers, or low grades. Where these evaluations are taken seriously, there is a tendency toward grade inflation, less-demanding assignments, and easy attendance policies, thus avoiding the risk of low ratings from vengeful students. The highest-rated professors are not necessarily the best teachers, and low ratings of those professors who are productive scholars don't really mean very much, so they don't have to be very much concerned about their evaluations. Some of those who deserve low ratings often enjoy the luxury of teaching only graduate students in small classes in courses in which the students have a vital interest in the subject matter and are not likely to give the professor a low rating for fear of possible repercussions. Only those whose primary function is teaching have to be really concerned about ratings, and they are the ones most likely to be teaching those classes for which ratings are most frequently low. The professors may feel intimidated by fear of low ratings from the students; whereas in the smaller and more specialized courses taught by those whose primary function is research, the students may feel intimidated by fear of retaliation from the professor, who could easily be a member of the student's doctoral committee.

If the quality of one's teaching is to be a major consideration when one is up for promotion or tenure, a better way must be found of evaluating it. More effort has gone into this at the primary or secondary school level than in higher education, because teaching is the primary function of the school teacher, who seldom engages in research. No really good means has ever been found, which is why most teacher organizations are resistant to merit pay schemes and most salary schedules are based on levels of certification and years of experience. Oddly enough, everyone seems to know who the really good teachers are. It is in documenting some sort of proof that the trouble lies, as teaching is as much an art as it is a science. Furthermore, a teacher who has good success with certain types of students in certain types of situations may fail to achieve the same success with other students in the same situation or with the same students in another situation. When a college or university faculty member is up for promotion or tenure, he or she is often provided an opportunity to make a case for his or her promotion or tenure. In addition to the evalu-

ations, which, if they exist, can hardly be avoided, faculty members sometimes present testimonials from a few of their better students. Strong
support from a student with a 4.0 grade point average can be quite impressive and may help to offset less-than-glowing evaluations from other
students. Another letter sure to impress one's colleagues is one in which
a student states that he or she decided to major in one's field as a direct
result of having taken one's course.

Faculty members sometimes document their teaching innovations and
submit this documentation as part of the package of materials submitted
for consideration when up for promotion or tenure. Videotapes, films,
slides, charts, graphs, and other visual aids may be used as well as games
and computer simulations. Getting input from colleagues or the department chairman and having them actually see and react to the use of these
innovations in an ongoing class situation may also be a good strategy.

Service, which is considered along with teaching and research in most
promotion or tenure evaluations, is a catchall category, including everything from service on local committees and speeches to the Rotary and
American Legion post to student advisement, direction of doctoral dissertations, consultantships, and service as an officer of a national organization in one's academic area. Service is not regarded equal in importance
to research, but it is an area that should not be neglected. Attending
national meetings in one's area of interest, reading papers, getting appointed to committees, becoming generally well known, and eventually
getting elected to office can be important. Attracting good graduate students and serving as their major professor is also important. These are
the people who help carry out the research activities that are so vital to
promotion and tenure, but their advisement and direction is usually clas-
sified as service. Reviewing significant books or serving as a referee for
important journals and, especially, serving as an editor for such a journal
can be impressive. Reading manuscripts for major publishers and doing
any sort of consulting may count for service. The important thing is not
to get involved in a time-consuming activity for which there is little or no
payoff. It will take about the same amount of time to read and review a
book for the local garden club as it will to review one for a major journal,
and a committee discussing local water rates may take as much time as
one revamping the core curriculum. There is only so much time, and it
must be used wisely, if one is serious about promotion and tenure. This is
not to suggest one should neglect one's wife and family and civic responsibilities, but one's family's welfare may be better served by a promotion
and tenure than a trip to Disney World. An assistant professor who fails

to win promotion in an "up or out" situation may soon be moving from the community he has served so well.

Publish or perish is not just an idle threat; it is a fact of life in most major institutions of higher learning, and no amount of high-quality teaching or important service is normally accepted as a substitute for research publications. There are institutions in which there are other kinds of tenure appointments for those with earned doctorates, not as professors, but in admissions, as house masters, deans of men or of women, or in other facets of administration. Promotion and tenure within the professorial ranks are ordinarily determined primarily by the amount and quality of one's research publications. Unlike teaching, this is something that can be counted. The professor who has brought in a million dollars in grant money has the edge on the professor who brought in only $500,000. The professor who has had 12 articles published in major journals will be ranked higher than the one who has had only 10.

Publishing in in-house publications, in Xeroxed form, or in nonrefereed or generally low-quality journals is largely a waste of time, so far as promotion and tenure are concerned. It may even count against a person. The same may be said of publishing a book through a vanity press. This is taken as proof positive of the fact that the work did not merit publication by a major publisher. A theoretical book or one reporting major research that is published by either a major commercial publisher or a university press should count for more than several articles, especially if it gets good reviews in major journals. The same cannot be said for publishing a textbook. Since this is primarily a commercial venture, the royalties are seen as an appropriate and sufficient reward. Such a book won't count for much when it comes to promotion and tenure. The main trouble with any book, of course, is that it takes so long to write it and have it published. With the pressure on young scholars today to get something published quickly, it is unlikely they will be publishing a sequel to *Origin of the Species*. Instead, they will be looking for something quick and sure, which may not really be very important but just good enough to get published.

If one's dissertation research is worthy of publication, this is, as has been stated previously, a good place to start. If one's major professor is a big name in the field and will consent to publish in tandem with the former student just starting out, this can be impressive. If, however, all one's publications are joint efforts and jointly authored, there may arise the suspicion that an individual is incapable of doing anything by himself. Unless the coauthor is a major figure in the field, an individually authored paper or article or book is likely to be more impressive than one that is jointly authored.

With all the pressure to produce and the very real threat of publish or perish and "up or out," one can assume there is a certain amount of cheating, that is, of fudging the data, or building a piece of research around an after-the-fact hypothesis. Several prominent cases have arisen in recent years in which researchers have been caught in the act: a heart researcher who fudged enough data to gain publication in *The New England Journal of Medicine* (which later filed a disclaimer) and an appointment to the Harvard faculty (rescinded) or the genetic researcher who painted black spots on white mice with India ink. With a computer, it is now possible to run everything against everything and then come up with some very creative after-the-fact hypotheses predicting any chance relationships that may have resulted. Is the amount of rainfall in Tibet actually related to the birth rate in Brazil?

Most of the legitimate work that is published is of little consequence. Libraries are filling up with junk, and, in some areas, all the research published in the last decade could be destroyed without setting the discipline back by more than a day and a half. How many doctoral students have gone to their major professor with a real problem only to be told that it was not researchable? This leads to doing research on problems of less consequence or of no consequence or on nonproblems if they are researchable. How do these things get published? Well, often they don't, for which everyone can be thankful, but sometimes they do get published. We have developed a fascination with research methodology, in which the research tail is wagging the disciplinary dog. It is a kind of operation overkill, where powerful statistical procedures are brought to bear on relatively inconsequential issues, often using an inadequate or poorly drawn sample. Referees for major journals are expected to separate the wheat from the chaff and thus guarantee some minimum level of quality, but they cannot be expected to replicate studies and have necessarily to accept much on faith alone. This can prove to be a mistake as in the cases previously cited. Unethical people easily succumb to existing pressures, and changing a few figures here and there may result in a publication.

In most fields, the journals are ranked in a more or less agreed-upon order of importance. Publishing in the better journals is, naturally, far more prestigious than publishing in others, as the competition is keener and the standards higher. Generally speaking, one should aim to publish an article in the highest-ranked journal likely to accept it, but this may mean a delay of many months in actually seeing it in print. A lesser journal may get it published sooner, so the author is faced with a hard choice.

Another problem is that long articles are usually harder to get published than shorter ones. Some authors take advantage of this fact by splitting one article up into two or three. This serves the double advantage of making them more publishable, because they are shorter, and at the same time increases the number of articles published.

In the final analysis, it must be said that there is a lot of politics involved in the promotion and tenure processes in most institutions. Administrators have their favorites, and many are not above manipulating the process to assure the promotion of those they favor and to deny it to those they don't. Jealous colleagues are often in a position to do the same. It may be important, therefore, to avoid controversy and to make friends and not incur the wrath of those who may appoint or serve on committees that may decide one's fate by recommending or failing to recommend one for promotion or tenure. One may pay a price for fighting for "truth, justice, and the American way," and although one should obviously stand up for what is right, sometimes regardless of the cost, one should be aware of the cost. An old professor once said that, while there were some things worth fighting for, they were on a very short list.

When it comes to promotion and tenure, there are some miscellaneous factors that are often taken into consideration that do not necessarily fall into one of the major categories of teaching, service, and research, for example, winning some kind of relevant honor or recognition, although these are usually for one's teaching, service, or research or writing. Obviously, anything that might improve one's chances of being promoted or granted tenure ought to be included if possible. In the final analysis, however, it is most likely going to be one's research publications that will turn the trick, so to speak. It has been observed that the two greatest teachers in our history could not have been promoted or received tenure in one of our major state or private universities, because neither Jesus nor Socrates published anything.

Finally, there is strategy to be considered in going up for promotion or tenure. If a sizable grant is likely soon to be approved, or a research in progress is about to be concluded, or an article or book is on the point of being published, it may be advisable to wait if that is possible. If a better-qualified colleague is going up for promotion or tenure, it may be best to wait if one is fearful of being unfavorably compared. If the present committee is made up of the members of an unfriendly clique, it may prove best to wait. If, on the other hand, a committee includes numerous close associates or people in one's field who are familiar with one's research, it may be best to go ahead and not to wait. Prepare carefully all the materials that are to be presented in support of a promotion or tenure evaluation. It is probably a mistake to assume that everyone knows how deserving one is. The burden of proof is usually on the candidate, and he or she must satisfy the requirements laid down by the committee or by the institution and as interpreted by the committee. If there are limited numbers of promotions to be made, one must meet the competition as well, not just come up to minimum standards but surpass them.

What is good progress? Much depends on the standards of a particular institution and the average time in rank of one's colleagues. With a doctorate in hand and an original appointment as an assistant professor, a promotion in five years would probably not be unusual, but a promotion sooner than that might be. Ten years, on the other hand, would be a long time in rank, if allowed. At the associate level, which often carries automatic tenure, another five years in rank would not be unusual, making a total of ten years to make full professor. Of course, some make it faster and some slower, and some never make full professor. A successful career normally leads to a full professorship.

Promotions are sometimes speeded up by moving from one institution to another, where a promotion in rank is often used as an inducement. Sometimes, the offer of a position at a higher rank in another institution can be used to speed the promotion process in one's own institution. Promotion and tenure provide job security and usually increased financial security. Today, there is growing resistance to granting formal tenure, and promotions have slowed to what they were in a time of expansion during, say, the 1960s, when positions were far more plentiful. Organizations like the AAUP are probably the best defense of tenure and reasonable promotion policies, but the strength and influence of professional organizations are determined by the size of their membership and the quality of their leadership. In some institutions, membership in AAUP, for example, is so small that its influence is nil. At the same time, no respectable institution wants to be censored by the national organization, as that is a black mark against the institution and increases the difficulty of recruiting.

The profession needs to retain reasonable promotion policies, tenure, and faculty control.

Committees, Associations, and Organizations: The Fine Art of Networking

In this essay we discuss more or less formal, structured interactions with other professionals, within the institution and outside, that new faculty should seek. Faculty have professional and ethical obligations to do this sort of service work, but this should not be considered just a burden. Networking with other colleagues within and outside the institution offers valuable support and potential collaborators on research and teaching. Networking can open paths to career advancement.

Committees

The university still retains much of its medieval structure, and although there have been increasing efforts to drag it into the industrial-technological age, the efforts haven't proved completely successful; hence much of the conflict between the faculty, which digs in its heels, and the administration, which insists, "yes, you will." While the industrial-model administration carries out the high-level management of the university, the medieval-model faculty committees carry out the low-level management. Furthermore, the faculty, either directly or indirectly through its committees, expects to be consulted on everything. A majority of these committees operate inside the university and are primarily concerned with curriculum and instruction and with faculty and student governance. There are student affairs committees, grievance committees, library committees, parking committees, steering committees, promotion and tenure committees, graduate committees, curriculum committees, allocation committees, and on and on. Theoretically, these committees help to make the day-to-day decisions that permit the university community to function with minimum friction. They are intended as a way for faculty to have meaningful influence on institutional affairs.

Getting to know other faculty members well, personally or professionally, is no easy thing, but committee work facilitates the development and continuation of such relationships. Committee assignments permit you to make interdisciplinary faculty contacts. You can learn far more about the behavior and attitudes of your peers in this way than in any other. You'll rarely sit in on other professors' classes or watch them doing research, so committee work gives you one of the few forums for observation. You should keep in mind that your conduct is also being carefully observed and analyzed by everyone else. You'll be under the academic microscope, and you can bet that the senior faculty and administration will come up with some form of evaluation of you as a result of your conduct on committees.

The committee system and its methods of functioning present you with one of the best opportunities you'll ever have to define your career goals, a fact that even experienced faculty members may not be aware of. You make a statement by the way you dress, but you make an equally clear statement as to what you are and want to become in your attitude and actions in committees, whether you want to or not. So be sure that you're making the statement you intend to. If your doctorate indicates that you're competent and have a legal right to enter academia as a professional, and your field of specialization indicates the direction you're likely to take, committee work permits you to project your more personal traits, ambitions, and desires. If, for example, you want your career to emphasize political reform, your committee work is likely to reveal this fact. If you want to emphasize your administrative ambitions, your work, attention to detail, and willingness to assume extra committee responsibilities will be quickly recognized by your colleagues and administrators. If you want to focus your career on research, your committee work will make that clear, even if only by the fact that you shun appointments and excuse yourself in committee meetings for lack of preparation by enumerating your research tasks. Your fellow committee members will sense your career orientation and perhaps even tend to forgive your lapses in committee attendance and preparation up to a point.

Depending upon your inclinations, different types of committee assignments will lead your career in different directions. Veterans of academia suggest that, as a beginner, you should be highly selective in committee assignments. Sit on no more than two committees. If you aren't careful, you rapidly become committeed to death. You might be flattered to be given a half dozen assignments, but it's likely that you'll soon find yourself running from one to another without the time to prepare adequately. One of the more frequently heard faculty complaints is the lack of time for other activities or for research due to committee load.

Types of Committees

There are high- and low-level committees, and you can readily determine which is which. Presidents, chancellors, and deans sit on high-level committees, where the most important decision-making and consulting is likely to take place. Such committees have impressive support systems, such as accomplished secretaries to do much of the technical work required. Low-level committees are apt to be concerned with day-to-day housekeeping duties and regulations and are rarely involved in policy-making decisions of any import. The library committee is usually low level, for instance. Often the members have sat together for many years, making decisions, for example, on what journals to order or to cancel and advocating increases in the purchase of microfilms or historic memorabilia. The head of the libraries may sit with the committee, but although the administration wants the library to function effectively, it doesn't want to be bothered with the details.

Another distinction in types of committees and their consequent importance to you is whether the committee is regular (on the books) or ad hoc. The regular committee is one that has probably existed for years—for example, promotion and tenure or financial allocation. A regular committee may be important, unimportant, high level, or low level, but it's essential to the continued functioning of the institution, and its mission is well understood. It solves managerial problems. The ad hoc crisis-type committee is one where critical or important matters are almost always on the agenda. The powers on the faculty often serve on these, and beginners are rarely asked to sit with them. Nonetheless, if you *are* asked, accept. Your work on that committee will draw far more attention than it's likely to on the regular committees. Another advantage of an ad hoc committee is that its life is brief, usually a month or two.

Finally, committees are either appointed or elected types. In the latter, faculty are given a list of faculty names from which to select the committee members, who are expected to represent faculty interests. Don't campaign for such committee assignments; it's bad form and almost guarantees that you'll lose. Appointments are made by a dean or administrator and are basically pats on the back—acknowledgement that you're either important or on your way.

So, if you want to travel in the academic fast lane (depending on your goals and career direction), ad hoc, high-level, and appointed committees are your best vehicles. A group of prominent university administrators recently noted that for women, particularly, committee work is the golden road toward administration, and it's hard work and the ability to compromise, accommodate, moderate, produce results, and be congenial rather than scholarship or political orientation that count most. In addition to giving you a high profile, committee work lets you discover whether you like administrative work or not, and you risk little in the process. You can always retreat gracefully to your duties as a professor. But if you find that administrative work does appeal to you, your committee work will let you move in that direction with considerable support because you'll have established yourself as an effective part of the faculty network. Those who enter the administrative ranks directly from business or with little academic experience rarely enjoy the faculty's confidence and trust to this extent.

To give an example of a committee success story, there was a young faculty member at a large state university who decided that he wanted to shift gears in his career and become an administrator. The legislature had mandated certain policy studies outside the university, and the man used his influence with some members of the board of trustees, who had known his father, a prominent politician, to gain an appointment to these study committees. He made it a point to cultivate his friendship with the board members and harvested the seeds of friendship over the years as he was often appointed to governmental-type committees—appointments that had a great deal to do with his eventual climb to the highest administrative positions at the university.

You'll inevitably come to realize that some committees are effective and powerful and some aren't. Some are only advisory while others are decision-making. For example, those that deal with grievances or injustices may make decisions that are final within the academic community (although the plaintiff may take the case to the civil or criminal courts).

For a committee to be truly effective, the administrator to whom the committee reports must be effective in delegating authority and clear and straightforward in communicating what he or she really wants the members to do. An autocratic administrator can make a committee into a charade of unproductive activity, but a good administrator can foster a feeling of faculty participation that will have rewards in increased creativity in the institution at large. It is depressing, although not unusual, to deal with an administrator who goes through the *pro forma* motions of appointing a selection committee for evaluating applicants for a position but who has already decided who the choice should be. If the committee doesn't sense this or refuses to go along with the sham, it may find itself dismissed and eventually replaced with a more amenable group.

Committee work helps you make lifelong personal and professional friends, looks good on your resume, shows you're involved, and fulfills a near-essential requirement for your promotion and tenure files. But be careful not to become a committee voyeur—a person who doesn't want to do any work but who pokes fingers in all the pies, preens plumage, and practices public speaking.

You may involve yourself heavily with committees, on which you work as hard as others do on teaching or research. As a superior committee member, you'll come thoroughly prepared, and you may become a highly valued assistant to the committee chair. But even though you're one of these industrious souls, there are some situations that can cause you problems. Some chairs see a committee as a means for carrying out their personal agenda—an agenda to which you may be completely opposed. As a new professor, think very carefully before you vocally object to the autocracy unless you have a martyr complex. Confrontations between you and the tenured faculty can poison your academic life for years. So before you jump in with argumentative sixguns blazing, consider quietly withdrawing from the arena and living to fight another day.

Associations and Organizations

National associations and organizations are generally discipline oriented. If you expect them to be of value to you, you must attend regularly, know the organization's structure and people, and be willing to travel. By becoming a *participating* member you can meet a wide range of significant people in your discipline, shed some of the parochialism of your job, and seek national recognition. Your participation in national or international organizations in your discipline can help you develop a cosmopolitan set of values and ideas. Professors who find themselves thinking that their institution will collapse if they don't stay home and mind the store are probably suffering from delusions of their own importance and not growing academically.

A second significant advantage to national organization involvement is that it encourages networking. As a member, you're likely to hear of job openings first, will probably have met faculty at the hiring institution, and may even know people on their selection committee—all of which gives you a head start. In addition, when you come up for promotion and/or tenure, your chair or dean may request a list of individuals who can evaluate your work—individuals who are expected to be nationally or internationally recognized academicians. Organizations provide you with a pool from which you can choose.

Taking advantage of the sometimes underused networking possibilities of committee work in national and international organizations can offer you cross-institutional research connections. Individuals often come together in joint research projects almost by accident: they were buddies in graduate school or did research together there; they were hired by the same institution and simply thrown together; or they've been appointed to projects organized by government or philanthropic organizations that want to collect the best brain power available for their project. But for you, as a new professor, national or international organizations may provide the best method of finding others interested in the same research area as you are through contacts at meetings.

One important national academic organization that is not discipline related and to which you should give some consideration is the American Association of University Professors (AAUP). This organization serves a vital role in providing a system of checks and balances in higher education. It acts on behalf of faculty in investigating charges of institutional misconduct. Although the number of the faculty who belong to this organization is relatively small, tightly knit local campus groups are vocal and committed and promote the use of the AAUP. Their clout varies from institution to institution depending on the number of faculty involved, and they do sometimes attract zealots who find getting involved with faculty causes irresistible. Nonetheless, they attempt to keep the academic community honest.

Consequently, you might give some thought to keeping a low profile in these organizations for a while to avoid being seen as too zealous, too rigid . . . or as the resident troublemaker. But if you're comfortable with your ability to compromise and strike a reasonable deal with the establishment, by all means get involved—you may end up being rewarded with an administrative position and permitted to join the very thing you initially opposed, the establishment. The administration will perceive you to be a "faculty leader we can work with."

Example: At a midwestern state university, a faculty member was branded a first-class troublemaker, alienating everyone in administration from department chair up, speaking out on every issue of concern, fighting in every battle, and regularly making the newspapers. Even though a faculty may like to fight, it also wants to be selective and take on only those battles it's likely to win. The professor in question waved the red flag on all occasions, and his colleagues and superiors began to resent his disruptive behavior. His only out—one you should consider if you ever find yourself in similar difficulty—was to have a cooling-off period. He chose to go to Europe for an extended period of study.

The temptation to champion the underdog may be too much to resist, but remember that you're creating your academic image and making a statement of your career direction. Just be sure you're saying what you mean. One professor on the West Coast was considered one of the best teaching professors on the campus and an academician of intellectual depth. Students flocked to hear his lectures. Having served the college in this capacity for some years, he began to redirect his academic career—to de-emphasize teaching and to participate in many campus and national committees, all of which were highly political and which provided him with a forum for expressing concern with underdogs, faculty members in difficulty, undemocratic procedures, and the rights of ethnic minorities. The committee system enabled him to transform his job and time allocation from that of fine teacher to that of seasoned politician within the institution.

Gaining National Recognition: A Place in the Sun

There are innumerable ways to attract attention and build a national reputation within and outside the academic world. Many academicians have done so. Woodrow Wilson as professor at Princeton University wrote an outstanding book on constitutional government and won national attention. B. F. Skinner at Harvard founded a major school of psychological thought. Alfred Kinsey earned a substantial reputation in studies of human behavior at Indiana University. The White House is constantly searching for the best and foremost economic advisors, who come largely from the academic ranks. But such successes require hard work.

The following seven career patterns may lead to your becoming a national figure. The patterns are organized in no particular order of importance but parallel the traditional professional concerns of research, service, and teaching.

Traditional Scholarly Publication

Gaining recognition through scholarly publications demands your perseverance and consuming effort. Accuracy is indispensable; you must support your theories with cogent and precise data. You must check and recheck, edit and re-edit, write and rewrite. Your publications will usually first appear in journals. You may produce a quality book—in fact, if you succeed in gaining some recognition, you'll almost invariably produce a book at some point. If the book is good enough, it may become a standard reference in the academic field, and it carries your reputation. The respected text may even go through eight or nine editions and may live longer than you do, giving you a kind of immortality. Work by an acclaimed scholar tends to unify the academic field, and you, as a beginner, will copy and emulate the teachings of traditional scholars, just as new professors later may emulate yours.

Specialized Expert

You can achieve a national reputation by becoming a recognized expert in a specialty area—"the" expert in a narrow field of endeavor. An expert is not an interdisciplinarian—just the opposite. For example, you may be the authority on Vincent Van Gogh; you may have spent a lifetime studying and becoming the expert on the politics of the Ming dynasty; you may be the expert on sodium compounds or a particular species of flea. Your knowledge within that limited area is so complete that your judgment is rarely questioned, and your advice is much sought. You have no equal in your field.

Example: On a state university engineering faculty, there was a recognized expert in the field of sanitary engineering. He had written "the" book on the subject. During the course of a day, he might receive a half dozen calls from urban sanitary engineers in all parts of the United States who were having a problem and who would invariably call his attention to a particular page of "the" book and question him further on procedures and processes. He almost invariably solved their problems. He had written the bible in the subject area, and many believed he was the only person in the United States who could solve their problems.

Dominant School of Thought

Over the past century, particular universities and colleges have attained pre-eminence in particular academic areas. They have, in a sense, attained something close to a monopoly. For example, probably no institution has ever exerted so much influence on professional education so long as Teachers College, Columbia University. Its dominance of teacher training was almost complete for 30 or 40 years. Other institutions tended to mimic it. Some state universities copied the name Teachers College for their teacher preparation divisions. Speech therapy at Iowa University has achieved a similar status, and Northwestern University is said to have become a mecca for academic journalism. There was a period when the University of Wisconsin's departments of social science were viewed as being the best in the United States because of their research production and influence in Wisconsin state government. Today, many state universities attempt to emulate this sort of influence and prestige by declaring certain programs to be an "area of excellence." By focusing on a specific subject area, they push for national recognition for the university.

When your institution clearly has dominated a field of endeavor, it's relatively easy for you as a faculty member, to gain national recognition. You belong to the club. You're in the academic fast lane; you're likely to be given special recognition and publicity when you read papers and have articles published. Other institutions that want to "get us one of them" may try to lure you away. As a graduate of such a dominant school of thought, you would also find yourself much sought after. You would be looked upon as having special knowledge and influence of considerable worth.

Many prestigious institutions and their faculties maintain far-flung networking systems that let you, as a graduate, collaborate with faculty at the "mother" institution for a considerable time and enjoy the rewards that come from your alma mater.

Such institutions use a feeder system to market graduate students who have studied within their excellent academic area. Perception of the school as influential fuels perception of graduates and faculty as influential, which further enhances the reputation of the school—a perpetual motion machine. This process works so well largely because institutions of higher education often feel insecure. By imitating the prestigious institution's policies or by hiring their graduates, they feel they'll build confidence in their own programs.

The Messiah and Disciples

Another pattern for achieving national recognition involves your building a competent and able staff of graduate students to carry out an extensive research effort and subsequent publication. This requires some skill in the art and practice of grant-getting. Graduate student assistance is expensive, and it's difficult to develop a coordinated team. The brilliant graduate student, like the prime college athlete, is much wooed. You must build your team with a specific goal in mind—your research agenda. Select only students who will contribute to your program. Toss out the prima donnas and grab the team players. The cost of putting your team together may eventually run into the hundreds of thousands of dollars. Recruit graduate assistants so you don't destroy the team structure with simultaneous graduation. Work in replacements gradually in order not to disrupt productivity.

Of course, you yourself will receive most of the national recognition. You can build a very productive career on this model. Most apprentice or journeyman academics will be more than willing to join you. The carrot for graduate students who contribute so much to your national recognition is that they learn the system of team research, program development, or experimental teaching and can apply it once they're hired at another institution.

You can thus establish a system that is self-perpetuating. The more productive your team, the easier it is to recruit new and able replacements and to attract grants. You may be able to publish at an astonishingly high rate. Frequently, your teaching duties, if you're involved in an extensive research program, are limited and often confined to the graduate level.

Synthesizer and Popularizer

If you want both national recognition and financial reward, your surest path is that of popularizer of innovative methods for dealing with academic or practical problems. You're the consultant who interprets others' theories, simplifies them, and combines them into a compact "application" methodology. Your market might include schools, businesses, hospitals, or the person in the street. If you have an academic background in which application plays a large role, you may naturally drift in this direction. You've been educated to be a practitioner, and this path to national recognition is a natural one for you.

While you might be condemned as something of a huckster in your consultant role, the real truth is that you serve a valuable role in synthesizing theories. You put ideas together as bits of this and that and come up with innovative action plans. If you're a natural synthesizer, you have a personality and performing ability that helps you sell your concepts or services in workshops, personnel meetings, self-help books, and so on. You are an entrepreneur of academia. You're quick to seize on ideas that fill a market gap, harvest existing theories, package them to meet a societal need, and create additional markets for your professional services. You occupy the top advertising role in academia; you're not generally attracted to administrative roles. You're a marketer, not a manager.

Your fees are often great and may, in fact, result in a doubling or tripling of your annual salary. Of course, the downside is that this sort of activity does not enjoy the prestige of other more traditional scholarship. That might not be a problem at some institutions. It might be at others, however.

Organizational Participant and Activist

As a new professor, you may elect to become involved in the professional associations sponsored by your academic field. All academic areas have their professional clubs, associations, or organizations. You must spend considerable time attending their meetings in the initial stage of your career. Institutions of higher learning usually recognize and appreciate the importance of these organizations and may even free you from teaching or service duties at the university so that you may attend. Almost all institutions provide travel funds, and if your name is carried on the program, your institution will often pay for all expenses you accrue at the meeting. If you decide on this route to national recognition, you'll quickly notice that certain activities go along with leadership in organizational meetings. You must meet and greet those who attend. Much politicking goes on at the meeting. There will be formal dinners and speeches, but most of the real maneuvering goes on at the far less formal dinners where the "Good Old Boys and Girls" get together and the insiders' business is done. You'll exchange valuable information and establish valuable relationships that may give you an advantage.

As a newcomer, you should go to such national or regional meetings regularly. The oldsters will shortly take heed of your presence, and name recognition will come before too long. Once you've got your foot in the door, your first rewards are likely to be committee memberships. There's a ladder system in these organizations, and you've usually got to begin on the lowest rung. You'll also quickly realize that many academicians who attend these meetings are there purely for a mini-vacation and to hear the major speakers. If they get one or two good ideas on teaching or developments in the field, they're happy. They leave for the airport after the last major speech, but the formal business meeting of the national or regional association almost always takes place after the crowd has left. New officers and committee members are appointed or nominated for the coming year, and recognition and rewards are dispensed.

If there's a national journal published by the organization (this may be its chief media vehicle), where and how it's published is of critical importance to you. The publication of the journal carries much prestige for editors and for the college or university that houses it. Many institutions are willing to pay overhead costs in order to gain the recognition that goes with being home to a prestigious journal. Realize that few, if any, such journals break even financially, but they are losers only in the financial sense. They gain national reputations for the institution and for their editors.

A variation on the organizational participant pattern involves your activity in associations that cover broad areas of interest. Examples are the American Association of University Professors, the American Educational Research Association, and the Modern Language Association. Such organizations have greater weight than the smaller, more focused ones. They, too, have a ladder system, and they frequently have political clout and recognition as well. Spokespersons for the groups may be called before legislative and congressional bodies to give testimony. Political organizations or candidates may seek their attention and support. They may have lobbyists of their own to promote their broad interests. The payroll of such associations may be quite impressive. Competition for high office will be more intense than that in the less powerful and less recognized associations. Indeed, high office in these very large organizations may require you to leave your teaching duties for a year or two to give full time to the national association. You may travel widely as a spokesperson for these organizations. Usually, universities and colleges are happy to grant sabbaticals for your efforts, because they, too, gain prestige and recognition.

Great Teacher

Can you achieve national recognition through great teaching? Some have. Think of such names as Kittridge with his Shakespearean course at Harvard, Poppy Buff at Cornell, and of course, the famous Mark Hopkins. These people wrote less than others, but their knowledge and lecture methods were so dynamic and so impressive they set the standards of teaching for several college generations. It used to be that few formal awards and honors were given to fine classroom teaching. Today, there are a few more. At many institutions, such awards are given by administrative units rather than being initiated and voted on directly by students. Consequently, and unfortunately, many have the stigma of political favoritism attached to them.

It is difficult to achieve national recognition through great teaching. Much depends upon the quality of your students. It may take years for your reputation as a teacher to penetrate beyond your college. There is always a certain amount of jealousy among your colleagues, who may not want to believe that your teaching ability is greater than their own. Sometimes, the only recognized distinction is between adequate and inadequate—and all adequate teachers are considered "gifted" teachers.

For the most part, teaching reputations are largely local—at most, state-wide or regional. A major problem in establishing your national recognition in teaching, as opposed to in research, is that criteria for measuring teaching are ill defined, often faddish and cyclic. What is considered an excellent teaching method in one period may be out of date in the next. Teaching criteria often reflect "good social relationships between students and professor," and the definition of social relationships may change radically.

Also, it is probably true that you'll have an easier time becoming a great teacher in some subject areas than in others. Traditionally, the social sciences and the humanities have been more fertile ground for recognition of great teaching than the natural sciences and mathematics. That trend might be changing, though. Much depends on what subject areas society tends to value. Presently, more emphasis is given to science and mathematics, so faculty in those areas may find, for example, that there are new prizes being given for outstanding teaching in those areas.

In the past, the Professor of the Year Award was considered prestigious and was recognized with a significant salary increase and occasionally with offers from other institutions. Today, every college within the university has some form of teaching award on both the graduate and undergraduate levels. These awards are often simply passed around to whoever has not yet won it. Frequently, they have been devalued and considered political—if no one hates you, you're eligible for a teaching award. When you retire, you might get the award simply because you've outlived everyone else rather than outtaught them.

Leaving Gracefully or Not So Gracefully

You might leave your position for any number of reasons. In some periods, there's enormous wanderlust in the profession, and in others there's relatively little migration. Obviously, you'll leave when you retire. You might simply resign and leave the profession to start your own business or be a bohemian. But the most likely reason you'll leave is to find another academic position—for health reasons; lack of opportunity, advancement, or adventure; or difficulties at your present institution. In this essay we discuss reasons for leaving a position and how to conduct oneself in the process.

Denial of Tenure

If you've been denied tenure, leaving is mandatory. If you're in a tenure-line position, in approximately your fifth or sixth year as assistant professor you must apply for tenure, surely the most critical period in your early career. If you're denied tenure, you'll receive a formal notice of the decision from the tenure committee or administration. After the formal notice, the dean or chairperson will probably call you in to explain the situation. It's not an easy decision for a faculty committee or administrators to make because they understand the consequences, and they'll be troubled even if the evidence overwhelmingly justifies the decision.

Denial of tenure might come as a shock. However, if the process works well, it should not be. If you are not performing as you need to, you should have been made aware of this well before the time for the tenure decision. Of course, the process does not always work well. As we have said before, one thing you should do to maximize your chances of success is to insist on a meaningful review process from faculty peers and department chair in the years leading up to the tenure application.

If you believe you deserve tenure and have the evidence to back up that claim, you may appeal the tenure decision. Typically, the tenure process involves several levels of authority. If the college tenure committee turns you down you can appeal to the dean. If the dean turns you down, you can appeal to the vice chancellor for academic affairs. We will say some more about this in the following pages.

If you are not granted tenure, usually you'll have a year in which to relocate. The ground is eroding under you and your time is limited, and although it won't help to panic, you've got to get moving.

Understand that it's easier to get another job when you already have one. If you opt out of higher education for a couple of years, you'll be looked upon with suspicion and have to explain not only the time lapse but also your reasons for wanting to change jobs in the first place. If you want to find a new job without a lapse into unemployment, you must be pleasant to the chairperson and others who are potential references. Everyone will know you're leaving—the grapevine will make sure of that—and their consciences often bother them a bit. ("There, but for the grace of God, go I.") So by all means seek the administrators' and faculty's help in securing another position. Many will be pleased to help if you behave gracefully. They'll sympathize and avoid rubbing your nose in the unfortunate mess. If they wish to help, certainly, let them. They won't lie in references, but they can avoid telling the full story of the denial of tenure. If asked specifically and directly about why you're leaving, they must, of course, be truthful, but they would usually much prefer to be vague and put the best possible face on the situation.

In a sense, if you choose not to fight the tenure decision, you have the opportunity to cast the situation in a better light than you could otherwise. If you definitely know in advance that you'll be denied tenure, you might have room to negotiate. You might be permitted to resign to avoid the stigma of tenure denial. Such a solution helps both administration and colleagues feel better.

Fighting the Decision

If you're convinced that the administration and the promotion and tenure committee members made a mistake or are really "sons of bitches" who are out to get you (and some people do reach that conclusion), you can, and sometimes should, fight them. But consider the possible consequences—you could end up as a sacrificial lamb; you could be committing professional suicide.

People who fight tenure denials often tend to run through the department and college bemoaning the unfairness of it all. If you do this, you'll likely attract people who hold their own grudges against the administration, and they may try to use you as part of their personal machinations. Most such "eggers-on" know full well that you'll lose the battle; however, they also know, and want the administration to know, it will have a real battle on its hands and that it too will lose something. The more public the battle, the more the administration is likely to lose.

Be aware of the fact that all that the administrators and promotion and tenure committee need do to sustain their negative decision is to create "reasonable doubt" as to your abilities. Of course, you can appeal to the next higher level to reconsider the decision. But even though it's true that such committees or persons are bound to act upon the question, they rarely reverse the initial decision. In almost all instances, all the lower-level administrator or committee need say (and it's a standard defense) is "In our professional judgment. . . ." This usually closes the case, because the further up the chain one goes, the more distant the administrator feels he or she is from the expertise needed to judge the professor's disciplinary abilities and accomplishments. In fact, the appeal typically must claim procedural errors rather than errors in evaluation of professional merit.

In an interesting case at a large university, a professor had graduated from a distinguished institution and had studied under one of the world leaders in his academic field. His credentials were blue chip; however, over the years he had become a burr under the saddles of his colleagues and the administrators of his college. True, he was a nonconformist—some would say an eccentric. There was a right way and a wrong way and his way. He insisted on the last. Although he had already achieved tenure, his colleagues signed a petition declaring him to be incompetent and demanded he be fired. A university-wide, blue-ribbon committee was appointed. All of his colleagues and administrators testified against him, and things appeared grim. However, at the last minute he produced a letter from his former academic adviser, who was now a major political figure in United States government as well as preeminent in the academic field, indicating in no uncertain terms that the professor was well qualified and among the leaders of the field. That did it. The university administration was caught in a difficult situation. If there's one thing a university fears more than anything else, it's publicity and legal entanglements. It will pay almost any price to avoid testimony and cross-examination. A jury may be inclined to see the lone professor as David fighting a well-financed and well-organized Goliath.

In the above case, the administration clearly knew when to back off. They cut a deal. But they also removed the professor from his college and teaching assignment and placed him in another one at the same institution. His career within the new college was still tarnished by the earlier conflict. He really didn't win, at least not much. The administration usually sees to that.

Doing Nothing

If you aren't granted tenure, you might decide you're bored with teaching, research, and service or that you're worn out by the struggle and decide to hell with the whole thing and chuck it. Several possibilities exist then. You might go into a business where you can use your knowledge, or you might try a switch to another profession. Or you might decide to go back to graduate school and reapproach academia through a side door, say by getting a second doctorate in a newly developing field. Indeed, returning to university teaching with a second doctorate, even if you didn't gain tenure with the first one, may be an incentive for hiring you. Postdoctoral work of any sort in your field will inevitably enhance your resume.

Ethical Misconduct

Even if you are granted tenure, that does not mean your job is absolutely secure. Professors still can be fired for cause. One such cause is ethical misconduct. (We will say more about ethics in our essay on that topic.) Ethical misconduct by a professor may involve such things as sexual harassment, drug or alcohol abuse, or academic dishonesty such as faked research. The faculty member is charged with soiling his or her nest.

These are extremely serious charges. If you ever are so charged, there are certain actions you should take immediately. First, find out the facts. Who is making the charges and under what circumstances? Of course, the question of your guilt or innocence comes first. If you're completely innocent, work furiously to prove it. For example, at one institution, a young professor was requested to be in the chancellor's office at 8:00 the next morning—told only that extremely serious charges were being made against him. When he appeared before the august group of administrators, he was asked whether he knew the student making the charges. Only when the administrators mentioned that the student was in his 10:30 section of a particular course did he understand what was going on. He didn't teach at that time and had not done so for two years. A secretary had simply misread the class schedule and supplied his name in error. Another individual was the true subject of the charges.

If the problem involves a minor indiscretion such as using vulgar or profane language to a student, perhaps your best bet is to go immediately to the dean or other superior and confess your behavior (assuming the charge is true). Be sure those in authority hear the complete story rather than bits and pieces and present the worst parts first. Such indiscretions are by no means condoned, but it's best to deal with them immediately before the situation becomes worse than it is.

At one time minor, and possibly major, indiscretions were swept under the rug as a matter of course by faculty committees and administrators and only private redress was sought. A wayward professor was quietly given the choice of resigning immediately or facing committee or administrative investigation—which usually satisfied the victim. Not so today. Public forums are used to spark reform or champion rights, forums which are often full of political intrigue and in which the accused has little chance of winning or even breaking even.

Of course, there are indiscretions and indiscretions. Alcoholism, once considered a crime or at least a moral lapse, is increasingly seen as a disease. Now, an alcoholic faculty member is punished less severely, especially if he or she seeks professional help and attempts to reform. Illegal drugs, however, are quite another matter, of course.

Much depends on where an indiscretion takes place. Once, faculty members were dismissed no matter where an incident took place. Today universities are less concerned about what you do off campus, but they are intensely concerned with your behavior on campus and with students. If you behave improperly with undergraduates on campus, you won't get a second chance, and the same is very often true with graduate students.

You must be able to identify potentially dangerous situations. For example, should you close the door when you speak with a student of the opposite sex? Students do have a right to privacy, but overexcited, angry, or vindictive students sometimes make accusations. Students have charged physical abuse when a professor merely intended to put a comforting hand on a shoulder. Your best course is to be consistently cool, detached, and objective in dealing with students even though such behavior does, to an extent, lessen the effectiveness of the relationship. On the other hand, if you and a student are long-standing friends, the situation is not as dangerous. You're likely to receive a multitude of warnings about covert or overt sexual harassment. Don't take them lightly.

If you are accused, whether you're guilty or not, seek legal help immediately—you have that right. If you're guilty, the lawyer probably won't save your job, but legal representation might get you a second chance. Some people in the academic world do believe in redemption. But don't count on that.

Two examples: A professor had taught for ten years at a small and exclusive private university and was a competent teacher. Although he was not going to achieve national recognition, he was not concerned. He had taken his Ph.D. at a nearby major state university—his dissertation had long since been approved and, like so many, was gathering dust on the library shelf. An inquisitive doctoral candidate at that institution plowed through the moldering manuscripts as part of the required review of the literature and discovered two doctoral dissertations exactly alike—word for word. And the aforementioned professor's thesis was of a later date than the other. The state university instantly revoked the degree and notified the private institution of its action. The professor had no doctorate, was accused of gross plagiarism, and lost his job. More embarrassing, he now had to go to school (at the private institution) and sit with his former students in order to get a degree and certification that would enable him to teach in the public secondary schools.

In a second case, a professor had achieved considerable standing at his private, conservative, sectarian university. He was well respected and might have remained there for the remainder of his career but for a major mistake. He was homosexual and had dropped by the local bus station and picked up two young transients. He took them home, and in the course of the evening, they beat him up, stole valuable items from the house, and took his new car. He immediately called the police and told them his house had been burglarized. The police apprehended the two young men who admitted the thefts but also charged the professor with criminal sexual behavior. The story could not be hushed up. The professor left the community instantly and found a job at a less distinguished institution in another part of the country.

Voluntary Moves

Of course, faculty members may change jobs because they want to and not just because they are forced to. For experienced faculty members as well as new ones, a career move may be a matter of career enhancement and revitalization. In an earlier period, it was usually considered to be sage wisdom that a faculty member should have three career moves after receiving the doctorate. Conventional wisdom suggests that, for their first job, faculty should not seek employment at the institution from which they received the doctorate. One distinguished professor noted that it took 20 years on the faculty to overcome being thought of as "my former graduate student" rather than "my colleague." Old habits die hard, and only under the most promising circumstances should you consider remaining at the institution from which you graduated. Get out and find something else. Come back some five years later, if you are addicted to the institution or locale.

The second career move probably should involve or revolve around the rank of associate professor. Coming to an institution at this rank means that faculty can overcome and put behind them the follies of their early career. Early mistakes can be erased and forgotten. (And people are apt to make them at the first job.) A cooler and more sophisticated approach is required in the second career move. Finally, the third move should take place at the stage of full professorship. This means that the faculty member arrives at that institution with a national reputation, clout, and prestige. The struggle to separate oneself from the crowd is over, and it is the third move that is probably the most enjoyable one in the faculty career pattern. But this sort of move also is fairly rare. Full professors are expensive, and in general, institutions only seek full professors if those professors are truly exceptional.

Career moves by established professors are brought about by various circumstances. However, they often involve some form of dissatisfaction. One must get annoyed before one gets up enough energy to make the moves for a career change. More is required than merely reading advertisements of university vacancies. It is always extremely unwise to reveal growing dissatisfaction. One can never know how many years later an institution to which one is applying comes back to an employer and asks questions. Every professor leaves a trail. Make sure there is no garbage left behind. Faculty members at this stage of job hunting should bite their tongue to avoid saying what may, in fact, be on their mind. Professors can always say that the position "has been a most interesting one, and I have learned a tremendous amount." This type of comment actually says little, but what one does not say does not have to be retracted. Be especially pleasant during the last six months at the institution. Mend fences. Leave in such a manner that some ten years later when the institution is called with regard to a recommendation for you the reply will be "he/she did an excellent job here and we only wish we could have kept him/her."

If you contemplate a career move, analyze the reasons for the move. Emotions should not dictate the move. You can easily jump out of the frying pan into the fire. It has been done.

One sort of move is an upward one to a more prestigious institution. Such a move doubtlessly results in a higher salary or rank. The move really serves as an evaluation of the job you are doing as professor. You are a success. The vertical move probably permits greater opportunity for research, more able students, and greater personal prestige. The library and other research facilities will be greater, and the support system will enhance the professor's productivity as well. However, the pressure to be productive will also be greater, more than likely. More time must be devoted to the job and less to family and private life. You have arrived professionally. More is expected of you. Although that has its benefits, it also has its costs.

A second sort of career move is horizontal. In this instance, the professor changes the job for one of equal rank and quality in a possibly different geographic region. Most such moves are made for personal reasons. The faculty member has just gotten a divorce. The former spouse has elected to remain in the community. Things are going to be rather uncomfortable. Possibly, the professor wishes to remarry. A good horizontal move would, it appears, give a new start. Not much gained, but not much lost either. In this case, it is not so much the setting that is being rejected as the personal relationships. A similar setting in another locale would be fine. Frequently, another reason for a horizontal move is that the family cannot adjust to the situation or the locale and going elsewhere seems desirable. Horizontal moves may also be made to change lifestyles or to make a desired lifestyle more of a reality. Some years ago, a distinguished professor, loaded with publications, sought an appointment at a similar midwestern institution when he was actually qualified for a position at a much more prestigious institution. His explanation for seeking this particular horizontal move was that he and his wife wished to have a ranch and sought a locale in which this would be possible.

Another sort of career move is downward. Here the faculty member leaves a more prestigious institution for one that is less prestigious. Moves of this nature are almost always forced upon the faculty member because of some kind of misconduct or poor job performance, such as we have discussed. However, on the other hand, some years ago a distinguished faculty member and former dean decided to become a faculty member at a southern predominantly black institution. He was strongly committed to the civil rights movement and felt he might make a positive contribution to the education of African American students. Retired faculty members at prestigious institutions often feel they are not yet washed up as educators and may join a good but less prestigious college to satisfy their need to gladly teach and gladly learn. Such faculty members may greatly enhance the teaching resources of these smaller institutions.

Let us turn now to another sort of move. It is not often mentioned, but it may be one of the major factors for experienced faculty member to seek or accept another position. It can be labeled as the "going-home" syndrome. In this instance, the faculty member feels a very strong pull toward home. We have cautioned against taking one's first position at the alma mater. But later in their careers, there might be reasons why professors would want to return to the old stomping grounds. There are a number of variations on this theme.

The small private institutions of higher learning often tend to claim a substantial number of their faculty members in this manner. The young professor has done his undergraduate work at the institution. He has enjoyed the honors and possibly has graduated as an outstanding student with *summa cum laude* recognition. Having now finished the doctorate and taught some few years far from the original school, he now may wish to return. Similarly, many professors want to return to the institution where they did their graduate work. They thirst for the intellectual excitement they remember so well at the graduate school. Indeed, in some instances, they may receive the call from their graduate adviser to join her on the faculty. There is a tremendous nostalgia attached to such a move. Sentimentality can be a strong force and motivating factor. This is the return of the native.

One must be cognizant of the pitfalls of such a move. One will leave one's present position without regrets, and the colleagues and administration are clearly conscious of the faculty member's emotional compulsion to make the move. However, many of these people will also note their own refusal to leave under similar circumstances and look down on a move made merely for the sake of "going home." Many who do leave for such positions may well find themselves back in the status of graduate student even though they hold professorial rank. They will be regarded as being in the pocket of their earlier academic adviser. It might be best to wait until the adviser is retired or dead.

An example comes to mind of two young professors who returned to a midwestern campus upon being requested to do so by their adviser. They spent many years as his assistants. At first they accepted this status; however, at fifty years of age, they still had not emerged from their adviser's shadow. Resentment began to be evidenced. It was always assumed that their major adviser controlled their votes in faculty matters and that a certain hegemony existed within the clique. In another such case, the faculty members who were outsiders without prior connections to the university tended to taunt the faculty member who had been brought back to his graduate school by his major adviser. It was pointed out to him repeatedly that without that help he would not have been hired. The faculty member hired under such circumstances may be regarded with suspicion by most of the others. They may never really accept him, and they regard the appointment as a form of academic nepotism.

On the contrary, one may wish to leave when she receives the call to return if a star of the first magnitude, an Einstein, a John Dewey, has formed a dynamic school of thought at an institution and is ready to expand the national and international influence of her or his philosophic or scientific thought and needs colleagues or disciples. In this instance, the faculty member can leave her present institution with the best wishes and congratulations of the full faculty and administration. Indeed, her advice on the successor to her present position may be avidly sought. They would like another just like her.

This may well be considered the passing of Elijah's Mantle. The faculty member is one of the chosen few. Enormous prestige accrues with the mere offer. In a sense, one attaches oneself to the tail of a meteor. The meteor blazes across the academic sky. One may, indeed, fall off but is certainly a great deal higher than she would be otherwise. The mere fact that the faculty member was "one of the last graduate students of Einstein and later one of his junior colleagues" will assure her of any number of positions at the highest ranked academic institutions.

The phenomenon of returning is interesting in itself. Possibly, the chief factor involved is that it provides the faculty member with the final and complete form of evaluation. Did you do well enough to be asked back? Are you as good as your old masters? Almost every professor has considered it at one time or another.

There are those faculty members who are asked to return home because they have themselves achieved stardom at another institution. The initial institution may court them assiduously. They have made a name for themselves in their academic field. The alma mater wishes to retain its status in the forefront of that field. Therefore, the faculty member is often bribed, in a sense, to return and lend her academic stature to the institution. Her present institution and the alma mater both seriously want her. Possibly several million dollars in research grants are involved. In such instances, the much-appreciated professor is likely to be very capable of marketing herself quite profitably. She did not get where she is by being dumb or naive.

There are instances in which the professor wishes to move back to the home area as a result of family business interests, real estate, aging parents, or in order to rear young children. Commitments and obligations aside from academia may play a major role in leaving the present institution. Although it is possibly preferable to move aged or infirm parents to the present location, this does not always work, and business interests can demand one's time and presence. It appears that commitments to back-home interests are especially powerful in swaying faculty members who are members of ethnic minorities. They may feel the need to go back to serve as role models in the broader ethnic community from which they have come. They may wish to have their children reared in the same environment. The current situation may not afford an ethnic community or group to which they can belong.

In a period of urban growth and chaos, it may be that this urge to go back into a familiar environment where one knows the rules and the limitations appeals to all ethnic and racial groups. The predictable has its appeal, and by returning to the home school or region, one can get confirmation of success among those who count the most—the neighbors and family.

One must be warned, however, to get one's priorities together and consider them in a realistic way. What may have appeared to be very appealing at an early period may, indeed, turn out later to be dull and downright boring. The "ideal" local environment may turn out to be parochial or provincial upon closer inspection. On the other hand, if you go to Los Angeles or New York City, you might discover that the "provincial" is pretty appealing after all.

The final scenario we will mention is retirement. Because new faculty likely are not actually planning retirement, at least not beyond the retirement account they set up, we will not say much about it. However, we do point out that the issue of retirement is important to new faculty in that, through retirement of current faculty, higher education will be undergoing a changing of the guard in the next few years. And this has enormous implications for younger faculty. The great expansion of university and college enrollments in the late 1960s created a need for many new faculty members. There was an employment boom. Today, this large cohort of professors has reached, or is about to reach, the age when retirement is imminent. Senior professors are expected to run the institution. The current group, who may have monopolized the institution for a considerable number of years, soon must be replaced. Something of a power and leadership vacuum will be created. This is both an opportunity and a challenge for you, as a new faculty member, to shape your career and lead your institution.

The Leaving Process

If you get an offer for a position that is clearly better in rank, pay, and prestige than your present one, you have to take it if you are at all ambitious. Your present institution may make you a counteroffer. If they like you and want to keep you, it's their last chance. If you're leaving only because of rank or salary, certainly you should listen.

Some use an offer of another position as a ploy to motivate the administration to make a counteroffer—at best, a dangerous maneuver. The administrators may congratulate you and promptly ask for your formal resignation. If you're bluffing, you're in trouble.

Some people with prime credentials fish continually for new and better positions, constantly testing their market value. Effectively, they're saying to the dean, "This is what I'm worth. I've proven it to you." This is a "put up or shut up" ultimatum. If you make it, be prepared to leave.

You might find yourself with two or more offers hanging fire and a home institution demanding to know your intentions. To buy time, you might suggest that you don't know yourself. You're playing poker. It's OK if you're willing to gamble and take the consequences. But if you start betting wildly by showing off the number of terrific job offers you've got, you'll eventually annoy the administration and your colleagues.

There are, of course, those faculty members who constantly keep their fingers on the up button all the time. They look constantly for the right job. In many instances, they orchestrate the process so that someone else is persuaded to submit their name for the job. Therefore, the actual candidate can merely say that "I really wasn't interested. Someone else submitted my name. I did go along with it. But I am not much interested." Of course, the truth is that the person is vitally interested, but the smokescreen tends to eliminate the necessity of explaining one's possible departure to colleagues or administrators. If one does not get the job, no great ego involvement is risked. After all the job sought the person and presumably not the reverse.

Let's say you have accepted a new position. How should you conduct yourself once the new job has been secured and the proper people at the present institution informed? Let us assume there are some months to go before one leaves the present job, and considerable teaching or assigned work must be accomplished. What should one do when one's job is advertised? How much advice and involvement is permissible in the selection of one's successor? Should one make oneself scarce?

The best advice from the veterans is that "when you leave the job, you leave the job." Maintain personal contact and by all means carry out your professional responsibilities in an able manner, but do not interfere or involve yourself in decisions that will govern the future of the institution. You may have some degree of authority in that decision-making process, but you will not have any future responsibility for those decisions, so refrain from the use of your present authority. Only upon repeated and sincere requests from colleagues or administrators should you voice opinions or attitudes toward your successor or the general program. Don't leave orders on what should be done. Some veterans will advise you to offer assistance on selecting your successor but that is all, and that should be done with a very light touch. Make such advice low key.

If one resigns in March but will remain on the faculty until the first of August, the situation is not always easy or simple. However, be gracious. Tend to your own business on the faculty. Begin to think and plan for the new job. Think of what you need to do at the next job. Be available to talk with the new person being interviewed. However, by no means should one dictate or become pushy. In fact, it is probably diplomatic to see and talk to the new person being interviewed only in the presence of others or members of the selection committee. Remember, if the faculty, administrators, others wish to consult with you about the person being interviewed, they know where to find you. There is an enormous temptation to meet with the person being interviewed with respect to the job and tell him or her everything. Don't!

In closing this essay, we suggest a few specific collegial actions as you are leaving gracefully.

1. Go out of your way to thank those who have supported your efforts as a faculty member: secretaries, colleagues in your department and outside it, dean and chairperson.

2. Give recognition to the individuals who deserve it for their own endeavors within the institution. You will probably never again have the opportunity.

3. Make sure you have adequately provided for the advisory needs of your graduate students. Negotiate with their new adviser to their benefit. If you intend to take graduate students with you to the new position, negotiate this above board with the university.

4. If you have received a grant, make very sure there is a clear under-standing of what portion of the grant, if any, goes with you. For example, what equipment or computer software is connected to the grant? What accounting should be made of that?
5. Be sure you return all property that belongs to the institution. Get everything in writing if possible.

When leaving an institution, there may be a temptation to say "good riddance." Resist that; show some class.

Part III

LEGAL AND ETHICAL ISSUES FOR FACULTY

Legal Rights and Responsibilities of College Faculty

Donald E. Uerling

As a new faculty member in postsecondary education, you should have some understanding of your legal rights and responsibilities as an employee. This essay sets out some of the basic principles of law that pertain to the employment relationship between the institution and you.

But note these two points. First, there is an extensive and complex array of laws that relate to your legal rights and responsibilities as a faculty member, and this short essay offers only a general discussion of a few major principles. Second, the outcome of a legal dispute over an employment matter will depend on the specific facts, the law to be applied, and the human element inherent in the judicial process, all of which vary from one situation to another. Put simply, the answer to many legal questions is "it depends."

The Employer Institution

Although there are some general principles that guide employment practices in postsecondary education, your legal rights as an employee will be somewhat situational, depending on the institution at which you're employed.

Employment relations at most postsecondary educational institutions are governed by the basic principles of contract law and by a number of federal statutes that prohibit various forms of discriminatory employment practices. However, the laws of the state in which the institution is located are of primary importance; each state has its own bodies of enacted and decisional law that pertain to the organization and operation of postsecondary education specifically and to employment practices in general. There is a significant difference, however, in the extent of state intrusion in the employment matters of different kinds of public postsecondary institutions. For example, state legislatures tend to exercise more control over the internal operations of a community college than over those of a major state university and little or no control over those of a private college or university.

A major distinction is that the protections afforded by the various amendments to the United States Constitution are a very important factor in public employment but are, for the most part, no factor at all in private employment. The Bill of Rights and the Fourteenth Amendment protect persons from actions of government, not of private entities. Public postsecondary educational institutions are creatures of state government, and their officials act under color of state law; in contrast, private institutions, although incorporated according to state law, are not government entities, and their officials are not government actors.

Regardless of the nature of the institution, most have a governing board with authority to adopt institutional policies and to employ necessary personnel. Although these policies and employment practices must be consistent with higher legal authority, they vary in significant ways from one institution to another. As a general rule of law, both the employer and the employee are expected to abide by the institutional policies that have been adopted. It's the institutional policies that initially define the nature of the working relationship between you and your employer, and it behooves you to have a working knowledge of these policies.

The Employment Contract

The employment relationship between you and the institution is defined primarily by your individual employment contract. The written documentation of this contractual relationship varies in form among institutions. Some are embodied in an exchange of correspondence between you and an authorized official of the institution; others are set out on a standard contract form signed by the parties to the agreement. At some institutions, a negotiated collective-bargaining agreement may establish many of the terms and conditions of your employment.

Insofar as the terms and conditions of employment are set out specifically in your employment contract, those provisions will be controlling. But many contracts don't include all the operable terms and conditions of employment; rather, other documents, such as institutional policies and collective bargaining agreements, are incorporated by reference. Also, institutional customs and practices, even if not specifically incorporated by reference, may be resorted to in instances where the specific meaning of a contract provision isn't clear.

Generally, you'll work under one of three kinds of contract. If yours is a special appointment not leading to tenure status, you may have a contract for a specific term, perhaps an academic year or a summer session. The duration of such a special appointment is easy to determine; when the contract term has ended, the employment relationship is over.

As a nontenured faculty member holding a regular appointment, you'll usually have a form of continuing contract, which is a contract for a specific term (usually one academic year) that is automatically renewed for a subsequent term unless institutional officials initiate dismissal procedures. It's important to understand that such a contract doesn't afford you any legal entitlement to continued employment. Although most institutions have some internal procedures they must follow before such a contract is not renewed, few institutions, if any, voluntarily extend any substantive rights to continued employment. Under this kind of contract, the institutional employer can unilaterally sever the employment relationship at the end of the contract term for any reason or no reason at all.

If you are a tenured faculty member, on the other hand, you'll typically work under a permanent contract that continues until you resign or the institution severs the employment relationship on grounds of either unsatisfactory performance or reduction in force. If your dismissal as a tenured faculty member is to be considered by the employer institution, extensive procedural and substantive protections come into play. Although the procedures vary from one institution to another, they usually involve several stages and might include such steps as an initial investigation, an evidentiary hearing before a committee of faculty peers, an administrative recommendation based on the results of the hearing, and a final decision by the governing board of the institution. As a tenured faculty member, you can be dismissed only for certain specified reasons. Although the terminology varies somewhat among institutions, dismissals for unsatisfactory performance usually are based on such grounds as insubordination, incompetence, neglect of duty, immorality, physical or mental incapacity, or "other good cause." Reductions in force may come about because of declining enrollments, discontinuance of programs, or deficiencies in funds for salaries. In any event, the burden will be on the employer to prove by evidence presented at a hearing that your dismissal is justified.

In terms of the employment protections afforded by institutional policies and employment contracts, the distinction between nontenured and tenured status is critical. If you are nontenured, you have little protection against dismissal; only minimal procedural protections must be provided, and no substantive justification need be established. If you are tenured, on the other hand, you have a great deal of job protection. The procedures that must be afforded prior to dismissal are extensive, and the institution must justify its reasons for your dismissal.

Few tenured faculty are ever dismissed for any reason; however, many nontenured faculty never acquire tenure status for a variety of reasons. Thus, the major point of decision as to whether you are to be retained generally comes at the time you apply for tenure. The purpose of your probationary period is to give you the opportunity to prove yourself. When you apply for tenure, your record of teaching, research, and service is reviewed to determine whether you've met the expected standards of performance.

Both the procedures to be followed and the standards to be met in granting tenure vary from one institution to another. Among the factors that may come into play are the public or private nature of the institution, the extent to which any state statutes apply, and the relative importance attached to the teaching, research, and service functions.

Regardless of what the procedures or standards are at a particular institution, most decisions to deny tenure are relatively invulnerable to a legal challenge. Although it's not unusual for faculty members to challenge denials of tenure in court, these challenges almost never succeed. A court may be willing to ensure that the proper procedures were followed, but it would be very unlikely, and indeed improper, that any court would ever second-guess a substantive educational judgment made by professional educators and set aside a decision not to award tenure.

In most instances, if you are not awarded tenure, you'll be dismissed. And, as noted, the chances of such a decision being overturned in court are minimal. Thus, the decision by the institution to award or deny your tenure will likely be the most important of your professional life.

Federal Law

You should have some understanding of the impact of federal law on your working life. To that end, a brief discussion of some major constitutional and statutory provisions follows.

U.S. Constitution

The Constitution protects personal freedoms but within certain limits. As noted, the primary impact of the constitutional protections of individual liberty is on the relationship between persons and their government; thus, the Constitution is relevant to what goes on in a public college or university but not in a private institution. Also, constitutional protections, whether substantive or procedural, are not absolute; in nearly every instance, a court will resolve a dispute by engaging in some balancing of the interests of the government and the interests of the individual.

The first ten amendments (the Bill of Rights) were adopted to protect the rights of individual citizens against the actions of the federal government. But through the operation of the due process clause of the Fourteenth Amendment, many of these protections also serve to constrain the actions of the states and their political subdivision and agencies. Of the protections so extended, those of the First and Fourth Amendments are most important to faculty in public postsecondary education.

The First Amendment provides that Congress shall make no law respecting an establishment of religion or prohibiting the free exercise thereof, or abridging the freedoms to speak, to publish, to assemble, or to petition the government.

The protections of freedom of religion are grounded in an establishment clause and a free-exercise clause. The basic requirement of the establishment clause is that government must be neutral with respect to religion; the sovereign should not sponsor, provide financial support, or be actively involved in any religious activity. The protections of the free-exercise clause recognize the right of every person to make individual choices about religion, free of government compulsion. To illustrate, the establishment clause would prohibit you from leading a class in prayer, and the free-exercise clause would protect your right to engage in private prayer.

Also, because of these two clauses, there are some situations in which constitutional law is relevant to private postsecondary education as illustrated by these two examples. If public funds go to support postsecondary education at a church-affiliated institution, an establishment clause issue is raised. If a state or federal law imposes some constraint on the way in which a private institution pursues its religious mission, a free-exercise clause issue is raised.

The First Amendment also serves to protect the freedoms of expression and association. These protections serve to ensure that you, as a faculty member, have the same rights as any other citizen to associate with others and to speak and write on topics you care about. Even though the government may impose reasonable regulations concerning the time, place, and manner in which you may exercise these freedoms, the content of your expression can be controlled only if the government can provide a strong justification for such a restriction. In the environment of postsecondary education, the extent of the Constitutional protections of freedom of expression are of special importance to you.

The basic Constitutional principles have been set out by the United States Supreme Court. A public employee does not relinquish First Amendment rights to comment on matters of public interest by virtue of government employment. However, the government's interest as an employer in regulating the statements of its employees is different from those it has in regulating the statements of the citizenry in general. The problem is to arrive at a balance between the interests of the employee, as a citizen, in commenting on matters of public concern and the interests of the government, as an employer, in promoting the efficiency of the public services it performs through its employees. Except in the most unusual circumstances, when you, as a public employee, speak not as a citizen on matters of public concern but as an employee on matters of only personal interest, the protections of the First Amendment are not likely to apply to a personnel decision made by a government agency. Part of the difficulty lies in determining whether your speech addresses a matter of public concern; that depends on the content, form, and context of a given statement. If your statements do address a matter of public concern and contribute to a government agency's personnel decision, then the protections of the First Amendment apply, and it must be determined whether the decision was justified. If your statement interferes with the operation of the agency or with close working relationships, then the agency's decision to prohibit that form of expression may be permissible.

Even if you have made constitutionally protected statements that could not be used as a justifiable basis for an adverse personnel action, that in itself doesn't necessarily insulate you from such an action if it's based on other permissible grounds. It's not unusual for public employees to challenge their discharge by contending that the employer's action violated their First Amendment rights to freedom of expression. If you follow such a course, the burden will initially be on you to show that your statements were both constitutionally protected and a motivating factor in your employer's decision. If you carry that burden, then your employer must be able to prove by a preponderance of evidence that it would have reached the same decision even in the absence of the protected conduct. If the employer can do so, its decision will not be overturned.

As a professor, you will make statements on many matters, possibly to the displeasure of your superiors. The content of your statements or the way in which you make them may sometimes become a factor in your performance evaluations or in decisions about your employment. The communications you make may be protected, but if you're prudent, you'll be cognizant of the limitations of these protections.

The Fourth Amendment protects people against unreasonable searches and seizures. This protection has been held to extend to a search of a public employee's office that was conducted by administrative superiors. To determine whether a search conducted by government officials is consistent with the mandate of the Fourth Amendment, the individual employee's legitimate expectations of privacy are balanced against the government's need for the search. Also, such a search must be reasonable in terms of both its initiation and its scope. For example, as a faculty member, you would have some expectation of privacy in your personal office, but that would not preclude another person from entering that office and opening a drawer to find a student file that was needed.

A major provision of the Constitution, insofar as public postsecondary education is concerned, is the Fourteenth Amendment. This Amendment operates through its due process clause and equal protection clause as a significant constraint on government authority.

The due process clause provides that a state cannot deprive any person of life, liberty, or property, without due process of law. Insofar as public postsecondary education is concerned, the due process clause functions in three significant ways. First, the fundamental concept of liberty embodied by the due process clause also embraces many of the freedoms guaranteed by the Bill of Rights; therefore, the actions of a state and all its creatures are subject to many of the same constraints that the Constitution imposes on the federal government. Second, this concept of liberty also embraces certain fundamental freedoms pertaining to matters of procreation, marriage, and family life as well as other personal interests, such as those affected by dress and grooming codes; thus, the authority of public officials to act in ways that affect such protected liberties is constrained by this protection at least to the extent that such actions must be reasonable and justifiable. Third, in many instances, the discharge of an employee or the exclusion of a student affects protected "property" interests in continued employment or education or protected "liberty" interests in one's reputation; if such interests are put at risk, due process requires that the individual be afforded the procedural protections of adequate notice and a meaningful hearing.

The equal protection clause provides that a state can't deny to any person the equal protection of the laws. The protections of this clause are sometimes invoked to challenge classifications of people or activities. Most such classifications are presumptively valid, and there need only be some rational basis for the distinctions made. But there are other classifications that tend to discriminate against certain groups of people or to limit the exercise of certain constitutionally protected freedoms; classifications such as these are often very difficult to justify.

Finally, you should know that most of these Constitutional protections are available to all faculty, both tenured and nontenured, as well as those on special appointments. The major exception is that a "property" interest in continued employment that would trigger the protections of procedural due process must be grounded in a contract, statute, or policy.

U.S. Statutes

Although Congress has no constitutional authority to directly regulate the governance and administration of postsecondary education, the impact of federal legislation on postsecondary education through less direct means is nevertheless substantial. Based on the powers delegated to it by various provisions in the Constitution, Congress has enacted a broad array of statutes that promote national policies of equal educational opportunity and fair employment practices.

A major prohibition against discriminatory employment practices in postsecondary education is found in Title VII of the Civil Rights Act of 1964. This federal statute provides that it shall be an unlawful employment practice to discriminate on the basis of race, color, religion, sex, or national origin. A major exception to this general prohibition is a "bona fide occupational qualification" based on religion, sex, or national origin.

Title VII is generally applicable to all employers—educational and non-educational, public and private, and its applicability is not tied to the receipt of federal funds. Its protections extend to applicants for employment as well as to those already employed. The statute allows for two kinds of claims: "disparate treatment" and "disparate impact." The former involves employment practices that are deliberately discriminatory; the latter involves employment practices that are neutral on their face but have a discriminatory impact. A relatively new development in the law that has arisen under Title VII is the protection against sexual harassment in the workplace.

A number of other federal statutes provide additional protections against unjustified discrimination in employment. Among these are: Title IX of the Education Amendments of 1972, which prohibits discrimination on the basis of sex; the Equal Pay Act of 1963, as amended, which prohibits sex discrimination in wage rates; Section 504 of the Rehabilitation Act of 1973, as amended, which prohibits discrimination against handicapped persons who are otherwise qualified; and the Age Discrimination Act of 1975, which prohibits discrimination on the basis of age if the person is over the age of forty.

Although the general prohibitions are set out in the federal statutes, the regulations and guidelines promulgated by various federal agencies pursuant to the authority granted them by the statutes are also "federal law" and may, in fact, be the more formidable protections against discriminatory employment practices in postsecondary education.

Within the general context of equal opportunity and fair employment practice lies the concept of affirmative action, but there is a difference that you should understand. The laws prohibiting discrimination do just that and no more. Affirmative action means what it sounds like it means; such programs are intended to take positive steps to enhance educational and employment opportunities for those groups who have been underrepresented in the past. The legal difficulties arise when the efforts taken on behalf of women and minorities begin to reach the point of reverse discrimination. The law in this area is complex and unsettled; however, a general rule seems to be that although admission, hiring, or promotion decisions should not be based solely on gender or minority status, it is permissible to take such characteristics into account along with other factors.

Academic Freedom

Academic freedom is generally thought to have some relationship to the legal rights and responsibilities of faculty in postsecondary education. There is some validity to this view, but the legal realities may be somewhat different than the general perceptions.

Whatever the concept of academic freedom may encompass, it clearly applies not only to the relationship between you as a faculty member and the institution but also to the relationship between the institution and its external environment.

Your academic freedom in relation to your employer institution must find its legal underpinnings in a contract, an institutional policy, a state statute, or a Constitutional provision. Any or all of these might be applicable at a public institution, but only contract and institutional policy provisions are likely to be relevant to your employment at a private institution.

Contrary to what seems to be a common perception, faculty who have invoked the protections of academic freedom to challenge adverse employment decisions have not fared well in the courts. Provisions in contracts, policies, or statutes that would afford specific and significant protections to faculty under the rubric of academic freedom are not common; this leaves the First Amendment protections of freedom of expression and association as the major recourse, and that one is available only to public employees. As a general rule, when you exercise these freedoms as a citizen and not as an employee, the constitutional balance will favor you; however, when you exercise these freedoms in the course of your employment function, the constitutional protections are much more limited, and the interests of your employer are likely to prevail.

The notion of academic freedom seems to have greater weight as a legal principle when the interests of the institution are at stake. For you, this is both good news and bad news. The bad news is that courts will be extremely reluctant to scrutinize the reasons for decisions about your hiring, tenure, promotion, or dismissal. The good news is that courts will be equally reluctant to review your decisions about academic matters, whether those pertain to the design and implementation of programs and courses, to evaluations of student performance, or to peer evaluations of other faculty.

Concluding Observations

As a teacher in postsecondary education, you work in an environment permeated by law. Those legal principles that define the employment relationship between you and the institution should be of special interest. As a matter of sound administration and ethics, institutional employers should abide by the requirements of the law; as a matter of professionalism, you should be as cognizant of their responsibilities as they are of their rights.

As is generally true for any relationship, an employment relationship must be nurtured or it will not remain healthy. Governing boards, administrators, and faculty need to work together. Each has a role to play, and each needs to understand and appreciate the roles of the others. You should view administrative superiors as sources of direction and support, not as adversaries.

Postsecondary educational institutions tend to be complex bureaucracies. Although that organizational characteristic is often looked upon with disfavor, it's precisely because many internal procedures have become routinized that both supervisors and subordinates know what to expect and are able to function together in relative harmony.

If you're prudent, you will learn what standard of performance is expected and meet that standard, develop good interpersonal relationships with students and other faculty, and abide by the valid directives of administrative superiors. If you do, your legal rights in postsecondary education will be a moot issue.

Academic Freedom
and College Teaching

Robert M. O'Neil

Several years ago I was asked to testify before a Virginia legislative committee, specifically in opposition to a bill which would bar the use by state employees of state-owned or leased computers to access sexually explicit material. Because the proposed law presented a serious and substantial threat to free speech, I eagerly agreed to take it on. To my surprise, I was the only witness on that side of the table. I was also surprised by the high level of hostility evident within the committee. When I warned them, by way of conclusion, "you cannot any more take this action than you could tell a custodian in the Capitol not to bring a personal copy of *Hustler* or *Penthouse* to read during his coffee break," I won few friends among the lawmakers.

The bill passed the committee unanimously later that day and soon received the acclaim of the senate and the governor's approval. Though the sponsors expected other states would follow with similar measures, none has done so, and the Virginia law remains unique. It was very soon challenged in a federal court suit, struck down by the district judge, upheld by a panel of the court of appeals, and eventually reconsidered by the full appellate court, whose judgment is anxiously awaited.

The Virginia experience offers two vital lessons about the current importance of academic freedom. It would have been difficult if not impossible to find an academic expert willing to testify against such a measure who did not have tenure or at least the protection of his or her academic freedom that a tenure-track appointment carries with it. Were I without such protection, I would not have expected to find a teaching job awaiting me on return to Charlottesville, much less still be teaching and writing as a member of the faculty several years later. Yet over the years I have always felt quite free to take such positions and express unpopular or unorthodox views, protected as I have always been by the safeguards of academic freedom.

The Virginia experience illustrates the value of academic freedom in a quite different way. Early agreement on the importance of a test case in federal court to challenge the law soon foundered on the reality that few state employees could risk coming forward as plaintiffs. To bring such a lawsuit, a person would need to show not only that he or she had a legitimate job-related need to access sexually explicit material on the Internet but that a request to a supervisor for permission—an exception which the law contained—would either have been a futile quest or would itself have abridged free expression. The absence of potential plaintiffs from the general state service roster came close to thwarting the test case.

Then the day was saved by six courageous state college or university professors—all quite clearly covered by the law—who were willing to let their names be prominently cited in court papers and who would allege not only that they needed for academic purposes to access explicit material but that a request to a "supervisor" would have burdened unduly their research and inquiry. Their role in the case invoked academic freedom at two levels—both in their ability to risk public identification with so highly suspect a cause and in their capacity to reveal, in court if necessary, the precise nexus between their scholarship and sexually explicit digital material. So the yet unfinished saga of the Virginia computer-use statute superbly illustrates the continuing relevance and meaning of academic freedom.

The need to explore and understand academic freedom has seldom been more urgent—an urgency intensified by the growing number of university teachers, many of them full-time teachers, who do not hold tenure and have no serious prospect of ever attaining it. The current debate over tenure and alternative faculty personnel systems deserves all the time and attention it can get. Central to this debate are a host of alternatives—means such as long-term contracts, most notably—which would allegedly protect academic freedom without the formal safeguards of a tenure or tenure-track system. Those who believe, as I do, that such alternatives are usually quite inadequate to the task and that tenure has proven its worth as a guarantor of academic freedom welcome as scholars any serious debate about issues so vital and so close to home, even as we view with some alarm the case being advanced to support a contrary view.

Anyone who is as deeply committed as I am to the system of faculty tenure in American universities is likely to have grave misgivings about any proposal that could, even if inadvertently, undermine or weaken the safeguards of tenure. Such misgivings are of several distinct types. The first concern is that even a system of formal, legally recognized, tenure does not always adequately protect academic freedom. A half century after the post-World War II anti-Communist hysteria, we have vivid reminders of the frailties of tenure, even in some of the most seemingly secure institutions. We have recalled the progressive purge of nearly 60 senior professors, starting with three members of the University of Washington faculty discharged summarily in 1948, on through three others dismissed by the University of Michigan several years later, and through a litany of truly horrible events for the American professoriate.

What makes these memories so poignant, even today, is that most of the faculty firings of the fifties reflected nothing firmer than suspicion of disloyalty (based typically on inference or conjecture), or refusal to reveal political associations or activities to external investigatory bodies. This sobering reminder of inherent limitations in even the best of tenure systems should give us pause—even in these calmer and much more secure times—in contemplating any changes that might weaken or dilute the safeguards which tenure affords.

Many critics of tenure suggest that McCarthyism is so long past and is so unlike anything of recent memory that current thinking about tenure should disregard such ominous antecedents. Apart from the question whether such terrible times could ever recur—a prospect no responsible policy-maker can ever gainsay—much more modern events illustrate the value of a system that protects an outspoken professor's freedom. Recall three events of the 1990s, hardly a time of witch-hunting or red-baiting. When Professor Lani Guinier was denied appointment as the U.S. Justice Department's chief civil rights officer because of controversial views she had expressed in law review articles about voting districts, she was able to resume her tenured professorship at Penn and later moved to Harvard, where she has continued to challenge complacent assumptions about voting patterns.

When Professor Joycelyn Elders was fired as the U.S. Surgeon General because of public statements she had made about teen sex education and especially about masturbation, she was welcomed back to her tenured post at the University of Arkansas, from which she has continued to speak out on important national health issues. And when Professor Christina Jeffrey was dismissed by Speaker Newt Gingrich as U.S. House Historian solely because in evaluating summer workshop proposals she had suggested the value of balance in treating the Holocaust, she promptly reclaimed her tenured position at Kennesaw State College and continued to challenge conventional assumptions about modern German history. These are cases of the 1990s, not of the 1950s. The professors protected by tenure in these instances were, of course, threatened not by their own institutions, but rather by external political forces. Yet there is little question that, absent tenure, although all three might have been welcomed back to campus after offending official Washington, others who held or wished to express unconventional views would have been less ready to follow their footsteps. So we might assume, at our peril, that tenure is valuable to protection of academic freedom and free inquiry only in times of crisis.

A second concern relates to the interests of those faculty whom tenure does not reach or protect. There have always been substantial numbers of university teachers without tenure. That group includes, of course, all who are on the tenure track but have not yet achieved tenure or reached the stage at which a tenure judgment must be made. It also includes visitors, full-time university employees who teach substantially less than half time, and many part-time faculty who hold adjunct and lecturer appointments, and would not be considered for tenure unless their time commitment substantially increased. The rub comes in the suggestion—central to current discussions of tenure alternatives—that there may be full-time teaching appointments which will never lead to tenure and will not even compel consideration of tenure status at the end of a probationary period because such a person is never on "probation."

Policies of the AAUP, most notably, and those of many universities as well, have always insisted that full-time teaching appointments be of limited duration, followed by a judgment about tenure. That limitation is typically seven years, though some quite reputable institutions have varied the number slightly—the University of California has long had an eight-year probationary period—and growing numbers of medical schools with faculty approval (and tacit AAUP blessing) have extended to ten years the period for those who must excel in teaching, research and clinical patient care as well as service. Such policies are rightly viewed as forcing the choice between "up" and "out." For those probationary faculty who do not merit permanent appointments when the probationary period ends, the only legally possible way to remain within the institution is by assuming a primarily nonteaching position.

While such policies may seem draconian and may, on occasion, limit flexibility both of institution and individual, they are vital to the integrity of the faculty personnel process. The requirement that so stark a judgment be made relatively early in a university teacher's career provides the most reliable form of quality control, an element that is almost inevitably lacking in nontenure systems such as those that rely mainly on renewable long-term contracts. To the extent that tenure alternatives presuppose an indefinitely extendable teaching appointment, without consideration of tenure—no "up or out" mandate, in short—they lack both the procedural safeguards of the tenure judgment and the substantive assurance of demonstrated academic and scholarly promise on the part of those who survive that process.

Equally troubling, such systems often lack rigorous safeguards for the nonrenewal of long-time university teachers. And to the degree that some such proposals clearly recognize the importance of due process to protect senior faculty from the pique of colleagues or political reprisal by trustees, they tend to become so tenure-like that a skeptic might well ask, "why not just call it tenure?" Indeed, one of the strengths and virtues of the term-contract alternative approach is claimed to be in precisely this area.

If a professor whose academic freedom has been threatened or abridged enjoys a right of appeal and review by a panel of peers as any reputable institution would presumably provide, the potential benefits of avoiding the perceived rigidities of tenure would seem to diminish in direct proportion to the enhancement of such safeguards. Quite simply, one can't have it both ways. The more a system looks and functions like tenure and the more it actually protects academic freedom, the less it creates that flexibility that many find appealing about tenure alternatives.

Finally, however, such proposals have one commendable quality that should not be lost in the debate. If they are less solicitous of the academic freedom of those who would be tenured or on a tenure track simply because the system does not confer tenure, they may at the same time be more protective of many faculty who fall outside the tenure-bearing matrix. Because such proposals are not tied to the formal status of tenure or tenure track, they might well do a better job of safeguarding the outspoken part-timer or nonteaching professional who is too often off the screen or below the radar of conventional tenure systems. Proponents of the soundest alternatives to tenure deserve commendation for their solicitude for a larger slice of the academic community and for their appreciation that such groups may encounter genuine academic freedom problems. The broader scope of potential protection afforded by such proposals does little to vindicate them at the core, but it certainly establishes credibility at the margin.

A third concern about such proposals involves their timing and rationale. Proponents of renewable contracts and other alternatives to tenure correctly note that recent years have brought unprecedented ambivalence about tenure, especially among younger faculty. Such uneasiness naturally leads to pursuit of alternatives. One would expect that mounting dissatisfaction would also spawn major change in personnel policies. Yet curiously, such change in actual institutional policy has lagged far behind what one would have predicted a decade ago, when a surprising number of institutions responded to a Carnegie Foundation survey that they were giving "some consideration" to altering or even abolishing tenure.

Little of that sort has in fact happened during the decade; if anything, practice has even moved in the opposite direction. Of three institutions which would, a decade ago, have been viewed as poster children for nontenure alternatives, two (Evergreen State University in Oregon and the University of Texas-Permian Basin) have embraced faculty personnel systems so closely resembling tenure that they clearly belong today on the other side of the ledger. Only Hampshire College, of the original three, remains fully committed (apparently to the complete satisfaction of its faculty) to long-term renewable contracts as a tenure alternative.

Meanwhile, the experience of several institutions at which nontenure alternatives surfaced during the past decade has not been wholly reassuring. Central Arkansas University's invitation to faculty to exchange tenure for substantially increased salaries received much national attention, especially among tenure critics, but had few if any takers on campus. Of two candidates to whom the trade-off was specifically offered, both of whom declined, one observing that "tenure offers prestige" and the other remarking simply that tenure was "the way it works" at a university. Meanwhile, the Central Arkansas proposal has drawn sharp rebukes from staunch tenure defenders; Professor Robert Gorman, who has been the AAUP president and has chaired its Committee A, terms it a "horrific proposal." In his view, "faculty members should not be encouraged, or permitted, to barter [the larger social end which tenure serves] for cash, particularly when they are likely to feel that their academic freedom will never be curtailed and that the trade-off is therefore of little consequence . . . [although] . . . [a]ll too often experience shows, that will prove not to be the case."

The experience at Florida Gulf Coast University, site of another widely heralded experiment, seems to inspire even less confidence. When this new campus opened several years ago, it had two classes of faculty—those who brought with them the academic tenure they had held on the parent campus of the University of South Florida and a majority of new arrivals who accepted term contracts in lieu of the tenure that was not available to them under the new structure. Three years later, nearly a quarter of the charter faculty had departed, most voluntarily, and some of them left because of concern over academic freedom. At least three of the founding faculty had been denied reappointment despite positive evaluations; two of those three argued that disagreements with administrators had caused their departure.

The absence of formal protection for academic freedom creates what the president of the Florida Gulf Coast faculty senate calls "an unstable environment that is unhealthy." Faculty groups have pressed for changes in the personnel structure—specifically, to add a "rolling horizon" to the contractual structure, amounting, in effect, to an automatic renewal of the very type that, as one skeptical regent observed, would deprive the institution of the very flexibility the plan was supposed to create—indeed, one might add, would actually leave Florida Gulf Coast with less flexibility than a regular tenure system provides, leaving only the worst of both worlds.

Finally, among the alternatives, mention must be made of Bennington College. Several years ago, Bennington's president, Elizabeth Coleman, earned attention and praise for effectively eliminating faculty tenure and substituting term appointments even for quite senior teachers. AAUP censure, condemnation by other faculty groups, and protracted litigation, ensued. All was fairly quiet on this bucolic Vermont campus for several years, suggesting that the new structure might be workable, even if clearly not optimal for the remaining faculty. But things changed when, in April 2000, a faculty critic of the administration was fired during the semester and a year and a half before the end of his contract term, allegedly because he had been tardy in submitting his student evaluations. (A later check showed that over a third of fall semester appraisals were not in on time.) Since he had been Bennington's only teacher of philosophy, his hasty departure—he was given three days to clean out his office and his college apartment—left that vital subject uncovered in the college curriculum. Meanwhile, the contracts of several other administration critics were not renewed this past year under less widely publicized conditions. Some Bennington faculty supported the administration's course in general and its handling of specific cases, including the *cause célèbre* in philosophy, noting that chronic tardiness in filing grades is especially inimical to student welfare at a small liberal arts college like Bennington.

There are doubtless other examples of alternatives to tenure. One that seems for three decades to have worked reasonably well is that of Hampshire College, which has never offered tenure but has relied entirely on long-term renewable faculty contracts. Hampshire is reliably reported to have denied reappointment or renewal beyond the seven-year period that would require an "up or out" decision at most tenure-track institutions.

Yet there is no evidence that abridgment of academic freedom or denial of due process has ever been validly charged against Hampshire, and there has been no formal AAUP investigation, much less censure. (Such a non-reappointment beyond the seventh year is not vulnerable, under AAUP standards, at Hampshire so long as the process comports with the college's own regulations and so long as the basis for such adverse action would not be deemed violative of academic freedom within a conventional tenure system.)

Hampshire thus remains the shining example—perhaps, indeed, the only example—of an institution at which academic freedom and due process appear to have been respected despite the absence of a formal system of faculty tenure. To understand better this anomaly, it would be helpful to know more than we do about the unique conditions under which Hampshire was founded—through a consortium of the four existing baccalaureate institutions in the central Connecticut River Valley, all of which retain traditional tenure systems while sharing faculty time and other academic resources with their new neighbor.

We do know at least two highly significant things: That from the very start, faculty members joined Hampshire without any expectation of tenure, so that those for whom formal protection of academic freedom would have seemed essential may simply have chosen not to teach there. Second, we also know that a generation of Hampshire presidents and governing boards have insisted on protecting academic freedom as fully without tenure as have their colleagues and counterparts at Amherst, Mount Holyoke, Smith, and the University of Massachusetts. What all this tells us is that it is not impossible, however difficult and unique the Hampshire model may be. The Hampshire experience, taken in context of Bennington and Florida Gold Coast, also tells us that a faculty personnel structure or system which relies mainly on renewable contracts is neither necessary nor sufficient as a guarantor of academic freedom.

Finally, if one concedes that tenure is not perfect—and to claim perfection, even for an unrequited defender, would be myopic—it is fair to ask how it could be made better. For one, the procedural safeguards in any personnel system can always be improved or enhanced—indeed, one of the virtues of some of the alternatives seems to be in precisely the area of procedures, presumably to some extent trading off a lowering of substantive standards for a raising of procedural safeguards.

Second, the role and mission of faculty tenure should be better understood as part of the case for its protection and preservation. Increasingly these days one hears from people who should know better—even within the academic community—that tenure exists to protect "job security" or salaries, perquisites, or pensions. Too easily lost in such casual assumptions is the central fact that tenure serves first and foremost to protect free expression and freedom of inquiry within the academic profession though it may incidentally (and not insignificantly) serve that end by preventing the arbitrary forfeiture of positions and benefits. But that is very different from asserting that the main function of tenure is to give college professors a high level of job security (which, the critics will often add, exceeds the security to be found in other professions.) Security is, of course, hardly irrelevant, but to recognize that fact does not and should not elevate employment security to the level of paramount value.

Third, it is crucial to recognize that tenure, even at its most secure, is not an immutable guarantee of lifetime employment. The termination of tenured appointments may occur in several ways, including but not limited to dismissal for cause—a severe sanction, imposed infrequently, but more often than critics of tenure would admit—and which is made unnecessary in a far greater number of cases where a faculty member's conduct would clearly warrant dismissal for cause, but an alternative course such as resignation or early retirement intervenes and moots the formal charges. Proof of a medical disability warrants termination of a tenured appointment if it demonstrates (in AAUP language) "that the faculty member cannot continue to fulfill the terms and conditions of the appointment"—a properly strict standard but one which is not impossible to meet.

Genuine financial exigency, reviewed by a faculty body, may also warrant termination of tenured appointments; although the standard is certainly not one to be invoked casually, proof of "exigency" does not demand that the institution have declared bankruptcy, forfeited all its material assets, or become unable to meet the next payroll.

Finally, there is that basis for termination which is probably least well understood and potentially subject to greatest abuse—the discontinuance for valid academic reasons of a program or department where exigency is not a factor but rather the decision is driven by (again quoting the AAUP language) a "judgment that the educational mission of the institution as a whole will be enhanced by [such] discontinuance." Here again the procedures are appropriately rigorous, but they can be and have in a number of instances been met to the full satisfaction of AAUP and other faculty organizations. In each of these ways, unrelated to personal "cause," institutions have long had the capacity to terminate tenured appointments. Thus the assertion that tenure represents an immutable guarantee of academic employment, regardless of the gravity of personal transgression or institutional need, is not only untrue but is also irresponsible.

A fourth concern is that tenure should not be viewed out of context. We easily forget that tenure is but one element of a sound faculty personnel policy. For example, the process by which tenure may be denied or tenure-track appointments not renewed is as crucial to the protection of academic freedom as are the limits on ways in which and reasons for which a tenured professor may be dismissed. For if an outspoken or unpopular teacher could simply be denied continuing appointment for any reason or for no reason, substantive limits on institutional policy would have considerably diminished value. Thus it was crucial three decades ago for the AAUP to declare policies and procedures for the nonrenewal of nontenured appointments which, on one hand, recognize that during a term a nontenured person enjoys essentially the same level of protection as does a tenured colleague, but on the other hand that the decision not to renew or extend such an appointment at its end is a quite different one.

Basic precepts of academic freedom apply at both stages, but they apply in different ways. Establishing that an unexplained denial of reappointment reflected political animus or desire to suppress criticism of the administration will perforce be more difficult, and in some situations may even be impossible if the decision-maker refuses to state reasons for the adverse action and institutional policy does not require any explanation. And in any event, the faculty member is likely at this stage to bear the burden of proof whereas a person facing dismissal may insist that the administration bear that burden.

Finally, as any good university attorney well recognizes, the importance of clearly stated and fair campus procedures can hardly be overstated in the disposition of academic personnel issues. Nor can the importance of consistently applying those procedures be emphasized unduly; lay persons understandably make the mistake of assuming that when the merits of a case seem clear—when, for example, the case to be made for suspension or dismissal of a faculty member seems beyond doubt—summary action is justified. In fact, as lawyers well know, precisely the opposite view should prevail: It is the easy case in which procedures must be scrupulous, for in the hard case, the temptation to relax and use shortcuts is far less likely to afflict decision-makers.

In these and other ways, the current debate over tenure and its alternatives may serve a valuable purpose. At the very least, such a lively debate forces us to reflect upon the basic interests of academic freedom to which any faculty personnel system must be committed and by which it must be judged. Probing the options as we have done here and as other forums have recently done may serve to strengthen the tenure system by enabling better understanding of what tenure does protect and, in some ways even more significantly, of what tenure does not always protect. Such a debate is also quite likely to make those who offer and confer faculty tenure more precise in defining its conditions and more careful and systematic in extending it. Finally, having to explain and defend the tenure system should make more resilient and resourceful those of us who believe that, despite its flaws and foibles, it is the best guarantor of academic freedom—or, to paraphrase Winston Churchill's defense of democracy—that "it is the worst system, save for all the others."

Affirmative Action: Myths and Realities

Mark R. Killenbeck

Affirmative action is both the most controversial and least understood aspect of the faculty hiring process. That is unfortunate, for there is very little about an affirmative hiring regime with which we should disagree. This assumes, of course, that we are speaking of the sort of programs the individuals who created affirmative action envisioned. For affirmative action, as conceived of by those who coined the term and as implemented in legally sound programs, is nothing more that a simple commitment to an evenhanded and open hiring process, within which the needs of the institution are clearly and honestly expressed, individuals are encouraged to apply without regard to race, ethnicity, or gender, and all candidates are given a full opportunity to present their credentials and have them assessed fairly.

Simply put, a true affirmative action program operates much like the formulation most of us encounter on the stationery of many institutions, the notation that declares that this university or college is "an equal opportunity/affirmative action institution." Appropriate affirmative action is a commitment to act *affirmatively* to ensure *equal* employment opportunity for all qualified candidates. Such a program may in certain circumstances take group identity into account, but it will do so only after carefully specifying the qualities and qualifications it is looking for in the position and ensuring that *every* finalist possess all of those attributes. And it will select an individual from a favored group only where it can fairly be said that group identity adds something real and positive to the educational mix.

There are, of course, two small problems with this formulation. This is not how most individuals understand affirmative action. And it is decidedly not the manner in which many affirmative hiring programs operate.

Contemporary discussions of affirmative action tend to play themselves out as conflicts between sharply divergent moral imperatives. Those who favor affirmative action view it as a necessary and appropriate mechanism for increasing the number of women and minority professors in the academy. The most common justification offered is that affirmative action will promote "diversity" in faculty composition. A less frequent, but in some respects more compelling, rationale is that affirmative action compensates individuals from favored groups for past discrimination, in the form of a "leg up" in the hiring process. Opponents, in turn, believe that affirmative measures operate as quotas or preferences for individuals that are granted solely on the basis of their group identity and, as such, violate the fundamental American constitutional precept that each individual is entitled to the equal protection of the laws. And they insist that such programs compromise higher education's historic commitment to merit as the abiding principle in all matters of appointment, promotion, and tenure.

The opposing views are vigorously expressed, philosophically and politically charged, and often the foundations for painful and protracted litigation. One of the deep ironies in all of this is that affirmative hiring programs need not pose these problems. And that most candidates for faculty positions, armed with a clear understanding of what affirmative action should be about, have little reason to worry about what the existence of such programs implies for their job prospects.

The Affirmative Action Debate: Definitions and Contexts

The first and arguably most serious problem in discussing affirmative action is that there is little if any consensus as to what the phrase actually means. Indeed, definitions of affirmative action are as varied as the agendas of the persons who articulate them. Some individuals, for example, claim that "affirmative action properly pursued seeks not the obviously unqualified, but the qualified and unobvious applicants" ("Reparation," 1977, p. 16), a formulation that emphasizes the need to establish simple but fair procedures. Others argue that such measures must have a more active dimension and treat affirmative action as a concept that "entails positive steps, rather than just passive nondiscrimination, to advance equality in education and employment" (Welch & Gruhl, 1998, p. 1). Still others speak of "a conscious effort to increase the representation of women and other designated groups in particular organizations, occupations, programs, and a wide range of activities" (Orlans & O'Neill, 1992, p. 7). And some actually deny that such programs involve anything that can even properly be characterized as differential treatment, maintaining that "affirmative action is not a preference; it is a modest effort to recognize the ways that standardized tests don't measure the potential of entire groups of people, particularly those who were not represented when these tests were developed" (Crenshaw, 1998, p. 146).

This ebb and flow of opinion is important, for it offers a perspective on why the debate about affirmative action is so philosophically and emotionally charged. But the real question for individuals contemplating an academic career and, in particular, those interested in a position at a given college or university is what appropriate affirmative action policies seek to achieve and how the institutions assessing their credentials go about meeting the objectives they have decided to pursue.

Most affirmative action programs define their ambitions in appropriately soothing ways. A typical policy will stress that the institution seeks simply to hire a candidate who meets all expressed qualifications and either enhances the diversity of the faculty or comes from an historically "underrepresented" group. In this context, diversity assumes very narrow and specific meanings. It is not, as some might wish, shorthand for creating an intellectual community within which all perspectives are represented, be they philosophical, political, religious, or experiential. Diversity is, rather, both intended to be and operates as an expression of a preference for hiring women or minority candidates. In a similar vein, the quest for individuals from underrepresented groups will generally operate in either of two ways. In its proper form, an affirmative hire undertaken for this purpose opts for a female or minority candidate when there is a disparity between the gender or racial composition of the total number of individuals available who possess the requisite qualifications (in legal terms, the "qualified workforce") and the proportion of such individuals within the department making the hire. In the alternative, a representational hire prefers an individual for that purpose alone, selecting a candidate on the basis of group identity as, for example, a "role model," even when it is arguably clear that it must lower its expectations regarding the relative qualifications of the individual chosen.

In many instances, both diversity and representational hires create the impression that a college or university is not in fact simply trying to draw distinctions between applicants "with similarly strong objective credentials." Accordingly, it often appears to both rejected applicants and the general public that thresholds are lowered, often substantially, when women or minority applicants are hired. Decisions of that sort, whether real or imagined, fuel the belief that affirmative action discriminates against individuals with superior qualifications. If, for example, the academic record and prior professional accomplishments of an applicant are appropriate measures of individual merit, on what basis can an institution justify interviewing or hiring candidates with what appear to be lesser objective credentials?

Individuals who support affirmative measures answer this question by trying to put the accepted understandings of merit in context. In particular, they emphasize that merit is an exceedingly fluid term and that it has historically been defined in ways that have operated to the benefit of white males and the detriment of women and minorities.

A compelling case can in fact be made that merit involves something more than objective qualifications. For example, the philosopher George Sher (1987) has noted that there are both moral and nonmoral dimensions of merit and that within each grouping there are variations on theme such that "the relevant desert-claims may seem to have no single justification" (p. 109). In particular, Sher emphasizes the complexity of the desert construct, stressing that it "is central to our pre-reflective thought" and that "most people find it simply obvious that persons who work hard deserve to succeed, that persons of outstanding merit deserve recognition and reward, and that persons harmed by wrongdoers deserve to be compensated" (p. ix). Viewed in this light, the argument for hiring predicated solely on objective criteria reflects a nonmoral claim, asking that we divorce individual attainments from the circumstances within which they were achieved. The argument for affirmative action, in turn, is premised on the assumption that context matters very much, both in terms of assessing individual worth and in assembling a group of individuals who will reflect in an appropriate manner the full range of institutional objectives, recognizing the crucial role that the composition of the academic community plays in the learning process.

There is, accordingly, a significant difference between affirmative action programs intended to be simple mandates for fair treatment and those that "challenge the sacred American myth that landing a job, or a seat in the freshman class, is a prize one deserves thanks solely to one's own efforts" (Sandel, 1997, p. 13). And that, as the history of affirmative action verifies, was not at all what those who created the construct had in mind.

The History: From Fairness to Entitlement

Modern affirmative action came into being in 1961, when President Kennedy issued Executive Order 10925. Most observers understood that this measure was intended to be a modest, largely symbolic first step in the new administration's efforts to eventually outlaw discrimination. To the extent they thought of it at all, they sensed that the phrase "affirmative action" was a shorthand expression requiring procedural fairness, a simple obligation to treat individuals appropriately by taking positive steps "to ensure that applicants are employed, and that employees are treated during employment, without regard to their race, creed, color, or national origin" (Executive Order 10925, 1961, § 301). As the person who introduced the phrase into the Order observed, "I put the word 'affirmative' in there" because "I was searching for something that would give a sense of positiveness to performance under that executive order" (Taylor, 1995, p. 40).

The term affirmative action was never defined in the measures mandating its adoption, and thoughtful observers speculated that it "presumably . . . meant such things as advertising the fact, seeking out qualified applicants from sources where they might be found, and the like" (Glazer, 1975, p. 46). As one contemporary commentary stressed, "read together" the various measures "indicate that the overarching policy . . . is to insure the neutrality of the hiring process—to ensure that hiring decisions are made on merit, with neither positive nor negative reference to minority determinative characteristics" (*Harvard Law Review*, 1971, pp. 1300-1301). A university or college might, for example, undertake aggressive recruitment efforts as part of the process of documenting a good-faith end to prior discriminatory practices. Hiring decisions would, however, be governed by the traditional assumption that individual merit was dispositive. Indeed, during the early years of affirmative action even its most ardent proponents maintained, vigorously, that "any institution that gives preference . . . on the basis of sex, race, or ethnic origin is violating the law" (Sandler, 1975, p. 402).

The term affirmative action was, then, a shorthand expression for the quest for procedural fairness. The mandate was narrow and specific and assumed that positive legislative commands not to discriminate could be paired with fair and open procedures to produce a society with "equal opportunity for all qualified persons." Accordingly, a university acted affirmatively when it took specific steps to broaden the pool from which it still selected the best-qualified candidate regardless of race, gender, or ethnicity. The basic decision was nondiscriminatory, and the affirmative matrix simply reflected a willingness to discard discredited assumptions about group characteristics—in this instance, the belief that certain professions were appropriately the exclusive province of white males—while aggressively seeking the most qualified applicants from a pool that would now include individuals previously excluded.

Compelling reasons supported embracing affirmative action as a matter of positive public policy. At the time Executive Order 10925 was issued, legally enforced discrimination against women and minorities was the rule rather than the exception in this nation, and individuals from disfavored groups were at much greater risk of being relegated to the margins of society. This was especially true, and troubling, in the nation's colleges and universities. Higher education has always been a central element of the American experience. Knowledgeable observers have, however, generally understood that the academy's public image masked a welter of contradictory realities and that the interests colleges and universities actually pursued were often at odds with their avowed intentions. The author of the Declaration of Independence, for example, seemed to have meant, quite literally, that "all *men* are created equal." In his *Notes on the State of Virginia* (1787) Jefferson proposed "diffus[ing] knowledge more generally through the mass of the people" by selecting the best *boys* for advanced instruction at public expense (pp. 146–47). Indeed, in his later years, he spoke disparagingly of any public role for women in his democracy, declaring "women, who, to prevent depravation of morals and ambiguity of issue, could not mix promiscuously in the public meetings of men" (1816, p. 72). Jefferson may have believed that education would create a "natural aristocracy among men" predicated on "virtue and talents," rather than an "artificial aristocracy, founded on wealth and birth, without either virtue or talents" (1813, p. 343). At Jefferson's University of Virginia, the aristocracy of men remained precisely that: a conclave of leaders, shaped by their educational attainments, to which women were denied access.

Minorities—in particular, African Americans—were in turn even less welcome in the inner circles of a nation that practiced a form of educational apartheid well into the twentieth century. Many of Jefferson's contemporaries believed he was too charitable when he observed that "in memory they are equal to whites; in reason much inferior," and that "never yet could I find that a black had uttered a thought above the level of plain narration" (Jefferson, 1787, pp. 139 and 140). These individuals and their descendants fashioned a nation in which slavery could be eliminated only through the Civil War, and the quest for equality would require massive and systematic intervention by courts and the Congress. Like most southern institutions, Jefferson's University of Virginia opened its doors to African Americans only when compelled to do so, albeit 20 years before it allowed women into the academic fold and just barely ahead of the force of the law. The image of Governor Wallace standing in the "schoolhouse door" would, accordingly, be etched indelibly on the national consciousness as an exemplar of an educational regime within which African Americans were, at best, second-class citizens.

More fundamentally, the totemic symbol of educational excellence, "merit," often assumed interesting dimensions with the university community. As the President's Commission on Higher Education observed in 1947, "the old, comfortable idea that 'any boy,'" much less, any woman or member of a minority group, "'can get a college education who has it in him' simply is not true" (p. 977). Privilege, it seems, remained an essential attribute in an educational system within which a series of seemingly impenetrable barriers denied countless individuals access to the perspectives and skills they needed and deserved. Even when colleges became more numerous, and a college education more affordable, the persistence of old assumptions about each individual's proper place in society would dominate a system that did little "to widen the horizons of ordinary students [so] that they and, still more, their children will encounter fewer of the obstacles that cramp achievement" (Harvard Committee, 1945, p. 11).

These realities made it quite clear that the procedural reforms envisioned within the original affirmative action mandates were necessary. At a minimum, they would provide one important means to "smoke out" inappropriate decision-making criteria and force institutions to articulate what they sought in the individuals they wished to hire. But the results of these initial policies were mixed, and although women and minorities made important gains, inequality remained the rule rather than the exception. These realities provided the foundations for a competing theory of affirmative action that emerged during the late 1960s and early 1970s, one that maintained that decades of discrimination made it necessary to seek both equal treatment and equal achievement.

Perhaps the most notable and important example of the new affirmative action rhetoric came in a commencement address delivered at Howard University in 1965 by President Lyndon B. Johnson, who declared that "we seek not just freedom but opportunity . . . not just legal equity but human ability, not just equality as a right and a theory but equality as a fact and equality as a result" (p. 635). This pledge, to frame a society within which "equal opportunity is essential, but not enough, not enough," eventually became a legal reality in regulations that spoke simply of the need for "good faith efforts" to achieve "equal employment opportunity" but in reality placed substantial pressures on employers to do more than ensure equal opportunity.

Under this new regime, an "affirmative action program" was "a set of specific and result-oriented procedures to which an [institution] commits itself to apply every good faith effort" (Revised Order No. 4, 1971). Such programs

> must include an analysis of areas within which the [institution] is deficient in the utilization of minority groups and women, and further, goals and timetables to which the [institution's] good faith efforts must be directed to correct the deficiencies and, thus to achieve prompt and full utilization of minorities and women, at all levels and in all segments of its work force where deficiencies exist. (Ibid., p. 152)

As a result, more and more institutions began to concentrate on the bottom line. And instead of serving simply as aspirations, goals became benchmarks against which performance was assessed, with institutions falling short deemed to have failed to meet their obligations.

The transformation of affirmative action from procedural mandate to substantive goal was the product of two complementary yet contradictory motives. One was the need to ensure that both the reality and effects of deliberate discrimination would end. An affirmative action mandate that did not in fact produce or at least was not in some sense required to produce measurable results invited the accusation that it was a "sham." A second, less commendable impulse was the need for organizations subject to the affirmative action mandate to demonstrate progress to both their government overseers and a skeptical public. The theory was quite simple:

> Neutrality on the part of [an employer], even open espousal of equal opportunity, will not overcome the years of job discrimination to which minorities have been subjected. Where no affirmative action is taken by employers, as was the prevailing situation prior to 1969, recruitment and upgrading of minority individuals proceeds at an extremely slow pace. (United States Commission on Civil Rights, 1970, p. 189)

Simply put, numerical objectives that were initially embraced as appropriate goals became very specific performance criteria against which progress was measured. The goals themselves were not, in any meaningful legal sense, quotas. Indeed, the regulations arguably forbade the adoption of such measures. They tended, nevertheless, to operate inexorably in that manner when administrators, often under intense political and public pressure, mistook statistical progress for appropriate accomplishment. As Laurence Silberman, Undersecretary of Labor from 1970 to 1973, explained, "we wished to create a generalized, firm, but gentle pressure to balance the residue of discrimination," but instead "our use of numerical standards in pursuit of equal opportunity . . . led ineluctably to the very quotas, guaranteeing equal results, that we initially wished to avoid" (1977, p. 14).

Affirmative Action and Higher Education: Reformulating the Quest for Excellence

Initially, affirmative action in faculty hiring seemed to be nothing more than a simple description of the manner in which higher education had always operated. In an early statement on affirmative action, for example, the AAUP (1973) stressed that the "first test of equal opportunity" is that there be "standards of competence and qualification . . . set independently of the actual choices made" (p. 156). At least in theory, any affirmative action that involved anything more than, for example, simply broadening the pool of candidates, would have been dismissed as fundamentally at odds with both the academic ethic and higher education's understandings of its legal obligations. The goal was the elimination of discrimination, and the assumption was that, to the extent positive actions were called for, higher education would correct its past wrongs by identifying and hiring minorities and women who were fully qualified and who had previously simply been overlooked.

Many parties to the educational compact had at least a basic understanding that hiring realities were infinitely more complex. Recognizing the need for changes, influential actors in the academy argued for a different approach. In 1975, for example, the Carnegie Council on Policy Studies in Higher Education defined affirmative action as

> actions to eliminate discrimination: creation of more adequate pools of talent, active searches for talent wherever it exists, revision of policies and practices that permitted or abetted discrimination, development of expectations for a staff whose composition does not reflect the impacts of discrimination, provision of judicial processes to hear complaints, and the making of decisions without improper regard for sex, race, or ethnic origin. (p. 2)

The Council's approach was arguably purely procedural. It spoke largely of how one treated individuals, and the operational theory remained, eliminating discrimination. However, the Council condemned only the "improper" consideration of group identity, a formulation that left open ample channels for a programmatic approach within which group identity would become a positive factor in the decision-making process. In a similar vein, the AAUP (1973) "commended" plans "which are entirely affirmative, i.e., plans in which "preference" and "compensation" are words of positive connotation rather than words of condescension or noblesse oblige—preference for the more highly valued candidate and compensation for past failures to reach the actual market of intellectual resources available to higher education" (p. 155). As a result, the position the AAUP embraced took matters to a new level, aiming directly at the notion that there were any defined, or even definable, dimensions to merit:

> We cannot assume uncritically that present criteria of merit and procedures for their application have yielded the excellence intended; to the extent that the use of certain standards has resulted in the exclusion of women and minorities from professional positions in higher education, or their inclusion only in token proportions to their availability, the academy has denied itself access to the critical mass of intellectual vitality represented by these groups. We believe that such criteria must thus be considered deficient on the very grounds of excellence itself. (p. 156)

To their credit, many colleges and universities recognized and accounted for the dilemma posed by policies that appeared to grant preferences based on group membership. They understood that under this approach in order to get beyond race or gender, institutions otherwise dedicated to decisions purely on the merits needed to expressly take race or gender into account. As one individual observed:

> Affirmative action can only have the effect that is hoped for (the effect that would justify it) if employers, boards of admissions, and the like are compelled (or compel themselves) to accept a significant proportion of applicants from minority groups—even if, after giving consideration to what would traditionally be regarded as their credentials, they must accept many whom they would otherwise have passed over. (Green, 1981, p. 14)

Asserting that an institutional initiative is designed to simply "level the playing field" so that all individuals may apply and be considered on an equal, nondiscriminatory basis is then quite different from maintaining that active consideration of group identity is consistent with accepted norms designed to simply distinguish between applicants with similarly strong objective credentials. This distinction became commonplace, however, when affirmative measures were transformed from a mandate for procedural fairness into some variation on what might properly be characterized as a substantive entitlement.

The Law: The Elusive Quest for "Equality"

Most of the legal issues that arise from affirmative hiring practices are grounded in the Constitutional command, expressed in the Fourteenth Amendment, that every individual is entitled to the "equal protection of the laws." That fundamental guarantee is supplemented by a variety of statutory enactments that impose various obligations on all employers, including the nation's colleges and universities. In each instance the threshold assumption is that same: Every person has a right to be treated equally in any instance within which comparisons are made between and among what the law refers to as "similarly situated" individuals.

That precept is supplemented by a series of understandings about the extent to which an employer may take group characteristics into account, most notably race, ethnicity, and gender. Courts (and, in particular, the United States Supreme Court) have long recognized that group identity has virtually no relevance for the purpose of making decisions about individuals. In legal terms, such characteristics are regarded as "suspect," and with very few exceptions, neither race, ethnicity, nor gender may be considered when making employment decisions.[1] The courts also understand that equality of treatment has not necessarily been the norm. In particular, they recognize that there is a substantial history of active, government-sanctioned discrimination against women and minorities for no reason other than their status as members of those previously socially disfavored groups.

At the same time, courts recognize that individuals are inherently different and that the equal protection command should not be understood to prohibit institutions from acknowledging distinctions that actually matter. These conflicting realities are perhaps best captured in a court decision that, although not about faculty hiring, nevertheless expresses eloquently the dilemmas posed by affirmative action. In the now famous or infamous (depending on one's perspective) *Hopwood* decision, the court indicated that preferential treatment of certain applicants—for example, the sons and daughters of rich alumni—was an appropriate institutional imperative, especially at private institutions, which depended greatly on the largesse of their graduates. The court spoke accordingly with approval of an admissions regime where

[a] university may properly favor one applicant over another because of his ability to play the cello, make a downfield tackle, or understand chaos theory. An admissions process may also consider an applicant's home state or relationship to

school alumni. Law schools specifically may look at things such as unusual or substantial extracurricular activities in college, which may be atypical factors affecting undergraduate grades. Schools may even consider factors such as whether an applicant's parents attended college or the applicant's economic and social background. (1996, p. 946)

Affirmative actions on behalf of women, African Americans, or other minorities were, however, dismissed by the court as risky exercises in social engineering.

Critics of *Hopwood* savaged the panel for suggesting that there was somehow a moral or legal equivalence between "affirmative action for the privileged" and preferences granted to "the race that was enslaved for 200 years and abused for another 100 and more" (Lewis, 1996, p. A27). In their estimation, "the plea for fairness based on 'merit' as measured by test scores appears to be confined to race—a plea that in our society should be regarded with some skepticism" (Katzenbach & Marshall, 1998, p. 45). Of course, the opponents of affirmative action saw things differently. For them, *Hopwood* "end[ed] the diversity charade" (Greve, 1996, p. A1), laying the foundations for the demise of "hated racial quotas [that] were foisted on an unsuspecting country by unconstitutional and extralegal means" (Roberts, 1996, p. A18).

These differences in perspective are understandable, especially when the decision-making criterion at issue is race, a characteristic that most of us believe simply should not matter when important individual decisions are made.2 The rhetorical touchstones are simultaneously familiar yet controversial. There is, for example, the first Justice Harlan's eloquent dissent in *Plessy v. Ferguson* (1896), in which he declared that "our Constitution is color-blind, and neither knows nor tolerates classes among citizens" (p. 559), an argument against the Court's shameful embrace of "separate but equal" that has now become a mantra for those seeking the end of affirmative action. There is Dr. Martin Luther King, Jr., whose vision of "a nation where [people] will not be judged by the color of their skin but by content of their character" (1963, p. 217) is embraced by both sides in the affirmative action debate. And there are the words of Professor Alexander Bickel (1975), who captured what appeared to be the central tenet of centuries of invidious discrimination when he declared that "the lesson of the great decisions of the Supreme Court and the lesson of contemporary history have been the same for at least a generation: discrimination . . . is illegal, immoral, unconstitutional, inherently wrong, and destructive of democratic society" (p. 133).

The common denominator in these statements is the belief that "distinctions between citizens solely because of their ancestry are by their very nature odious" *Hirabayashi v. United States*, 1943, p. 100) and that "all legal restrictions which curtail the civil rights of a single racial group are immediately suspect" (*Korematsu v. United States*, 1944, p. 216). Unfortunately, matters are not quite as simple as they seem. As Justice O'Connor stressed in *Adarand Constructors, Inc. v. Pena* (1995), "suspect" does not necessarily mean unconstitutional. Thus, although every affirmative action policy and program is measured strictly against the promise of individual equality before the law, the Court has recognized repeatedly that the equality guarantee is conditional, a personal right of the highest order that an entity may nevertheless modify or set aside when pursuing a sufficiently important goal. That was, tellingly, the lesson of the Japanese exclusion cases, the decisions that first labeled racial classifications "odious" while nevertheless sanctioning a massive deprivation of the civil liberties of Japanese Americans during World War II. And it has been a consistent theme in the Court's jurisprudence ever since. Indeed, even Justice Scalia, who rails against "the concept of racial entitlement" and has argued that "in the eyes of government, we are just one race here, [i]t is American" (*Adarand*, p. 239), concedes that there might be occasions where race can properly be taken into account.

The proverbial bottom line is that there are circumstances in which affirmative measures granting some sort of preference will be deemed constitutional, provided the program in question pursues in an appropriate manner public interests and social policies of the highest order, generally by offering remedies or compensation for past, legally enforced discrimination. The balance is a delicate one, and there is no simple, mechanical way to determine which social policies justify granting preferences based on group membership. Consider, for example, the Court's landmark decision in *Regents of the University of California v. Bakke* (1978). In many respects, the core of that case is its continued skepticism about the use of group identity—in this instance, race—as an appropriate criterion in the admissions decision. Even Justice Powell, whose opinion came to be viewed as the judgment of the Court, expressed considerable reservations about the use of such criteria, stressing that "racial and ethnic distinctions of any sort are inherently suspect and thus call for the most exacting judicial examination" (p. 291).

There are two principal reasons for this. The first reflects a simple reality previously noted: In general, group identity has little, if anything, to do with actual qualifications. Even Justice Brennan, whose willingness to tolerate the approach taken by the University of California, Davis Medical Center would divide the *Bakke* Court in unfortunate ways, stressed in his opinion that "the assertion of human equality is closely associated with the proposition that differences in color or creed, birth or status, are neither significant nor relevant to the way in which persons should be treated" (p. 355). The second reason is instrumental. Invoking group identity as a decision-making, or even decision-influencing, criterion carries definite risks, because use of a group-based preference will tend to perpetuate the stereotype that certain ethnic groups are incapable of achieving success without special race-based programs.

At the same time, preferential treatment or simply taking group identity into account in some arguably nonpreferential way might well serve a variety of very important educational and social interests. Some of these considerations are properly denominated as compensatory or remedial and are realized through court orders entered against individuals or entities that have engaged in deliberate, invidious discrimination. Thus, as even the *Hopwood* panel conceded, the Supreme Court has approved numerous measures that "remedy past wrongs" in a race-conscious manner. Indeed, support for such programs is sufficiently pronounced that the Court has approved formulaic remedies that can only be properly described as quotas. In *United States v. Paradise* (1987), for example, the Court imposed, in the light of a history of especially invidious discrimination, a "one-black-for-one-white" promotion regime for state troopers in Alabama. The Court has also barred the use of arguably innocent academic mainstays when there is even a colorable risk that their use will perpetuate prior discrimination, holding in *United States v. Fordice* (1992) that public universities in Mississippi could not, among other things, require a certain minimum composite score on a standardized test as an admissions criterion, given the policy's origins in an era of legally mandated discrimination.

In addition, the Court has intimated that other needs and interests may well suffice, even in the absence of a finding of overt, illegal discrimination. In *United Steelworkers of America v. Weber* (1979), for example, the Court sustained a voluntary affirmative action measure, even though the entity adopting it had not itself engaged in, or been found guilty of, discriminatory hiring practices. The Court noted that the plan was "designed to eliminate conspicuous racial imbalances" that were the "vestiges" of discrimination. Stressing that simply ending overt discrimination would not be enough, the Court declared that it "would be ironic indeed" to read the federal civil rights laws as a "legislative prohibition of all voluntary, private, race-conscious efforts to abolish traditional patterns of racial segregation and hierarchy" (p. 204). And, even though the *Hopwood* panel disputed the significance of the observations, various members of the Court have spoken of affirmative measures with approval, especially when these reflect the nature of the educational process. The most notable instance came in *Bakke*, where Justice Powell stressed that "the attainment of a diverse student body . . . clearly is a constitutionally permissible goal for an institution of higher education" (pp. 311–12). Similar sentiments are evident in *Wygant v. Jackson Board of Education* (1986), in which Justice O'Connor spoke with approval of the "goal of promoting racial diversity among the faculty" (p. 288 n.*), and observed that, "although its precise contours are uncertain, a state interest in the promotion of racial diversity has been found sufficiently 'compelling,' at least in the context of higher education, to support the use of racial considerations in furthering that interest" (p. 286). And, in its most recent foray into the affirmative action thicket in *Adarand*, the Court emphasized, without saying precisely what it meant, that "when race-based action is necessary to further a compelling interest, such action is within constitutional constraints if it satisfies the 'narrow tailoring' test this Court has set out in previous cases" (p. 237).

It is in this last respect, the requirement that the means selected be appropriate, that most affirmative measures challenged in courts have failed. The legal requirement is deceptively simple. If an institution decides to use an otherwise suspect characteristic as a basis for making a decision, it must do so using the "least restrictive means." That is, if there is any other way to make the determination that does not involve using group identity as a factor, that alternate approach must be embraced. It is on this basis that most affirmative action challenges have been resolved. In *Bakke* and *Hopwood*, for example, the universities used race and ethnicity as substitutes for rather than as simply one aspect of the "qualifications" sought in applicants for admission. Two-track admission systems were created, within which applications were segregated by race and ethnic origin. That approach allowed the courts to easily and appropriately hold that these characteristics had become dispositive rather than simply one permissible plus factor in a regime within which similarly qualified individuals were treated equally.

A legal affirmative action program is then one within which the primary emphasis is on fair procedures. A college or university will fashion a program requiring that all necessary steps are taken to guarantee that qualified applicants are aware of the position and will be considered carefully and fairly when they apply. Such programs may, in appropriate circumstances, add race, ethnicity, or gender to the decisional mix but only after they have defined clearly the threshold qualifications for the position and have identified an appropriate educational reason for taking these otherwise suspect characteristics into consideration. It is in this respect that an affirmative action program might treat race or gender as a plus factor, tipping the balance in favor of a female or minority candidate who clearly meets all other required qualifications but only when the institution can show that race, ethnicity, or gender actually matter.

This does not mean that every program, or every decision, will operate in the same way. Acting affirmatively might mean that an institution creates a fair and open hiring process, characterized by advertising the position widely, actively encouraging and seeking out applications from a wide range of candidates, and assessing each individual objectively in the light of a clear job description and expressed institutional needs. To the extent such a system affords any competitive edge to certain candidates, it is only in the sense that a threshold decision is made that all finalists meet the standards articulated and that compelling educational reasons exists for making the decision in favor of one particular applicant.

It could also involve attempting to cure an imbalance in the faculty. Under this approach, an affirmative hire might involve opting for a woman rather than a man in a department whose current gender composition does not reflect the relative proportion of individuals holding the qualifications sought. That is, in a discipline in which the potential pool of qualified faculty is evenly split between men and women, a decision to favor a woman over a man would be appropriate if the current departmental split was skewed in favor of men. A final possibility is that the institution believes it is important in and of itself to hire an individual possessing a particular group characteristic. In this sense, affirmative action becomes a true substantive obligation, characterizing race or gender as an important qualification for the position.

In each instance, there must be evidence that supports the decision. A college or university cannot, for example, simply assume that its gender composition does not reflect the norm within the discipline. It must, rather, have a sound evidentiary basis for believing that the paucity of women within its ranks does not in fact reflect their availability within the potential applicant pool. Nor can it simply assume that diversity is a good thing, or that race or gender is an intrinsic aspect of the position it seeks to fill. It must, rather, be prepared to prove that these beliefs comport with sound educational practice. And, most importantly, it must have that evidence in hand before it crafts a policy or makes a decision, for if there is one thing the Supreme Court has made absolutely clear in these matters, it is that post-hoc justifications will not be accepted in support of an affirmative policy or affirmative hire. In some instances, such evidence will be readily available, if for no other reason than that the applicable federal regulations impose considerable justification and record-keeping requirements on all employers. In others, it is now incumbent on the higher education community to conduct the necessary studies, as courts and the general public have become increasingly skeptical regarding the justifications that have been offered in the past.

Conclusion

A purely procedural affirmative action program poses no real issues for potential faculty either as a matter of principle or a matter of law. Such regimes are simply a means for insuring that the hiring process is open and fair. Affirmative action programs that involve some sort of preference on the basis of group identity, on the other hand, assume that characteristics such as race, ethnicity, and gender serve as legitimate proxies for a variety of individual attributes that may appropriately form a part of a hiring process that evaluates individuals in the light of unique institutional needs and priorities. Such policies are conscious of the individual applicant's group identity and, for purely educational reasons, willing to take it into account in order to fashion a faculty that offers the range of skills, characteristics, and interests necessary to create the critical mass required to enrich the learning process.

The assumption is that affirmative action policies are necessary and appropriate in a society in which inequality of opportunity remains a pervasive reality. There is much to be said for this belief, especially when one examines not just the composition of current college and university faculties but also the demographics of those individuals attaining terminal degrees in their fields. Unfortunately, affirmative action as it is now commonly practiced has accumulated considerable negative baggage, as pervasive public support for the fair and equal treatment of individuals collides with an equally widespread belief that affirmative action inevitably involves granting preferences predicated solely on group membership. This is especially the case in higher education, in which a variety of noneducational concerns have led universities to adopt affirmative action policies that, when tested in the harsh light of litigation, have been exposed as legally and philosophically bankrupt.

The challenge for an institution making an affirmative hire is to articulate clearly an appropriate vision of what it means to be affirmatively active and then adhere strictly to professed values, forms, and procedures, regardless of consequences. This requires that each affirmative action program reflect the sound and considered judgment of professional educators about educational concerns rather than matters of institutional prestige, political comfort, or any of the myriad other realities that have distorted and destroyed what was once an appropriate impulse. It also means that the hiring process should be a principled one, in the sense that the institution must be honest and open regarding what it is doing and why, articulate its goals and procedures within a matrix of sound educational policies, and exhibit patience.

The goal of a proper affirmative action program is not to make a hire for its own sake, and college and university administrators should have the integrity to recognize that it may sometimes be better to leave a position unfilled or to opt for a candidate from a nonpreferred group rather than compromise academic standards. Both sound educational practice and a proper understanding of what affirmative action should mean require that an institution hire the best candidate for the job, assuming that in some instances that individual may well be a member of a preferred group. That tracks, in a very important way, the goal of all applicants: To find a position for which they are suited, not as a matter if individual entitlement but rather because training and skills have prepared them for the important obligations they are about to undertake.

Author Note

Portions of this chapter are based on and drawn from my article "Pushing Things Up to Their First Principles: Reflections of the Values of Affirmative Action," which appeared in Volume 87, Number 6 of the *California Law Review* at page 1299, and appear with the permission of the California Law Review, Inc.

Notes

1. The primary example of the exception to this rule is what the law refers to as a "bona fide occupational qualification," a notion that captures the common understanding that gender is a relevant consideration in selecting individuals who work in gender-sensitive environments like prisons, in which privacy concerns are pronounced. The Supreme Court has also drawn a distinction between classifications based on race or ethnicity, which are deemed "suspect" and are subjected to "strict scrutiny," and those that are based on gender, which are described as "quasi-suspect" and examined under a form of "intermediate" review. These distinctions are largely irrelevant for present purposes.

2. There are exceptions, with scholars like Herrnstein & Murray (1994) maintaining that there are important distinctions between and among the races.

3. *Bakke* remains the only case involving higher education in which the Court has discussed these issues (the reference to faculty in *Wygant*, for example, is an allusion to the composition of a primary and secondary school faculty). Many of the constitutional rules that are applied in such settings are not appropriate in a postsecondary environment. Nevertheless, there is little reason to believe that the Court's analysis on these matters will change when a university case eventually reaches it. Indeed, if anything, the Court's sensitivity to the academic freedom concerns that permeate university faculty decisions about educational matters make it likely that it would be more inclined to accept an argument for affirmative action from a college or university.

References

Adarand Constructors v. Pena, 515 U.S. (1995).

American Association of University Professors (1973). Affirmative action in higher education: A report by the council committee on discrimination. In *AAUP policy documents and reports* (1995) (pp. 155-56). Washington, DC: AAUP.

Bickel, A. M. (1975). *The morality of consent.* New Haven: Yale University Press.

Carnegie Council on Policy Studies in Higher Education (1975). *Making affirmative action work in higher education: An analysis of institutional and federal policies with recommendations.* San Francisco: Jossey-Bass.

Crenshaw, K. (1998, July). Fighting the post-affirmative action war. *Essence,* p. 146.

Executive Order No. 10925 (1961). *Federal Register,* 26, p. 1977.

Glazer, N. (1975). *Affirmative discrimination: Ethnic inequality and public policy.* New York: The Free Press.

Green, P. (1981). Affirmative action and the individualist principle. *Social Policy,* 11, p. 14.

Greve, M. (1996, Mar. 20). Quoted in Biskupic, J., Texas diversity policy overturned; U.S. appeals court rules campus admissions plan unconstitutional. *Washington Post,* p. A1.

Harvard Committee (1945). *General education in a free society: Report of the Harvard Committee.* Cambridge, MA.: Harvard University Press.

Harvard Law Review (1971). Developments in the law: Employment discrimination and Title VII of the Civil Rights Act of 1964. *Harvard Law Review,* 84(5), pp. 1109, 1300-1301.

Herrnstein, R. J. & Murray, C. (1994). The bell curve: Intelligence and class structure in American life. New York: The Free Press.

Hirabayashi v. United States, 320 U.S. 81 (1943).

Hopwood v. Texas, 78 F.3d 932 (5th Cir. 1996), *reh'g denied*, 84 F.3d 720 (5th Cir. 1996), *and cert. denied*, 518 U.S. 1033 (1996).

Jefferson, T. (1787). *Notes on the State of Virginia* (Peden, W., ed., 1954). Charlottesville: University Press of Virginia.

Jefferson, T. (1813, Oct. 28). Letter from Thomas Jefferson to John Adams, in Vol. 11. *The works of Thomas Jefferson* (Ford, P. L., ed.,1905). New York: G.P. Putnam.

Jefferson, T. (1816, Sept. 5). Letter from Thomas Jefferson to Samuel Kercheval, in Vol. 15. *The writings of Thomas Jefferson* (Lipscomb, A. A. & Bergh, A. E., eds., 1905) (p. 343). Washington, DC: Thomas Jefferson Memorial Association of the United States.

Johnson, L. B. (1965, June 4). To fulfill these rights: Commencement address at Howard University, in Vol. II. *Public papers of the presidents of the United States* (p. 635). Washington, DC: Government Printing Office.

Katzenbach, N. de.B. & Marshall, B. (1998, Feb. 22). Not color blind: Just blind. *New York Times Magazine*, p. 45.

King, M. L. Jr. (1963). I have a dream, in *A testament of hope: The essential writings and speeches of Martin Luther King, Jr.* (Washington, J. M. ed., 1986) (p. 217). San Francisco: HarperCollins.

Korematsu v. United States, 232 U.S. 214 (1944).

Lewis, A. (1996, Mar. 22). Abroad at home: Handcuffs on learning. *New York Times*, p. A27.

Orlans, H. & O'Neill, J. (1992). Preface to affirmative action revisited. *Annals of the American Academy of Political and Social Sciences*, 523, p. 7.

Plessy v. Ferguson, 163 U.S. 537 (1896).

President's Commission on Higher Education (1947). Higher education for democracy: A report of the President's Commission on Higher Education, in Vol. 2. *American higher education: A documentary history* (Hofstadter, R. & Smith, W., eds., 1961). Chicago: University of Chicago Press.

Regents of the University of California v. Bakke, 438 U.S. 265 (1978).

"Reparation, American Style" (1977, June 19). *New York Times*, § 4, p. 16.

Revised Order No. 4: Affirmative Action Programs (1971). Federal Register, 36, p. 23, 152.

Roberts, P. C. (1996, Mar. 22). Waterloo for quotas in landmark ruling? *Washington Times*, p. A18.

Sandel, M. J. (1997, Dec. 1). Picking winners. *The New Republic*, p. 13.

Sandler, B. (1975). Backlash in academe: A critique of the Lester Report. *Teachers College Record,* 76, pp. 401–402.

Sher, G. (1987). *Desert.* Princeton: Princeton University Press.

Silberman, L. H. (1977, Aug. 11). The road to racial quotas. *Wall Street Journal*, p. 14.

Taylor, H. Jr. (1995, June 11). Quoted in Lemann, N., Taking affirmative action apart. *New York Times Magazine*, pp. 36, 40.

United States Commission on Civil Rights (1970). *Federal civil rights enforcement effort.* Washington, DC: Government Printing Office.

United States Commission on Civil Rights (1978). *Social indicators of equality for minorities and women.* Washington, DC: Government Printing Office.

United States v. Paradise, 480 U.S. 149 (1987).

United States v. Fordice, 505 U.S. 717 (1992).

United Steelworkers of America v. Weber, 443 U.S. 193 (1979).

Welch, S. & Gruhl, J. (1998). *Affirmative action and minority enrollments in medical and law schools.* Ann Arbor: University of Michigan Press.

Wygant v. Jackson Board of Education, 476 U.S. 267, (1986).

Ethics of the Profession: Complexities of Collegiality, Professionalism, Morality, and Virtue

Karl Hostetler

In one way or another, many of the questions we and our contributors have explored can be summarized as asking, "What is the right thing for a professor to do?" or "What is a good, worthwhile life for professors and other people involved in higher education?" In other words, many of the most important questions you must face as a professor are ethical questions. At root, college teaching is an ethical enterprise. Hence, discussing the ethics of the profession is a highly appropriate way to end this book. With our ideas of what is professional and ethical, right and wrong, good and obligatory, we make statements about what is most important in our lives as professors. We and the public use these ideas to understand ourselves and our colleagues, to evaluate, to censure and commend, and to set ideals for which to aspire in our teaching, research, and service. We need to be thoughtful about them.

However, currently, it is rare for graduate programs to require that graduate students receive any sort of systematic and significant instruction regarding the ethical aspects of faculty life in higher education. Perhaps this is beginning to change. At any rate, whether or not you have done work in it, ethics is a vitally important but complicated dimension of your work that you will face throughout your career. We cannot do a whole lot with this broad and complex topic in the space of one essay. What we aim to do, though, is bring some issues to your attention and prompt you to do some thinking about them. We already have considered some of these questions before, and we will not repeat those discussions. What we add here are some basic ethical concepts and examples you can use to think further about these questions, to think about them *as* ethical questions.

Collegiality

Ethics is a huge topic. It is helpful to carve it up into some different territories. Let's start with an area that can be called "collegiality." Basically,
collegiality means being a good colleague, being decent and civil with
other people. We have talked about this earlier in this book, although we
did not identify it as an ethical concern. Collegiality might not seem like
an "ethical" concern at all. Sometimes people have the idea that ethics
involves only those things that either are exceptionally good or exceptionally bad. In light of that sort of understanding, collegiality, although it
might be nice, does not count as "ethical." What's correct in this interpretation is that collegiality, indeed, is different from other ethical concerns.
For example, some ethical standards or values are absolute requirements,
so that when people violate them, those people are subject to ethical
condemnation. Not sexually harassing students and colleagues would be
an example. Collegiality is not like that. It is desirable, and, other things
being equal, we should expect people to act collegially; yet when professors aren't collegial, they are not subject to the same sort of censure as
the harasser. This does not mean collegiality is not an ethical concern;
just because professors do nothing awful does not mean they have ful-
filled all they should, ethically. The point is that collegiality is important,
but it is not as strong an ethical requirement as some other things.

We are not just splitting hairs here. Saying of a person, "He is not
ethical," is a powerful statement; it can be a ground for dismissal from a
faculty position. We need to be careful when making such a claim. While
we want to encourage ethical behavior in ourselves and colleagues, we do
not want to be moralistic. Collegiality is a desirable and admirable trait in
professors; it is not optional in the same way wearing a tie to class is.
However, thinking that lack of collegiality is as great an ethical violation
as harassment of students cheapens the whole enterprise of ethical judgment and evaluation.

Perhaps some examples will help illustrate what we are getting at. For
instance, as we have said before, be decent to secretaries and other staff.
Staff should not be treated as servants. Perhaps it is not ethically required
to thank them for their work or to take a bit of an interest in their lives, but
ethical action is not about doing only what's absolutely required. Giving
staff thank-you notes or small gifts once in a while are collegial things to
do and have ethical value.

Or to take another example, in faculty meetings it may not be clearly
unethical to raise your voice or lose your temper, but those are not especially desirable actions, either. Your colleagues may be stubborn and un-

reasonable, and it is understandable how one can lose patience with them. Even so, there is value in responding civilly, in maintaining reasonableness even in the face of unreasonableness.

Again, though, let's be careful here. John Dewey once said that ethics too often is thought of in too "goody-goody" a way.[1] We emphatically are not saying that collegiality and ethics in general are about being "goody-goody." For instance, there can be times when it is ethically acceptable or even required to lose patience, say, for the sake of achieving some more pressing good that is being thwarted. Collegiality is a two-way street, and when others are not doing their part, you have to consider other routes. Be aware that this has its dangers. As a new professor who likely lacks power relative to senior colleagues, your actions can come back at you. Prudence is not necessarily a vice. (But then courage can be a virtue, too. We'll talk about virtue below.)

Collegiality (and ethics in general) is not about being a saint. There may be times when it is ethically acceptable not to be "good." But then, as we say, collegiality is a two-way street, so you need to expect that others will not always be "good" either. Part of being collegial is giving people space for being less than perfectly admirable. Likely, you will have colleagues who are crotchety old geezers. You can either condemn them as crotchety old geezers, or you can look for ways (which you might not find, of course) to achieve and maintain some sort of collegial relationship.

This isn't always easy. For example, a new professor joined a department in which there were five former deans, each of whom had been instrumental in getting his predecessor fired. Their infighting and shifting alliances were Machiavellian. How do you deal with a situation like that? Sometimes the best course is the path of avoidance. If you find yourself in a similar situation, you could let it be known that you're deeply immersed in research and have no spare time to get into the issues.

To take another example, senior faculty have a natural tendency to advise newcomers. (This book reflects that disposition.) They insist, "I wouldn't do that if I were you." Humor them. Their advice may actually be worthwhile! Listening to advice doesn't mean that you have to take it. Most people won't ask you if you did. If they do, and you haven't done as they suggested, just say that complications arose that forced you to change your approach. Eventually, the advisers will accept you as a club member and turn their attention to the new crop of greenhorns.

A final example. If you indicated interest in a professor's research, projects, or programs when you were interviewed, the professor may try to involve you in them. Avoid an outright refusal or total avoidance, or you'll leave the individual feeling betrayed. Showing an interest in colleagues' work is part of your collegial responsibilities, and if you indicated an interest during the interview, a sudden reversal will leave you looking like an opportunist.

Our advice here might strike you as being fishy ways to wiggle out of the problems. But our position is that seeing higher education as a matter of art and politics is consistent with seeing it as an ethical endeavor. For example, even if our advice implies that you bend the truth, remember that you have at least two basic ethical concerns in difficult situations like these. One concern is ethical ideals. Certainly we would like to deal with colleagues in an open, forthright way; that would be the ideal. But then you need to ask, what would be the result of acting more forthrightly, for example, saying that you simply do not want to get involved in departmental infighting? Perhaps your colleagues would admire you for that. On the other hand, maybe they would see you as siding with the enemy, or as being wimpy. In any event, it is legitimate to think about the consequences of acting on ideals. Max Weber described this as a tension between an "ethic of intention" and an "ethic of responsibility."[2] The point is that our principal intention is to serve ethical ideals but that there can be times when acting on the ideals is irresponsible, when it can lead to more harm than good. The point is not that it's acceptable to act unethically once in a while. The point is that you act unethically if you act only on ideals and ignore the possible consequences. And the particular consequence we are concerned about here is collegiality. Honesty is an important part of collegial relationships, but if being completely honest has the potential to destroy collegiality, you need to consider other options.

Professionalism

Collegiality involves the sorts of commonsense things we would expect of any person. But there are other ethical concerns, which we will call professional concerns, that are more specifically connected to the role of professor. There can be a good deal of overlap between the collegial and the professional. For example, ranting and raving at secretaries is not only uncollegial but also unprofessional. So, these are not necessarily distinct categories. However, there is a point in the distinction because there are some things with ethical significance that can be expected or desired of professors just because they are professors.

We cannot get into a prolonged discussion of what it means to be "professional," but we will note two pretty basic aspects. First, as a professor, you have a certain status about which you need to be concerned. For example, it is not a good idea to get too friendly with students. At least, you need to be careful that students understand what your friend-ship means. As their professor you have the professional responsibility to evaluate their academic work in a critical and fair way. Similarly with your professor colleagues. When as a faculty you and your colleagues debate the merits of a department policy or of the work of a colleague applying for tenure, you need to be able to evaluate those things on relevant crite-ria and not just speak and vote as your friends do. We are not saying that no sort of friendship with students and colleagues is acceptable ethically. However, you do need to be careful that the sorts of friendships you have do not hinder you from maintaining your professional status.

Another element of your professional status is that you represent other members of the profession. For example, if you write letters to the editor of the local newspaper, you might need to make clear that you are pre-senting your own opinion and are not representing the profession or your institution.

The second aspect of professionalism we'll note is that as a professor you have certain professional activities other people do not have. Involve-ment in professional organizations is one obvious example. Serving on the program committee for a professional conference or simply attending such conferences can be thought of as a professional obligation. Or people outside your college or university might approach you to be a consultant because of your expertise in your field. You might not always prefer to do such things, but these sorts of activities come with the territory of being a professor. This does not mean you can never decline to be involved in these areas. Indeed, as a new professor, you should be cautious about devoting too much time to activities outside your teaching and scholar-ship. However, you have to acknowledge that you legitimately can be called upon to participate in these sorts of professional tasks. Finally, to recall an example we used before, publishing is a distinctive part of most professors' work, and there are also ethical considerations there, such as not submitting an article to more than one journal at a time.

Once again, we are not advocating a "goody-goody" view on these things. Faculty have rights to their private lives and their personal eccen-tricities. Avoid taking professionalism to an unreasonable extreme. But do keep in mind that professionalism is a legitimate and important ethical concern for you.

Morality and Virtue

We have two more territories to identify before we're done mapping the "ethical." First we identify a domain we will call the "moral." This word can mean a number of different things, but we use it to mean something like moral obligations. Our example of not sexually harassing students would be a moral concern in this sense. Not harassing students goes beyond collegiality and professionalism in two ways (although it also overlaps those things). First, it is a requirement in a much stronger way. Being civil is not just something to do or not do as you wish, but we can cut people some slack if sometimes they act uncivilly. Not so with harassment. Similarly with academic freedom and affirmative action. Concern for academic freedom is a professional concern other professions do not have, but it goes beyond professionalism in that academic freedom is particularly important. People disagree about how and to what extent academic freedom should be protected, but professors have at least some sort of moral obligation to protect and exercise academic freedom. Likewise with regard to affirmative action. People disagree on the desirability of affirmative action, but they cannot deny that it raises very basic moral issues of equality. Whatever their particular views on affirmative action, faculty need to acknowledge that it is an ethical issue and that they have an obligation to do their part to serve equality in hiring, teaching, and other areas.

Second, morality goes beyond collegiality and professionalism in that it involves more fundamental ethical values, and this goes some distance toward explaining our first point that these are stronger requirements. Respecting people is a very basic ethical value. Sexual harassment violates that obligation. Incivility is not a good thing, but neither is it so clearly a violation of the duty to respect people. Similarly, freedom is a very basic ethical matter. Not every restriction on a professor's freedom is a violation of morality, but academic freedom is at the core of what a professor does, and so has a moral weight other things do not have. It might be uncollegial to take a senior colleague's favorite seat at a faculty meeting, but that is not a moral violation of the colleague's freedom. Being an ethical professor includes having due regard for fundamental ethical values.

We cannot leave things there, though, because there still is a piece missing. Morality, as we have been describing it, does not exhaust the ethical domain that exists beyond collegiality and professionalism. Take courage, for instance. Courage is not a matter of collegiality, although being collegial sometimes can require courage. Nor is courage just a matter of professionalism although acting professionally can require courage—as when you confront controversial issues in your classes. Courage is something akin to respect in terms of being ethically fundamental. Being courageous rather than cowardly says something quite significant about an individual's very identity as a person. Courage—and similar attributes such as generosity, kindness, and patience—have ethical significance on the magnitude of moral duties. Yet they are different than moral duties in that we cannot mandate them in the same way we can conformity to the duty not to harm persons. Ethically, we can require of anyone that they not harm other people. It is less clear that we can require courage or generosity, at least not in the same way.

We will call this the domain of ethical virtue—virtuous traits of character and virtuous actions. As virtues they have significant ethical import. But as virtues they go "beyond the call of duty" in a sense.

From this some people conclude that traits such as courage and generosity are less important than, for example, respect for other persons. But that conclusion is too hasty. It is not so much that generosity is less important than that it is less clear what generosity requires of any particular person. For instance, if professors have a family, it might not be possible or desirable for them to be as generous in giving time to students as it is for a professor without family. Even so, it is possible for them to be generous with what time they do have. It is not that being generous is unimportant ethically or that it cannot be expected to some extent; the point is that we need to be careful when we consider what generosity means in the case of any particular person.

Why the Distinctions Matter

In the preceding pages we began to explain the importance of these distinctions between ethical concerns. We want to say more about that. Again, one reason we identify these different categories simply is to point out that there are differences. You need to be sensitive to the difference between something that simply is undesirable and something that really is evil. Just as we do not want to treat every ethically significant infraction as just unwise or in poor taste, neither do we want to treat all infractions as morally egregious. On the one hand, we risk being wishy-washy; on the other hand, we risk being moralistic and self-righteous. As you think through the difficult situations you will face, you need to keep in mind the complexity of ethical concerns.

But this brings us to another point. How do you handle this complexity? In pointing out the several categories we mean to show that there are a number of different concerns that you will need to juggle. Part of the difficulty of ethical judgment is that oftentimes relevant concerns conflict or are in tension. Recall our examples when we were discussing collegiality. There we saw a tension between the ethical ideal of honesty and the desire to maintain collegial relationships with other faculty.

One strategy for dealing with these sorts of tensions is to establish a priority rule. For instance, we might say that when moral duties conflict with collegiality or what's "merely" professional or virtuous, the moral duties should take priority. There is some point to that position. If a colleague really is harming a student, that needs to be stopped, whatever the consequences for collegiality.

However, the problem is, many situations are not so clear-cut that this sort of priority rule provides helpful guidance. What if you sincerely believe a colleague's grading policy is too severe and so unfair to students? You have a moral obligation to see to it that students are treated fairly. So does that mean fairness must be your overriding concern? Perhaps there are ways we could see collegiality taking priority. If your department already is rent by in-fighting, would adding this other problem to the mix fracture relationships beyond repair?

Perhaps we could reply by saying that the real problem is not so much collegiality as that a fractured faculty would lead to harm to additional students in one way and another, and so collegiality is not really the issue. That might be a good way of looking at it, but far from resolving the conflict, that presents us with a different sort of conflict, a conflict about morality. We would have a conflict between preventing harm to the particular colleague's students and preventing harm to students more generally. Perhaps we could try saying that because more students are involved in the latter case, they should have priority. The problem is, quantity is not the only relevant issue. For example, what if many students were harmed only slightly, whereas fewer students were harmed a great deal? In that case it is not so clear who should have priority.

Our point is not that you cannot work out an ethically sound solution to such a conflict. Arriving at a solution cannot be reduced to following any sort of simple priority rule. There is no simple priority between the different categories we identify, nor is there any simple priority within the categories. You need to use judgment and not just follow a rule.

Dealing with Difficult Issues

Again, let us emphasize that our point is not that good decisions cannot be made in ethically difficult situations, nor is it that just any decision is as good as another. Although we cannot get into all the arguments for our claim, we would argue that there can be better and worse decisions in these situations; these decisions are not just matters of opinion. People will point out that different people will arrive at different decisions. That may well be. (Although, just how frequently do people disagree really? Do people disagree about all ethical issues?) But that still does not mean every decision is as good as another. A bigot might arrive at a different decision about a case, but that hardly requires we accept his decision as being just as good as any other.

In turn, the response might be that, setting aside the bigots, it can be difficult to decide what decisions are best. People can have good arguments for differing views. That also is true. But even if there is no one right answer to an ethical problem, that does not mean there are no wrong answers. Our point is not that people must agree on what should be done in ethically difficult situations. Our points are, first, you should realize that these issues are complex, and second, realize that these are issues where decisions need to take account of relevant concerns that you cannot just take or leave as your opinions incline you.

What are these concerns? We have suggested a number of them although we admit we have not been especially thorough or systematic. We are arguing that you need to take account of collegiality, professionalism, morality, and virtue. You need to take account of ideals of fairness and respect and of the consequences of your action and inaction. Yes, sometimes you will find that knowledgeable and well-meaning people disagree with you about what concerns are most important and what should be done to serve those concerns. Still, and this is the important point, you can agree that these are relevant concerns that require attention from all of you. This will not yield easy answers in difficult situations, but easy answers are not the aim. The aim is good answers, ethically justified answers. The trick is to maintain conditions in which you and your colleagues can work together to find ethically acceptable answers. Those conditions will not be achieved if people take the attitude that any old view is just as good as any other.

This might seem to be a daunting task. It certainly is, at least in some important ways. But remember, too, that you do not operate in an ethical vacuum. For example, professional associations of which you are a member may have ethical codes. These can be specific to some discipline, or they may be broader than that. For instance, the AAUP has statements on professional ethics.[3] Also, your particular college or university may have its own ethics code. These sorts of documents are just some examples of resources for thinking through the ethical decisions you face.

But remember that they are only *resources*; do not expect them to provide easy solutions to difficult problems. For one thing, no code can anticipate all possible problems. For another thing, even when a code does anticipate a problem, you face the task of determining what the code requires of you. For example, the AAUP Code says professors should "make every reasonable effort to foster honest academic conduct" in students.[4] But what counts as a "reasonable effort"? And what about other ethical concerns you must have besides honesty? For example, it's ethically good to develop trust between yourself and students. But if you are overconcerned with student cheating, how can you get students to believe you trust them?

There's no magic formula for deciding these tough ethical questions. No one has a monopoly on ethical wisdom in such cases. You yourself need to ponder these issues. Read what people have to say about them.[5] And call upon your colleagues to help you think through them. Other people cannot make ethical judgments *for* you, but more often than not, they should do it *with* you.

Some Cases

To conclude this essay we offer a couple of brief examples of ethical judgment. The discussions will be too brief, but maybe they will at least suggest how judgment is possible and what it might look like.

Granting a Ph.D.

A senior professor guided a fifty-year-old graduate student from a Third World country through the Ph.D. process. The student had to rewrite her comprehensive examination repeatedly. Her adviser not only gave her all the questions in advance but also graded all of them himself, contrary to accepted policy. The student's supervisory committee merely was shown the essays after the fact. At first, they requested that the specialist professors who wrote the questions be permitted to grade them. However, eventually the rest of the committee deferred to the senior professor, indicating that they would sign for the comprehensives if it meant getting the student graduated and out of the institution. The faculty felt the graduate student was a genuine nuisance—for example, making many demands on the secretarial staff and generally being impolite.

On the dissertation work, the senior professor himself found the student's initial attempts at writing to be extremely insufficient. He therefore set about not only suggesting revisions to the student but also doing most of the writing himself. In the oral examination, the student answered no questions. Instead, the senior professor ran interference for her and proceeded to answer the other committee members' questions himself. All signed, approving the granting of the Ph.D.

The senior professor's junior colleagues on and off the committee were all well aware of the problem and considered it to be near fraud. You are the most junior member of the faculty within the department. Ethically, what should you do?

This situation illustrates a basic conflict between concern for academic standards and concern for a human being—the student. Earlier, when we discussed students, we considered the tension between maintaining traditional academic standards and curriculum and serving equality in the context of an increasingly diverse student body. That is a real ethical issue. On one hand, there is the legitimate concern that standards of scholarship are not being maintained. The case appears to involve academic dishonesty, which may be considered wrong in itself and wrong because of the consequences it might lead to. For example, it isn't too far-fetched to think that the professor's actions are wrong in that they threaten to undermine the academic quality of the institution or at least the public's perception of academic quality, with the possible consequence that public support for the institution will erode, harming both faculty and students.

On the other hand, there is merit in the idea that concern for a human being should come before concern for an institution's image. It might be argued that the professor acted rightly in putting this human concern before academic concerns, particularly for a student from a Third World country who might not have had all the advantages enjoyed by other students.

However, the conflict here is not clear-cut. We might ask whether the student's well-being really was being served by her advisor. Perhaps compelling her to do more of her own work, even if that meant struggling and perhaps failing, would have been of greater benefit to her. We might also argue that the adviser was being paternalistic and, if not thereby showing disrespect for the student, at least overstepping reasonable bounds. Paternalism sometimes can be ethically correct (say, when preventing a drunken person from walking out into traffic even though the person insists that he really wants to do that), but it can be carried to the point that the object of the paternalism is sold short so far as her ability and right to determine and carry on her own activities.

But then this case raises the issue of whether the activities demanded of the student are the proper ones. Ethical reflection includes examining the purposes we have in order to test whether they really are good. Are academic standards are being upheld here? *Should* they be upheld? Is the committee operating with a proper conception of scholarship? For example, the case focuses on the student's inability to present her learning orally and in writing. But does that inability show she has not learned? Isn't learning the really important thing?

That's an important question. Professors should be concerned to avoid overly narrow views of scholarship. But in this case, it is not clear that the student really was learning much of anything at all. Plus, this student's learning is not the only important thing here. If the student was preparing for a faculty position, that sort of position requires some significant ability to communicate with students and colleagues. It isn't clear that the committee's professional and scholarly expectations were unreasonable. But even if there is a real question about that, it is difficult to see how the advisor's actions contribute to really tackling the scholarship issue. He seemed more to dodge the issue than confront it.

To this point, we've focused on the adviser, but there is also the issue of the complicity of the remainder of the supervisory committee. The information suggests that they were motivated to rid themselves of a nuisance. We can attach some ethical weight to this if we see the student's actions as violating collegiality. The case says the student was "impolite" and a "nuisance." How serious are those infractions ethically? The argument would be stronger if this nuisance was so extreme as to harm or place excessive burdens on the professors, other students, or the secretarial staff. In any event, it is clear that there are other ways of dealing with a nuisance besides rubber-stamping her dissertation.

Although it seems not to be a concern of the committee in this case, support for the committee's complicity might exist if they were truly concerned for the student's well-being or for maintaining a positive collegial relationship with their faculty colleague. But again, it's not clear that the student's well-being was best served in the action taken, nor is it clear that their (in)action was necessary for or worth maintaining a positive collegial relationship. Why couldn't the committee collegially yet firmly resist their senior colleague's actions? Maybe that would require some courage. But that could be a reason to do it rather than avoid it.

We have posed a lot of questions here. What might all this show about your obligations as a junior faculty member in such a situation? Certainly, any professor has the sorts of ethical obligations considered above. The fact that you are new on the job doesn't absolve you from the necessity of ethical thought and action. Still, you may have special circumstances that could make your ethical obligations different from those of your more senior colleagues. For example, as a new professor, you wouldn't have been involved in the development of the situation. It could be argued that the situation should have been dealt with long before and that the onus of culpability rests with those who have turned a blind eye to the problem. Even so, although it may be ethically acceptable not to take action in this case, that's different from ignoring the case. The situation calls for the attention of relevant parties, and even you are a relevant party.

As a junior faculty member, probably you have more to lose by becoming involved than do senior faculty members. By taking sides or even appearing to take sides, you risk being pulled into a political power struggle in which you lack power. Prudence might call for remaining neutral. But the prudential action is not always the best (often risky) action. Of course, there is ethical value in courage in the face of such risks, but we can't say that it is ethically illegitimate to ever consider personal well-being in such a case. Still, you need to ask what best serves your well-being here. Perhaps your short-term interests are served by steering clear of the controversy. But how about your longer-term interests? For example, if your department gets a bad reputation because of your colleagues' actions, what will that do to your chances of attracting students, grant money, and so on?

So what should you do in this case? It appears that there's nothing to do about this particular student; she's gotten her degree. Of course, if she were to ask you for a reference, you could write a letter that reflects doubts about her ability. But then you'd need to think about whether you should write such a letter. That's an important issue, but space doesn't allow us to get into that aspect. What we will consider is what you might do to prevent such a situation happening again, which seems to us to be a reasonable and important aim.

Several things seem pretty clear to us. First, this seems to be a case you should be concerned about. You can't be intimately concerned with all the innumerable ethical problems in the world, but this case is near enough and significant enough to warrant your attention. Second, there are a number of issues you must consider if you're to make an ethically appropriate decision—issues such as respect for the particular student, other students, and colleagues; concern for academic standards and honesty; and concern for yourself. Third, these considerations appear to rule out certain actions. For example, it's not ethically appropriate to cavalierly dismiss difficult students from the university, and it's not ethically appropriate to cavalierly limit your concern to what is most likely to help you get ahead.

Beyond these rather obvious things, though, the question of what to do becomes less clear. It's important to know students' well-being should be considered, but it's another thing to know what best serves students' well-being. It's also another thing to know how students' well-being fits in among the many other relevant concerns that must be faced.

A response to the situation and the issues it raises requires judgment, not a formula. We've ruled out a couple courses of action, but beyond that we cannot say what ought to be done. For instance, it would help if we had more information about such things as how other faculty think about the situation, what sort of support they might give you for differing actions you might take. Here's a place where our point about exercising judgment with other people comes in. A reasonable course of action would appear to be to talk with colleagues to get a sense for how things stand with them. By doing so, you would not be ignoring the problem. Talking with people might not appear to be decisive action, but ethically appropriate actions are not always decisive.

Even though it's important to recognize that answers to ethical problems are not always clear, it's also important to realize that some situations do have fairly straightforward responses. The next case is such an example.

A Question of Coercion

A senior woman in an undergraduate class in English composition appeared at 5:20 P.M. to turn in her paper to her young, unmarried male professor's office. She explained why she was late; her computer had failed at the last minute. He reminded her that there had been a 5:00 P.M. deadline as was specified in the course syllabus. He could not accept any papers after 5 P.M. She pleaded. To get a passing grade for the class, she needed to hand in the paper and receive a decent grade on it. Still the professor refused.

The student continued to plead. Finally, the professor said that there was a large Homecoming party on campus that evening, and if she would go with him to the event, he would accept the paper. The student was stunned. She said that she had a date flying in for Homecoming and that she had to meet him at the airport and take him to the party. The professor shrugged his shoulders and said it was up to her; either she go with him or he would not accept the paper. At last, knowing the academic consequences, she agreed. She arranged with her roommate to pick up her date and take him to their apartment while she went to the party with the professor. Later, she indicated to her friends that she had a lovely time and really did not regret going with the professor.

You are a new professor in the English Department. The woman's roommate reports the incident to you. What should you do?

The obvious issue here is a professor's relationship with students—particularly social relationships. We might maintain that in this case nothing of a sexual nature happened, so it was an innocent episode. Besides, we might say, the relationship consisted of only one date and is over now. Even more to the point, the woman said she had a nice time.

But that is far from the end of the story; there are serious ethical problems with the professor's behavior. First, it's questionable whether professors and students should have such relationships at all, even for one evening, and whether such a relationship is in the student's best interests. Certainly the professor has an obligation to be concerned about the well-being of the student here, not merely his own pleasure. The fact that the woman didn't express anxiety about the date later doesn't mean all is fine.

This case raises questions about the professor's impartiality in dealing with this student and other students. In his professional role as teacher, can he be objective in his judgments of this woman's academic work? Is he being fair to his other students when he accepts her paper after the deadline, a deadline to which the rest of the students were apparently held?

Moreover, clearly there is some significant degree of coercion involved because the professor is using the promise of academic reward to influence the student. Whatever we feel about faculty-student social relationships generally, to coerce a student in this way is a misuse of the professor's power and ethically wrong.

In the professor's defense, we might consider that the student had some part in creating the situation. After all, she approached the professor and repeatedly pleaded for an extension, and when he tried to refuse, she persisted. In the end, he was only doing her the favor that she herself asked for. Plus, she appears to have waited until the last minute to do her assignment, and in that way created a problem that she should have avoided.

Although it may be that the woman has to bear some responsibility for the situation, this does not absolve the professor of his responsibility. She may have acted poorly, but he is the professor and needs to act professionally. It's not clear that he was doing the woman a service by giving in to her, and it's wrong to take advantage of her anxiety in order to get a date with her. Giving the student an extension for such reasons is mistreatment not only of the particular student but also of the other students in the class, who were not given a similar extension. This is not to say that exceptions to rules must never be made (take the case of accepting a late paper from a learning disabled student, for example), but to be fair, differential treatment must be based on relevant reasons, and in this case the reason ("I'd like a date with this student") is not relevant ethically.

Another pertinent issue here is the propriety of the professor's deadline policy. It's appropriate to assign some due date for work, but to set an absolute time limit may be too severe. Such policies must be considered with care.

In this case it's clear to us that the professor has done something ethically wrong. It may not be clear that attending the party was egregious in itself. It may not be clear that the professor can't be objective in his grading of the woman's paper or the other students' papers. However, to use his power and position to coerce the student is wrong regardless of her initial overtures and her later lack of regret about the matter. Furthermore, to grant a student a special privilege for such reasons is unfair to other students.

Now we come to the issue of what you should do about this. We have just said there is a serious problem here. But how serious is it? And is the problem your problem? For example, why did the roommate report this and not the woman herself? You might want to contact the woman to see if she wanted you to pursue this. But then, as we have argued, this is not just the woman's problem. The professor's behavior affects other students, too. So, even if the woman were to say she does not want you to pursue the issue, you could not let that be the end of things.

You might wonder if this should be passed along to someone else, your department chair, say. That is a possibility to consider. On the other hand, the roommate did come to you. This suggests you have some responsibility here, at least to the extent of finding out the roommate's reasons for coming to you. It would be too easy if you were merely to say it isn't your problem.

Also, you might be slow to report the incident because you are not sure just how bad your colleague's actions were. How severe was the harm done? It is clear that he needs to stop doing this sort of thing. But must he be reported in order to achieve that? Would reporting him be a collegial thing to do? In addition, if you are concerned for the student's well-being, as you should be, perhaps making an issue out of the incident would adversely affect her. The professor might retaliate. Or the student might be embarrassed if the incident became public.

As in our first case, we would need to have more information before we could make any really detailed recommendation. Even so, this case does appear clearer to us in that you would need to take steps to ensure that, at the very least, the professor not repeat his action with the student or any other student. Perhaps we could chalk up this first incident to poor judgment rather than an ethically vicious character, but that doesn't change the fact that this behavior must cease. One reasonable course of action would be to talk with the professor about this. That would be a collegial and professional thing to do. The professor might not see it that way; he might say it's none of your business, but you would have good grounds for saying it *is* your business. Keeping the issue between you and him like this would guard against possible embarrassment to the student. Here's a situation in which it might *not* be a good idea to talk about the incident with other colleagues, although there might be ways you could do that and still protect the identities of the individuals involved. And so far as guarding the student from retaliation, there would be ways to do that, say by checking with the student or her roommate from time to time.

It could be that these initial steps do not work well for one reason or another. If so, you would need to consider additional steps. But that can happen in any situation. The point is not to come up with the one sure-fire solution but rather to formulate justifiable actions that can be revised and improved as events require.

What do you think of our suggestions? You might disagree with us. Our point is not that you should agree. What we do ask, though, is that you take our claims seriously and attempt to respond. It's in such serious give-and-take that we make progress in serving the ethical aspects of our profession.

To close we offer one more case for you to think about. In addition, you might try creating your own cases and sharing them with colleagues in order to generate some helpful discussion.

Questionable Research

A senior colleague is renowned for her research. Because of her reputation, she has brought great prestige to your department. The professor attracts graduate students from across the country. She has secured a number of large grants and uses this money to support a half dozen graduate research assistants. You are a new professor who has just joined the department. The professor was instrumental in getting you hired. During your interview, she told you she was impressed with your dissertation research. The professor has invited you to collaborate in her research. This appears to be a great opportunity. Having heard about this invitation, one of the professor's graduate students comes to you and tells you that the professor has asked him to alter data on several occasions. What should you do?

Notes

1. John Dewey, *Moral Principles in Education* (Carbondale, IL: Southern Illinois University Press, 1975), p. 43.

2. Max Weber, "Politics as a Vocation," in *Weber: Selections in Translation*, W.G. Runciman, ed. (Cambridge: Cambridge University Press, 1978), pp. 212–25.

3. American Association of University Professors, *Policy Documents and Reports* (Washington, DC: American Association of University Professors, 1990).

4. Ibid., p. 76.

5. There are many worthwhile texts and articles you might read. We will note just a few. For a good discussion of the basics of ethical judgment that is not overly technical, we suggest Wayne C. Booth, *The Company We Keep* (Berkeley: University of California Press, 1988). Karl Hostetler, *Ethical Judgment in Teaching* (Boston: Allyn and Bacon, 1997) is written for K–12 teachers, but the discussion and examples of judgment could be interesting for professors. For discussion of ethical issues in higher education, some texts to try are Steven Cahn, ed., *Morality, Responsibility, and the University* (Philadelphia: Temple University Press, 1990); William May, ed., *Ethics and Higher Education* (New York: American Council on Education, 1990); Steven Cahn, *Saints and Scamps* (Lanham, MD: Rowman and Littlefield, 1993); Peter Markie, *A Professor's Duties* (Lanham, MD: Rowman and Littlefield, 1994); and Linc Fisch, ed., *Ethical Dimensions of College and University Teaching* (San Francisco: Jossey-Bass, 1996).

Contributors

Editors

Karl D. Hostetler
   Professor, University of Nebraska
   Columbia University, Ed.D.
   Northwestern University, M.A.T.
   Dartmouth College, B.A.

R. McLaran Sawyer
   Professor, University of Nebraska
   University of Missouri, Ph.D.
   University of Illinois, M.A.
   Southeast Missouri State College, B.S.

Keith W. Prichard
   Professor, University of Nebraska (emeritus)
   Harvard University, Ed.D.
   Columbia University, M.A.
   Indiana University, B.S.

Contributors

Anthony S. Abbott
   Professor, Davidson College

Kenneth E. Anderson
   Deputy Vice Chancellor for Academic Affairs, University of Illinois

David H. Bergquist
  Dean, Becker College

Lamore J. Carter
  Vice President for Academic Affairs and Research,
  Grambling State University

Gregory P. Clayton
  Director of Insurance and Benefits, University of Nebraska

John A. Glover
Professor, Ball State University

Linda Haverty
  Assistant Professor, Ohio State University

Paul E. Kelly
  Professor, University of Georgia

Mark R. Killenbeck
  Professor, University of Arkansas

Mary E. Kitterman
  Dean of Faculty, Stephens College

Linda J. Koenig
  Assistant Professor, Emory University

Robert M. O'Neil
  Founding Director, Thomas Jefferson Center for the Protection of Free
  Expression; former Chairperson of AAUP Committee A

Constance J. Pollard
  Assistant Professor, University of Idaho

Richard R. Pollard
  Assistant Professor, University of Idaho

Norman Rempel
  Registrar, Administrative Faculty, Fresno Pacific College

Jay W. Rojewski
    Visiting Professor, University of Illinois

Gargi Roysircar Sodowsky
    Associate Professor, University of Nebraska

Donald E. Uerling
    Associate Professor, University of Nebraska

Roy Weaver
    Dean of Teachers College, Ball State University

Dean K. Whitla
    Director, Instructional Research and Evaluation,
    Harvard University

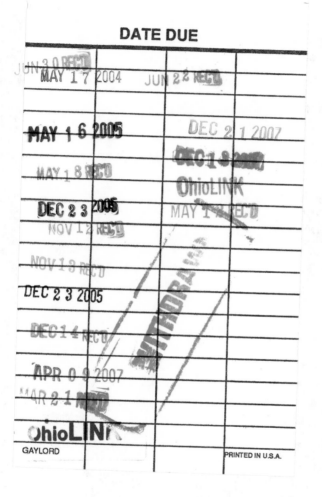